PEER PROGRAMS

An In-depth Look at Peer Helping
Planning, Implementation, and Administration

Resource book for the following:

Peer Power, Book 1, Workbook: Becoming an Effective Peer Helper and Conflict Mediator, Third Edition

Peer Power, Book 1, Strategies for the Professional Leader: Becoming an Effective Peer Helper and Conflict Mediator, Third Edition

Peer Power, Book 2: Applying Peer Helper Skills, Second Edition (workbook)

Peer Power, Book 2, Strategies for the Professional Leader: Applying Peer Helper Skills, Second Edition

Peers Helping Peers: Program for the Preadolescent, Student Workbook

Peers Helping Peers: Program for the Preadolescent, Leader Manual

Problem Solving (Resource Audio Tape)

Judith A. Tindall, Ph.D.
Psychologist, L.P.C., Consultant, Trainer, Author

Rohen and Associates
Psychological Center
St. Charles, MO 63301

ACCELERATED DEVELOPMENT
A member of the Taylor & Francis Group

PEER PROGRAMS: An In-depth Look at Peer Helping Planning, Implementation, and Administration

1 2 3 4 5 6 7 8 9 0 BRBR 9 8 7 6 5 4

Technical Development: Virginia Cooper   Marguerite Mader
                         Delores Kellogg   Janet Merchant
                         Cynthia Long   Sheila Sheward

Cover Design: Gail Shultz

A CIP catalog record for this book is available from the British Library.

∞ The paper in this publication meets the requirements of the ANSI Standard Z39.48-1984 (Permanence of Paper)

Library of Congress Cataloging-in-Publication Data

Tindall, Judy A.
    Peer programs: an in-depth look at peer helping: planning,
implementation, and administration/Judith A. Tindall.
        p. cm.
    Rev. ed. of: Peer counseling. 3rd ed. c1989
    Includes bibliographical references and index.

        1. Peer counseling 2. Peer counseling—Study and teaching.
    I. Tindall, Judy A.   Peer counseling.   II. Title
    BF637.C6T557   1994   94-20448
    158'.3—dc20   CIP
ISBN 1-56032-378-7

For additional information and ordering, please write or call:

ACCELERATED DEVELOPMENT
A member of the Taylor & Francis Group
1900 Frost Road, Suite 101
Bristol, Pennsylvania 19007-1598
1-800-821-8312

DEDICATION

Peer Programs: An In-depth Look at Peer Helping is dedicated to my husband Arburn and sons Jarrett and LaMont. They have given feedback on the material and offered support as the material was developed. They have participated in the development of support audio and videotapes and other materials. They have been a stabilizing influence in my life. As LaMont moved into our lives and became an additional family member, he helped me truly understand cultural differences and the rewarding aspects of those differences.

PREFACE

Peer Programs: An In-depth Look at Peer Helping—Planning, Implementation, and Administration, a resource book to accompany peer helper exercises entitled *Peer Power, Book 1, Becoming an Effective Peer Helper and Conflict Mediator, Workbook* and *Strategies for the Professional Leader;* and *Peer Power, Book 2, Applying Peer Helper Skills, Workbook* and *Strategies for the Professional Leader* grew out of my interest in helping nonprofessionals learn to help others one-on-one, in small groups, and in groups of classroom size. When I looked for ways to teach lay helpers in the late 1960's, I found very few ideas or models that would do the job of training well. As a result, I was faced with the dilemma of wanting to teach helping skills to nonprofessionals and not having any model or program that I felt would be effective for this task.

When I first started training peer helpers in a middle school, I served as a counselor and was overwhelmed by needs of students. At that time, I was running several counseling groups each week and seeing many students faced with academic and drug problems, pregnancy, loneliness, and family issues. Simply not enough help was available to go around. As a result, I decided to train youth in helping skills to assist in leading rap groups, one-on-one helping, classroom groups, and cross-age tutoring.

I also found that youth often did not go to adults for help. Their friends seemed to be the ones to whom they turned first. Sometimes, misinformation or no help resulted. It appeared to me that the natural helping was between peers. Therefore, I decided to build on this natural process.

In the research that I had conducted, I found that group counseling alone was not sufficient to teach effective helping skills. Other studies supported my conclusions that group counseling did not do what I wanted it to do. Therefore, I decided to investigate other ways of imparting helping skills to the layperson.

I discovered through collaborative research, which used highly structured step-by-step training procedures, that I was able to teach helping (communication) skills to nonprofessionals to a degree of effectiveness that was statistically significant. Because of these findings, I decided to refine the training program so that a professional social worker, Employee Assistance Program person, teacher, counselor, psychologist, nurse, or minister could use the program to train peer helpers, lay helpers, peer facilitators, or tutors.

In 1973, I presented to a national convention the first mimeographed copy of a training program that Dr. H. Dean Gray and I developed. Since that time, I have presented this model at local training centers, professional meetings, and state and national conventions, and consulted and trained many peer helping professionals internationally. I estimate that approximately 20,000 individuals have indicated an interest in training peer helpers by attending those various meetings and training sessions. In addition, many have corresponded with me to request help in training peer helpers and to share their successes and failures in these ventures.

From my experience in these workshops and meetings, I decided that I had an obligation to other professionals to put my ideas and training procedures into a form that they can use effectively. In my presentation of how to set up and implement peer programs, I not only use personal experience, but draw on what others have reported as being effective in administering a program.

In my training procedures I have used ideas and concepts developed by Dreikurs, Carkhuff, Sprinthall, Jung, and Myers and Briggs. As a result, a step-by-step model for training peer helpers forms the basis of exercises for trainees and is organized into two sets of books for effective skill building. They are *Peer Power, Book 1, Becoming an Effective Peer Helper and Conflict Mediator, Workbook* and *Strategies for the Professional Leader;* and *Peer Power, Book 2, Applying Peer Helper Skills, Workbook* and *Strategies for the Professional Leader.* Also available are an audio tape on *Problem Solving* (Decision Making) and a videotape demonstrating communication skills.

Two books that have been developed for preadolescents also may utilize *Peer Programs* as a resource book. These are *Peers Helping Peers: Program for the Preadolescent, Student Workbook,* and *Peers Helping Peers: Program for the Preadolescent, Leader Manual,* coauthored by Shirley Salmon-White, Ph.D., and myself.

In the *Peer Programs* book, I wanted to include some of the rationale behind peer helping, how peer programs can impact some of the problems of society, some of the research data, and some of the sample programs to give a more complete understanding of nonprofessional human relations training. This is to help those who are responsible for planning, implementing, and administering peer programs. The purpose of these five books—*Peer Programs: An In-depth Look at Peer Helping—Planning, Implementation, and Administration; Peer Power, Book 1, Becoming an Effective Peer Helper and Conflict Mediator, Workbook* and *Strategies for the Professional Leader;* and *Peer Power, Book 2, Applying Peer Helper Skills, Workbook* and *Strategies for the Professional Leader*—is to meet the need for written materials on peer helping for professionals who want to train others but need a format to follow.

The *Peer Programs* book is intended for interested professionals such as administrators, managers, teachers, counselors, ministers, religious educators, social workers, EAP counselors, mental health professionals, prevention specialists, corrections workers, support group leaders, human resource professionals, and others in the helping professions. The exercises in the *Peer Power* books are intended for those interested in learning human relations skills (communication, crisis reduction, peer helping, leadership). The strategies for the peer professional and the exercise workbooks for trainees are neither panaceas for trainers nor a replacement for effective existing programs, but they can serve to open wider the exciting developments in human relations training and will identify an effective procedure for the implementation of a peer helping training program. Specific program skills will truly empower others to be more effective helpers.

I would like to thank all the teachers, administrators, counselors, and supervisors in the Pattonville School District, Rockwood School District, and at Southern Illinois University who helped to form a basis for the first edition.

I personally want to thank H. Dean Gray for his expertise, clear thinking, and hard work that put together the first edition of *Peer Programs* under the title *Peer Counseling* (1978). Since the first edition, the following people have taken the time to read the material and given me feedback: John Canale, M.D.; Jan O'Neil, M.A.; Shirley Salmon, Ph.D.; Karen Johnson, M.A.; Hazel Sprandel, Ph.D.; Gail Horn, M.A.; Jeannie Rohen, M.A.; Elizabeth Foster, Ed.D.; and Rose Holt. I want to thank board members of *Missouri Peer Helpers Association* and the *National Peer Helpers Association* for continuing to challenge and impact my thinking, which gives me the energy to continue this work in the peer helping field. Those *Missouri* and *National Peer Helpers Association* members who come to conferences and share their programs have added to the material reflected in these books.

The hope is that these materials will assist trainers and others who are designing, developing, and delivering peer helping programs as they move ahead in their peer helping activities.

Judy Tindall

TABLE OF CONTENTS

LIST OF FIGURES

LIST OF FORMS

Chapter I

AN OPEN LETTER TO THE PEER HELPING PROFESSIONAL

Dear Peer Helping Professional,

The goal of this book is to provide a program designed to teach peer helping professionals a method and rationale for training peer helpers. Peer helping programs are a major delivery system of affective education or deliberate psychological education. Peer helping programs can provide prevention, intervention, and support systems for people. Strategies in this program are to give away helping and counseling skills and attitudes, or, more specifically, to teach helping skills to laypersons. This program will enable the trainer to teach interpersonal communication skills and techniques. The training will enable lay helpers to work with others, either formally or informally, in a variety of helping roles. This training program will also assist you to help laypersons apply these skills. Often lay helpers learn skills but do not have a system to apply these skills.

The philosophy of a counselor "giving away" skills and "training" others in peer helping requires a specific plan, strong commitment of energy, self-awareness, and time, and probably additional training. This resource book and accompanying student workbooks entitled *Peer Power, Book 1* and *Book 2, Workbook,* along with *Peer Power, Book 1* and *Book 2, Strategies for the Professional Leader,* will help you become aware of the scope and tasks of a successful peer training program. The program design has been developed and field-tested by myself and others for several years.

Peer programs have been shown to be an effective strategy to meet some of society's problems such as falling academic standards, loneliness, health problems such as AIDS, teenage pregnancy, smoking, substance abuse, eating disorders, conflict, cultural diversity, stress, lack of support groups for individuals and families facing chronic illness, aging parents, genetic disorders, addictive problems, suicide, and neighborhood and work related problems. The research indicates that a peer is often the most effective in influencing behavior of others.

Several personal attributes are essential before a peer helping professional can deliver a peer helping program successfully. This success of training lay helpers depends upon five attributes:

1. A high level of awareness of one's own values, personality type, feelings, goals, and aspirations.

2. An awareness of time and effort involved.

3. A commitment to developing and completing a program.

4. A willingness to take creative risks.

5. An ability to trust trainees.

The peer helping professional must be both dedicated to the concept of the value of training lay leaders in affective interpersonal communication skills and competent in designing a curriculum using and teaching such skills. A trainer who is functioning at high levels of effective communications skills enhances the chance of trainees functioning at high levels of effectiveness. Even though the trainer may have had experience in counseling or teaching, this experience does not assure effectiveness in peer helping teaching. Research by Carkhuff (1969) warrants the conclusion that oftentimes a counselor has lower helping skills as a result of that counseling experience. One very easily can develop habits and behaviors that are destructive and ineffective for peer training and not be aware of it. Therefore, trainers for peer training programs need to improve continuously and add to competencies in their personal helping skills before and throughout the process of training others.

The first requirement for being effective in training peer helpers is *possessing a high level of awareness of one's own values, personality type, feelings, goals, and aspirations.* A trainer must have a strong and accurately developing awareness of self and others in order to carry out an effective training program. Without this ability to know oneself accurately, a high probability exists that the trainer will exhibit behaviors that can detract and damage an otherwise effective program. The leader of any program of this nature exerts a tremendous influence, either negative or positive, on trainees learning the basic communication skills. Unless trainers are cognizant of personal feelings and emotions and how these feelings are communicated to others, their impact on trainees will be haphazard—sometimes destructive, sometimes beneficial—but never will the impact be consistently helpful in the growth of the individual trainee.

A second attribute is *an awareness on the part of the trainer of the significant amount of time and effort required to organize people in an educational system, workplace, church system, hospital, youth facility, or community system that is neither geared nor oriented to include peer helping training.* As is true with other requirements of peer training, if the time, effort, and energy are not given willingly, or if the trainer is not able to give the time to organize a program adequately, the probability of success will be reduced.

The third attribute is that *the time commitment to develop and complete a program requires high levels of physical and emotional energy.* A peer training program requires energy levels that enable concentration over relatively long periods of time. For example, a key training procedure that relates directly to this energy need is found in the feedback process of the program. The feedback process requires that the trainer both identify the effectiveness of a trainee's communications skills and feed that appraisal back to the trainee. To do this consistently and well requires a high enough level of energy to concentrate for significant periods of time. High expenditures of energy require that one be in good physical condition. Otherwise, difficulty will occur in maintaining energy levels sufficient to be an effective rater or trainer.

Fourth, the **willingness to take creative risks is important.** The *Peer Programs: An In-depth Look at Peer Helping* book is only a resource book, and for a specific program to be effective, each person must use personal creativity to develop needed modifications. Although it is important not to change the skill building pattern, the program design needs to be adapted to the unique conditions existing in the system being served. Because each system operates somewhat differently, adaptations require creative thinking and planning to fit the program design into the structure of the setting in which the training takes place. For example, an open school could have peer helpers located in many parts of the building, whereas a traditional school may have to fit a training program into an often rigid physical and curricular structure. The program design needs to be adapted also to the developmental level of those being trained.

Fifth, **the competency and integrity of the trainees must be trusted.** An element of risk always exists when one is training helpers because possibly they will go beyond skill limitations in helping other people. Experience shows, however, that trainees become acutely aware of their limits as the result of training. Considerable time and effort in the training program are spent in clearly identifying the responsibilities of the helper when dealing with material that may be confidential or beyond the helper's capacity. The final requirement, then, is to trust the lay helpers, after giving them a thorough training, to have the integrity that will support that trust.

When using the training procedures described in this book, the experience has been that no inappropriate helping behaviors of any consequence have occurred. Apparently, the training helps to establish the qualities of competence and integrity needed to be able to trust trainees. To date, this trust has been supported by thousands of peer helpers.

One caution to you, the peer helping professional, is not to use this resource book as a "cookbook" process. The program design demands a high degree of structure for success, and the resource book should provide a disciplined structure rather than a recipe for your program. A trainer is urged to blend personal creativity into implementing the program to specific needs without destroying the integrity of the process and the program design.

To you, a potential trainer, an invitation is issued to participate in a highly exciting program for increasing competencies in the helping skills. *Peer Programs: An In-depth Look at Peer Helping* has been developed to assist people interested in an action program for training peer helpers. The accompanying four books entitled *Peer Power, Book 1, Workbook: Becoming an Effective Peer Helper and Conflict Mediator* and *Strategies for the Professional Leader;* and *Peer Power, Book 2, Workbook: Applying Peer Helper Skills* and *Strategies for the Professional Leader* contain content and activities to assist trainees in gaining and applying the essential skills under your supervision. There are accompanying audio and video training tapes available for certain populations. Those of you working with preadolescents may want to consider *Peers Helping Peers: Program for the Preadolescent, Student Workbook and Leader Manual.*

Sincerely,

Judith A. Tindall, Ph.D.

> *A man becomes virtuous*
> *by performing virtuous acts;*
> *He becomes kind by doing kind acts;*
> *He becomes brave by doing brave acts.*
>
> *Aristotle*

Chapter II

PEER HELPING
AND ITS COMPONENTS

Interest among counselors and other persons in the helping professions has been growing significantly over the last several years; interest in teaching nonprofessional skills, attitudes, and concerns of effective human interrelationships has also expanded. Training programs are relatively new and terminology is in the formulative stage. By reading this chapter you will be exposed to the frequently used terminology in peer helping and the meanings commonly associated with these terms.

PEER HELPING

The most important term is the concept of *peer helping.* For the purpose of the program, peer helping is defined as *a variety of interpersonal helping behaviors assumed by nonprofessionals who undertake a helping role with others.* Peer helping includes one-to-one helping relationships, group leadership, discussion leadership, advisement, tutoring, service learning, conflict mediation, peer education, and all activities of an interpersonal human helping or assisting nature.

AFFECTIVE EDUCATION

Because the trainee's experience is one of learning how to teach, the trainer must be aware of the concept of *affective education* or *deliberate psychological education.* The terms "affective education" and "deliberate psychological education" (DPE) essentially are interchangeable, and both refer to educational concerns that deal with feelings. References to DPE strategies relate to procedures or programs that teach or train people in the concepts and skills involved in improving interpersonal affective psychological behaviors and attitudes. Feelings become the central focus of DPE programs, and peer helping training becomes a core concept of these programs. Teaching people to become more facilitative and effective in interpersonal relationships is the goal of DPE programs, and peer helping training is one of the major delivery systems to that goal. In other words, DPE strategies attempt to aid in developing counseling skills and attitudes or, more specifically, to teach helping skills to laypersons.

Affective education includes all educational experiences in which the major emphases are related to understanding feelings, emotions, and interpersonal relationships. Teaching interpersonal skills is related directly to affective education parameters.

DEFINITIONS

Learning peer helping requires a training program. The program requires peer professionals, trainers, trainees, support from staff and administration, and a training format and procedures. Certain terms may be new to you. So you and others can communicate easily, terms used in your program will be used as explained in this section. The following terms and meanings frequently are associated with the training aspect.

Trainer. The trainer—a professionally educated counselor, psychologist, teacher, nurse, clergyperson, social worker, human relations specialist—is any person in the field who assumes the responsibility for basic and advanced training. This process includes organizing, developing, implementing, and following through with procedures for a complete peer helping program. A more complete description of the trainer's responsibilities will be found in Chapters VII and X of this book. The profile and development pattern of a trainer are provided in Chapter VI.

Peer Helping Professional. This person serves in the following roles: trainer, supervisor, grant writer, administrator, facilitator; or any role that involves being in charge of peer helpers and their projects.

Trainee. The trainee is a person who is involved in a peer helping training program. This person is learning to function as a peer helper.

Participants and Group Members. These collective terms are used to refer to trainees. Each term is used as appropriate in the context of this book and the trainee book *Peer Power, Book 1, Workbook: Becoming an Effective Peer Helper and Conflict Mediator.*

Program Design (Model). A specifically designed program to prepare helpers. This program follows an age appropriate curriculum.

Role-playing. Role-playing refers to a training procedure in which a trainer or a trainee assumes the role of helper, helpee, rater, or any additional role that enables a training technique to be demonstrated.

Feedback. Feedback is the process by which listeners communicate to others the reaction that they have to the quality of communication of the speaker. The format of this program requires that trainers and trainees act as raters to give feedback to trainees who are practicing various skills.

The terms "helpee," "helper," and "rater" are used to describe roles that trainees assume during the training period.

Helpee. The helpee is any trainee who is functioning as the individual with a concern.

Helper. The helper refers to any trainee who is functioning as an individual assisting the person with a concern.

Rater. The rater is any person whose function is to give constructive feedback as to the quality, accuracy, and effectiveness of the helper's helping responses.

Peer Helper. The term "peer helper" refers to a person who assumes, either by choice or conscription, the role of a person helping contemporaries. This definition excludes professional counselors but can include all paraprofessionals when they function as interpersonal peer helpers. The term "peer" denotes a person who shares related experiences, values, and life-style.

The terms "helper," "tutor," "lay helper," "mentor," "peer helper," "peer mediator," "peer leader," "peer health educator," "peer facilitator," peer counselor," and "paraprofessional" often are used interchangeably in the literature. Peer helpers are nonprofessional persons who have learned interpersonal skills so as to aid peers. Peer helpers may either assist or work independently of professional counselors.

Paraprofessionals. Persons who have completed satisfactorily a peer helping program are referred to as paraprofessionals. They are considered important members of the team when peer helpers work with professional counselors. Peer helpers are often able to help do things that professionals alone either could not do as quickly or could not do at all.

Helping. Helping has many ramifications. In the peer helping literature, helping refers to giving assistance to a person who is in need of personal psychological assistance. The helper is the peer helper who provides the assistance; the helpee is the one who receives the help. On completion of a basic skill training, a trainee assumes the role of peer helper.

The peer helper has the skills and the psychological strength to provide the helpee with the assistance needed. Thus, helpers must in some manner communicate concerns, feelings, problems, or other human needs for which the helpee wants assistance. The helping process could occur in a group setting as well as on an individual basis. Helpers, therefore, offer interpersonal human assistance to helpees.

Communication. As used in these peer helping books, communication refers to verbal and nonverbal (body language) messages involving two or more individuals. Specifically, the communication is between the helpee and helper. The purpose of the communication is to facilitate self-exploration and/or understanding. Because helpees must communicate concerns, feelings, problems, or other human needs, peer helpers must possess skills necessary to enable an understanding of what is being communicated.

Helping Process. The helping process is the composite of all activities associated with the helper's helping the helpee. The helping process may be summarized diagrammatically as shown in Figure 2.1.

Responding. Responding is the process by which the helper provides constructive information concerning the helpee's communicated behavior. Feedback enables helpees to know that they have been understood and that the helper is able and willing to assist them.

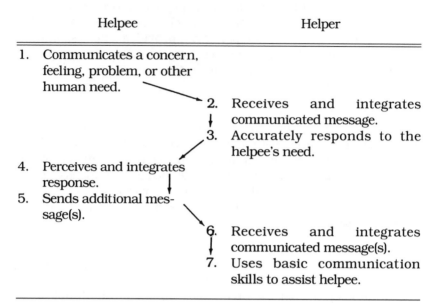

Helpee	Helper

1. Communicates a concern, feeling, problem, or other human need.

2. Receives and integrates communicated message.
3. Accurately responds to the helpee's need.

4. Perceives and integrates response.
5. Sends additional message(s).

6. Receives and integrates communicated message(s).
7. Uses basic communication skills to assist helpee.

Figure 2.1.   Diagrammatic summarization of the helping process.

Empowerment.   The process whereby leaders strengthen and develop followers. The leader does this through the process of
• sharing information and making it possible for followers to obtain appropriate kinds of education,
• sharing power by developing initiative and responsibility,
• building the confidence of followers so they can achieve their own goals through their own efforts,
• removing barriers to the release of individual energy and talent,
• seeking and finding the various kinds of resources that followers need, and
• providing organizational arrangements appropriate to group efforts (Gardner, 1990).

Service Learning.   Service and learning goals blended in such a way that both occur and are enriched by each other is called service learning. Service-learning projects emphasize both sets and outcomes—the service and the learning—and the projects are designed accordingly. Programs that emphasize learning always include a strong reflective component in which students utilize higher order thinking skills to make sense of and extend the formal learning from the service experience (Toole & Toole, 1992).

Prevention. Caplan (1964) defined three categories of prevention. Primary prevention attempts to prevent a disorder from occurring. Secondary prevention attempts to identify and treat a disorder at the earliest possible moment so as to reduce the length and severity of the disorder. Tertiary prevention attempts to reduce to a minimum the degree of handicap or impairment that results from a disorder that has occurred already.

Peer Counseling. This is also called peer helping, but with the particular focus on one-on-one helping with social issues.

Peer Helping Program. This is an implemented system for recruiting, training, and supervising youth to provide a variety of helping services to peers, schools, agencies, businesses, and communities.

Peer Ministry. This refers to a peer helping program implemented in churches with a focus on theological relevance to daily life.

Pro-social. This refers to acts and services that are motivated by regard for and a commitment to interests and needs of others.

Youth Service. This is also known as community service, volunteerism, and service learning.

BASIC COMMUNICATION SKILLS TO BE TAUGHT

The format for training follows patterns that were introduced originally by Carkhuff (1969, 1987a, & 1987b),

Egan (1986), Gazda (1973), Gordon (1970, 1978), Ivey (1971, 1973), Ivey, Gluckstern, and Ivey (1982), Ivey and Gluckstern (1984), Jakubowski-Spector (1973a, 1973b), and others and are modified to teach interpersonal helping skills to nonprofessionals. Various terms are used in the literature today to describe the helping process and helping skills. For example, Active Listening utilized by Gordon involves teaching others empathy and acceptance skills to help facilitate problem solving with others. Carkhuff described the Responding process, which includes empathic questioning, listening for feelings, meaning, and personalizing facilitating understanding. Carkhuff also described the initiating process, which involves helping the person move into action.

For the purposes of teaching interpersonal helping skills to nonprofessionals, the following terms will be used in this program. The program teaches the basic interpersonal skills presented in Figure 2.2; that is, communication skills that have been identified by eight areas: attending, empathizing, summarizing, questioning, genuineness, assertiveness, confrontation, and problem solving. These eight skills are used frequently in the *Strategies for the Professional Leader* books and the two *Peer Power* books. They are defined for future reference as follows:

BASIC COMMUNICATION SKILLS

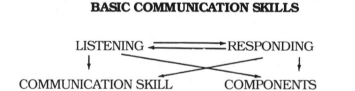

Figure 2.2. Basic communication skills.

Attending behavior relates most directly to the concept of respect, which is demonstrated when a helper gives the helpee undivided attention, and which by means of verbal and nonverbal behavior expresses a commitment of focus completely on the helpee. The term connotes an active behavior on the part of the listener and is a prerequisite to effective helping. Learning about verbal and nonverbal communications and their effects is essential for peer helping.

Empathy or "empathizing," as used here, is equivalent to Carkhuff's (1969) "minimally facilitative level of empathic response." Empathizing responses must communicate an accurate awareness of the feeling and meaning of the helpee's statements and of the conditions that generated those feelings and statements. Empathic responses do not go beyond the helpee's demonstrated level of understanding. In other words, the helpers respond with an accurate identification of what the helpees have communicated and do so in such a way that the helpee may perceive the helper's understanding easily. To utilize empathy skill the peer helper needs to be able to discriminate among messages from the helpee and to paraphrase the meaningful ones.

Discrimination is a part of empathy. It is the ability to separate effective and facilitative interpersonal communication from ineffective and destructive behaviors. Discrimination of effective behaviors precedes any other communication skill.

Paraphrasing, expressing the feeling and meaning of what the helpee communicates, is also a part of empathy.

Summarizing is any helpee behavior that organizes several helpee statements into one concise statement. Initiative responding is listening so as to be able to respond in a manner that sheds new light on and adds new dimensions of awareness to the solution of a problem.

Questioning is the process of inquiring so as to prompt a reply. Questioning pertains to a subject under discussion and oftentimes an area of concern to the individuals present. Effective questioning from helpers prompts the helpees to consider their concerns in greater depth, to identify, to clearly understand a problem, and to consider alternatives.

Genuineness is communicating honest feelings in such a way that the relationship between two or more individuals is maintained or enhanced. Helpers must be genuine in all behaviors.

Assertiveness involves the ability to express thoughts and feelings in an honest, straightforward fashion that shows respect for the other person.

Confrontation is communication that identifies discrepancies in another person's behavior.

Problem Solving is the process of moving a person through phases of exploring a concern, understanding the reason for that concern, and evaluating behavior that affects solving the concern.

Conflict Mediation is an informal, problem-solving, nonadversarial proceeding. It is a form in which an impartial person (the mediator or helper) facilitates communication between parties to promote reconciliation, settlement, or understanding between and among them.

The basic skills taught in the program are fundamental communication helping skills. A summary outline of the communication helping skills is provided in Figure 2.2.

APPLYING PEER HELPER SKILLS

After learning the eight basic peer helper skills as outlined in *Peer Power, Book 1*, participants are provided with an opportunity to utilize those skills and learn additional ones in *Peer Power, Book 2: Applying Peer Helper Skills*. In *Book 2* are several modules for applying the peer helper skills in areas where peer helpers frequently are utilized. Any or all of these areas may be appropriate for your situation and your peer helper training program. Information for the trainer to offer both introductory and advanced programs is contained in this *Peer Programs* book. For the trainees, two separate books are provided so that you may select the book most appropriate for trainees with whom you are working at the time. There is one book for pre-adolescents: *Peers Helping Peers*.

Drug and Alcohol Abuse Intervention and Prevention

Chemical abuse is one of the leading problems in America today. Most of us are not aware of the types of chemicals available, the kinds of problems that these chemicals create, the extent of these problems, or how to treat individuals who have chemical abuse problems. This training will increase helpers' awareness of these issues.

Wellness/Stress Management

Wellness implies leading a healthy life—having the body, mind, and emotions in balance with each other and with the human environment. When these components are out of balance, a condition of stress ensues. Stress management techniques enable peer helpers to help individuals find and change or control their own stressors.

Enhancing Self-esteem

Helpers learn to focus on the group members' strengths to help them gain or regain self-confidence and to emphasize the positive rather than the negative side of personality.

Leadership Training

Group and organization leadership training involves determining and balancing task-type and people-type styles of leadership, communication skills, mediation and judgment skills, and leadership expertise.

Facilitating Small Discussion Groups

At times peer helpers are asked to lead small discussion groups with peers. Some of the groups are open-ended groups and others are problem-solving. The module will give the participants practice in leading small discussion groups.

Leading Classroom Groups

Peer helpers for classroom groups are often needed to assist in distributing information to large groups because information given by a peer is often better accepted than when provided by professionals. Topics include health issues, getting along with friends, value clarification, and others.

Peer Helping through Tutoring

Peer helpers are often called on to assist others in learning a new skill, to help with formal teaching, or to work with students who have difficulty learning. This module will assist peer helpers as they work in their role of tutoring.

Recognizing Eating Disorder Problems

Eating Disorders have become an increasing concern with emphasis on thinness and achievement. Anorexia, Bulimia, and Compulsive Overeating are problems at all ages. Peers are often the first to notice odd eating behavior. This module will assist peer helpers in assessing their own eating habits and recognizing eating problems in others.

Suicide Prevention

Peers are often the first to know of someone considering suicide. This module will assist the trainees in recognizing the symptoms of suicidal behavior and some action steps to take. Activities to assist those left behind also are presented.

Coping with Loss

All people cope with loss, and some losses have more impact than others. Coping with loss is part of the life cycle. This module will assist the trainees in understanding reactions to loss and also will help them cope with their own losses and assist others who are coping with loss.

Ethical Considerations in Peer Helping

This is still one of the most important modules for the peer helper. This might be addressed prior to starting any training and addressed throughout each activity and later as the peer helpers are delivering their activities.

> *I don't care what*
> *you know*
> *Until I know that*
> *you care!*
>
> —*K. C. Hunt (1988)*

Chapter

WHY PEER HELPING NOW?

> *At the end of life we will not be judged by...*
>   *how many diplomas we have received*
>   *how much money we have made*
>   *how many great things we have done.*
>
> *We will be judged by...*
>   *I was hungry and you gave unto me*
>   *I was naked and you clothed me*
>   *I was homeless and you took me in.*
>
> —Mother Theresa's *Words to Live By*

The traditional "treatment" model of the past has not been effective in preventing and solving some of today's complex problems—problems like conflict and violence, gangs, drug abuse, eating disorders, HIV, loneliness, school dropouts, low academic achievement, teen pregnancy, abuse, lack of understanding of others different from us, stress, accidents on the job, lack of care for the elderly, and health problems.

The traditional "treatment" model implies that people are to be treated by professionals—sometimes at a cost of $1,000 per day—and if this doesn't work, some are placed in prison at the cost of $20,000 per year. This treatment model means that a professional must first identify the problem, intervene, and move toward treatment. The financial support for this traditionally has come from individuals, private insurance, and the government. The facts are that in the United States, between 9 and 12 million American children have no health insurance (Children's Defense Fund, 1990). As resources become scarce or disappear altogether, a new paradigm is emerging. The new paradigm involves utilization of people as resources to deliver services at dramatically reduced costs.

PEOPLE AS RESOURCES

People in the peer helping model become resources who can contribute to schools, businesses, committees, and churches. The idea is that peers become resources to each other. This model would move people away from a "me-ism" to a more caring society. According to Piaget and other developmental psychologists, empathy (or perspective-taking) is one of the most critical competencies for cognitive and social development (Attili, 1990). Johnson and Johnson (1987) stated that all psychological development may be described as a progressive loss of egocentrism and an increase in ability to take wider and more complex perspectives—an empathic process that takes place with peer helping.

The term *peer resource* is used to refer to any program that utilizes nonprofessional people to work with other people in schools, communities, churches, business, industry, and intergenerational programs. Included in this peer helping model are such programs as youth service, cooperative learning, peer tutoring, peer health education, cross-age tutoring, peer helping, peer mediation, peer leadership, self-help groups, mutual aid groups, neighborhood helpers, intergenerational programs, and volunteers in businesses.

It is common knowledge that the first person to whom someone will turn in trouble is a friend. The first person to notice that someone is experiencing difficulty usually is a friend. According to Johnson and Johnson, "The primary relationships in which development and socialization may take place may be with peers" (1987, p. 126). Friendship is very important to youth. One of the values youth have is to be a friend and have friendship. Failure to develop social and relationship skills is a powerful predictor of later substance abuse, delinquency, and mental health problems (Kellam et al., 1982).

The connotation of peer pressure has in the past been negative. As a result, schools adopted the "just say no" campaigns. Peer helping emphasizes and builds on the opposite side of that phenomenon—the positive side.

For several reasons, peer helpers are a particularly effective means of reaching youth, particularly those whose behavior puts them at risk for the problems mentioned above. (Best, Thomas, Santi, Smith, & Brown, 1988; Botvin & Wills, 1985; Flay et al., 1985).

1. Peer helpers can have more credibility with the target audience than can adult professionals (Finn, 1981; Klepp-Knut, Halper, & Peery, 1986).

2. Peers may have a better understanding of the concerns and the pressures facing the target group than an adult professional might. This understanding enhances their ability to engage the target group in a discussion for purposes of changing behavior or transmitting information (Finn, 1981; Perry, Klepp, Halper, Hawkins, & Murray, 1986).

3. Peer educators can be effective role models of desired behaviors (Flay et al., 1985; Perry et al., 1986).

4. Peer helpers are more likely to interact with the target group on a daily basis outside the more formal setting

such as a classroom. This gives an opportunity for peers to be of influence in day-to-day living.

5. Peer helpers can learn lifelong skills. Once peer helpers learn to teach and model positive health behaviors, they may continue beyond the program and generalize what they learn to new situations (Finn, 1981).

6. The greatest changes take place with the peer helpers themselves.

A significant study conducted by the Search Institute of Minneapolis, involving over 49,000 6th-12th graders across the Midwest, gives evidence why peer helping programs should be an integral part of every school, campus, and community. This systematic study of youth perspectives, values, and behavior looked at external assets of support, control, and structure and the internal assets of commitments, values, and competencies that are needed to stimulate and nurture healthy development. It also looked at the deficits, or liabilities, that can interfere with healthy development, such as hedonistic values, T.V. overexposure, drinking parties, stress, social isolation, and negative peer pressure. Each of the deficits is associated with at-risk behavior, and those students who reported the deficit also reported a significantly higher number of at-risk indicators—such as frequent alcohol use, cigarette use, attempted suicide, school absenteeism, driving and drinking, sexual activity, and bulimia—than those who did not report the deficit. The study also found that the more assets a student reported, the fewer deficits were indicated.

One of the results of the study showed that students who engage in projects and programs to help others, defined as pro-social behavior, on a weekly basis are less likely than non-helpers to report at-risk behaviors.

The study also found that helping behavior decreased from 6th grade to 12th grade as hedonistic behavior increased (Benson, 1990). It would seem that peer helping programs do provide opportunities for youth to develop pro-social skills.

In prevention programs, peer helpers and peer leaders provide more than factual information; they teach pro-social skills, demonstrate decision-making skills, and enhance self-efficacy through role-playing and appropriate behaviors. Peer-led programs anchored in social learning theory (Bandura, 1977) build on early social inoculation approaches (McGuire, 1964). If schools, businesses, and communities viewed peer pressure as a way of life and saw people as resources with peer helping training, then peer pressure would move from negative to positive. "Just say no" campaigns tend to emphasize the negative.

PROBLEMS OF SOCIETY TODAY

For just a few minutes, open your mind and look at the following picture. In the 1940's the seven leading causes of discipline in California public schools were

1. talking in class,
2. chewing gum,
3. making noise,
4. running in the halls,
5. getting out of line,
6. wearing improper clothing, and
7. not putting paper in the wastebasket (Mendel & Lincoln, 1990).

Today, at many schools, common problems are drug abuse, gang related violence, teen pregnancy, assault, arson, murder, vandalism, venereal disease, suicide, bombings, absenteeism, and abortion.

A small town in Pennsylvania named Rosetto was founded in 1883. The men in that community worked in the quarries along the Delaware River. The women maintained the homes and reared their families. The people lived in tightly knit Roman Catholic families, and their children learned traditional values. Rosetto became famous in 1961 as the "miracle town" because, despite eating traditions that featured meals amply piled with the high cholesterol content of cheese and fatty meats and citizens who tended to be on the plump side, the incidence of heart attacks was only one-third the national average.

By 1971, the town of Rosetto had made dramatic changes. Men no longer worked in the slate quarries but commuted out of town; families joined country clubs in the nearby Poconos; new homes were being built; the sale of Cadillacs increased; women had gone to work; church attendance had dropped; and television antennas were everywhere. The divorce rate was equal to the national average, and of course the incidence of heart attacks was similar to the national average. Fast-paced living had changed this town and its citizens.

A dangerous myth is that most American youth can muddle through their teens and become productive adults largely on their own. Few do. The statistics paint a grim picture for youth.

- If a child is born to a single mother, chances are one in two that she or he will live in poverty. Further, if that teen happens to be a parent, chances are 70% that she or he will live in poverty (Children's Defense Fund, 1990).

- Because of abuse of alcohol by women, every year about 40,000 children are born with alcohol-related birth defects, such as attention disorders, hyperactivity, speech-language disorders, and, the most serious disorder, fetal alcohol syndrome (Newman, 1990).

- For every 1,000 infants born alive in the U.S., 13 will not live to see their fifth birthday (Children's Defense Fund, 1990).

- About 1,000 young people attempt suicide every day (Children's Defense Fund, 1990).

- One in every four homeless Americans in our cities is a child (Children's Defense Fund, 1990).

- The dropout rate is equally alarming. Every day, an average of 1,512 youngsters drop out of school (Children's Defense Fund, 1990).

- Of the young people who stay in school, studies show that one-half graduate without reading, math, and science skills that would allow them to perform moderately complex tasks, such as summarizing a newspaper editorial or calculating decimals (Children's Defense Fund, 1990).

- Every 12 seconds of the school day, an American child drops out (Children's Defense Fund, 1992).

- Projections for the year 2000 are that new jobs will require a work force whose median level of education is 13.5 years (Johnson, 1987).

- Every 53 minutes in America, a child dies of poverty (Children's Defense Fund, 1992).

Taken together, these and other circumstances place children and their families in at least difficult and often impossible situations.

Conflict and Violence

The days of *West Side Story's* "Wine, Women, and Song" have exploded into today's violence, crime, and some heavy metal music that seems to glorify conflict and violence.

From the fighting and name-calling on the playground to the stabbing in the halls, to the shooting in the schools, to the street gangs, to the riots in Los Angeles, to the inability of business to negotiate a "fair deal," to unions and global wars, conflict seems to be the theme of the present day.

Our children live with the threat of violence on a daily basis. In fact, on an average, 135,000 children bring guns to school every day (Children's Defense Fund, 1990).

School safety was among the top concerns of the nation's governors when they crafted the six national educational goals of 1990. Goal 6 states, "By the year 2,000, every school in America will be free of drugs and violence and will offer a disciplined environment conducive to learning" (The National Association of Elementary School Principals). The Association focussed on violence and punishment at an annual meeting in 1994 (*USA Weekend,* February 25-27, 1994).

Youth between the ages of 13 and 18 constitute about 11% of the population. Recently, the same age group was responsible for 41% of the arrests for offenses such as homicide, rape, robbery, aggravated assault, and burglary (Federal Bureau of Investigation, 1989).

Between 1953 and 1986, the violent crime rate rose almost 600% and the property crime rate 400% (Skogan, 1989). Crime statistics for 1988 and 1989 reveal an overall increase of 5% for violent crimes in the U.S. (Federal Bureau of Investigation, 1989).

Business and industry see violence on the increase. Jones (1991) reported that violent crimes cost American businesses $50 billion each year. For example, in supermarket chains in 1989, a survey of employees indicated that 37% admitted being angry with customers, 4% reported fighting with customers, and 7% reported fighting with coworkers.

What Can Peer Programs Do? Peer programs that emphasize conflict resolution and mediation in schools, communities, and businesses need to be developed. Those schools that have developed conflict resolution programs have shown fighting reduced by 75% and referrals to the office reduced by 50% (Salmon, 1992a). Wilson (1992) summarized the data from 15 districts in California to establish that peer helping or conflict resolution programs also reduce the high incidence of school crime in middle and junior high schools. He reported that campus violence was reduced greatly because students learned to deal with problems in a nonviolent manner.

Gangs

Immigrants formed groups to protect themselves and their neighborhoods from other groups. Like their present-day counterparts (gangs), these groups were made up mostly of underprivileged minorities. They supported themselves through street crime and fought turf wars with rivals (Goldstein, 1991). Today the street crime is drugs, and the wars are fought with high-powered weapons bought with the huge proceeds of the narcotics trade.

By 1989, Spergel, Ross, Curry, and Chance reported that delinquent gangs were located in almost all 50 states, with the possible exception of a few north central mountain states and perhaps some northeastern states. Collectively, 35 surveyed cities reported 1,439 gangs. California, Illinois, and Florida have substantial gang concentrations as do Los Angeles County (600), the City of Los Angeles (280), and Chicago (128).

The general profile of gang-related youth consists of the following:
low motivation,
low self-esteem,
behavior/discipline problems,
chemical use and abuse,
poor peer relations,
negative police involvement, and
poor internalization skills.

The six basic self-esteem needs of gang-prone youth are

1. identity—the need to be unique and be special;

2. bonding—the need to be accepted by others and to be included;

3. competence—the need to feel successful;

4. safety—the need to feel both physically and psychologically secure in one's environment in order to grow healthy;

5. change—the need for variety and positive changes in one's daily life; and

6. meaning—to have life mean something. (Gonzales, 1991).

Understanding the profile of gang members and the self-esteem needs of gang members can be the first step to assisting youth in becoming resources.

What Can Peer Programs Do? Most peer programs offer opportunities for youth to experience a sense of accomplishment, gain acceptance by others, obtain a feeling of belonging, and learn guidelines for safety. Peer programs bring meaning to one's life. Therefore, involving youth in peer programs provides youth with some of the same self-esteem needs as involvement in gangs does. The key element of self-esteem, as Hendin (1987) stated, is the experience of being needed, valued, and respected by another person, which produces a new view of self as a worthwhile human being (p. 43).

An example of how one school district utilized an older peer to help elementary children resist gang pressure was seen in Missouri's Ferguson-Florissant School District. The elementary children were being lured by local gang members until the older trained peer helper worked with the elementary children on a regular basis, with the result being that gang activity began to seem less glamorous.

Bernard concluded from a 1988 survey of the literature, "There is no better way to ensure that prevention is empowerment. . .than to make peer programs. . .in their truest sense of providing opportunities for meaningful participation and responsibility. . .the major approach in prevention programs for children and youth."

Falling Academic Standards and Dropping Out

Students graduating from today's schools have fewer academic skills than generations past. Falling ACT and SAT scores tell us that higher education will have to teach basic skills if students are to succeed in college.

The *St. Louis Post Dispatch* (Sept. 10, 1992) reported that the American College Testing scores of the class of 1992 were unchanged for the fourth year in a row. The report stated that students were not taking math and science in high school in order to prepare for college work. Bob Schaffer, Public Education Director of Fair-Test, a national watchdog group opposed to most standardized testing, pointed out that the strongest trend in the ACT and other tests is family income. Students with family income of less than $60,000 a year scored an average 5 points lower than students with family incomes of $60,000 and above.

The same kind of disparities occurred among students of different races. Blacks, Hispanics, and Native Americans scored lower than Whites and Asians. The different averages underscore the social and economic inequities in American culture.

Businesses in Missouri promise to support taxes for education if the schools will make changes and truly "educate" youth. Currently businesses spend millions in teaching workers basic skills.

In 1967, 41% of all jobs in America were held by high school dropouts, while college graduates held just 13.2% of all jobs. In 1987, dropouts held only 14.9% of the jobs; college graduates held 25.3% (Mendel & Lincoln, 1990). These facts are very alarming when we recognize that in some inner city environments the dropout rate can reach as high as 40%.

Many youth today have very low performance at school because of lack of motivation and negative attitudes toward learning. Some of these students come from disadvantaged families, and some actually have some kind of learning disability—among those the dropout rate is often higher.

What Can Peer Programs Do? Peer tutoring programs have flourished in this country in the last 25 years. You can find these programs at all levels of elementary, middle, and secondary school, higher education, and in the community. A variety of research indicates the success of peer tutoring programs. The tutors must go through training as a tutor for them to be successful and for the tutees to learn. Sprinthall and Blum (1980) found that in one cross-age teaching program in which untrained pupils tutored other pupils, the untrained only program produced no effects at all. In the case of untrained children tutoring recently mainstreamed pupils, the results were negative; tutors developed more negative attitudes towards mainstreamed children and employed greater criticism in their teaching techniques than in their initial teaching strategies. Therefore, if students are left simply to tutor without training, negative effects happen not only for the tutors, but also the tutees.

Some inner city schools have started peer tutoring programs to reduce dropout rates. The St. Louis Public School System has tutoring in all of its middle schools as part of the regular school day and in some after school programs. Therefore, providing training for peer tutors is essential if they are to be helpful to others (Foster, 1991).

Riessman (1990) stressed the negative impact on students that may come from dividing the peer helping program into tutor and tutee categories; tutees may be resentful and feel inferior. Riessman believed that a system in which all students take both tutor and tutee roles is fair and effective. Students in the tutor role unfailingly gain significantly, both academically and personally. After experiencing the tutor role, students more readily and profitably accept also the tutee role. Cooperative learning models, or schools that are set up where everyone is a tutor *and* tutee, are ideal.

Some of the service learning programs in our schools have helped youth become interested in helping others and their communities.

A variety of community efforts are directed toward working with adults to learn to read and write. Some of the programs need help to formalize their programs and train the volunteers more fully.

Schools of today must move to a new paradigm. Schools must be restructured so that students have an opportunity to be helpers and helpees in some form through cooperative learning, service learning, peer helping, peer leadership, conflict mediation, and other peer programming.

Drug and Alcohol Abuse

The abuse of alcohol and drugs is one of the biggest problems facing society today. The impact of alcohol and drugs on society is devastating. The cost of substance abuse to business and industry is in the billions.

Youth often follow the model of the adults in society, by thinking a party is "getting high" time. Prescribed drugs at times are abused by youth and adults in suicide attempts.

Substance abuse can be the reason for costly accidents, both individually and ecologically. For example, the oil spill in Alaska a few years ago was caused by a ship whose captain was found to have been abusing alcohol. Business and industry report that 40 billion dollars is lost each year because of alcohol abuse (Jones, 1991).

It appears that some prevention efforts are beginning to have an impact. Secretary of Health and Human Services, Louis W. Sullivan, M.D., announced that the federal government's 17th annual survey of high school seniors showed significant decreases in drug use from 1990 to 1991, with the rate of "any illicit drug use within the past year" down from 33% to 29%—or approximately one-half the 1980 rate. The survey was conducted by the University of Michigan's Institute for Social Research. These researchers surveyed 15,483 seniors from public and private school graduating classes of 1991. They compared the results to a similar survey in 1990. They found significant decreases in use of

cocaine, down from 1.9% in 1990 to 1.4% in 1991, and a drop of 73% since 1980, and

alcohol, down from 57% in 1990 to 54% in 1991, and a 25% drop since 1980;

and in "lifetime" use of

any illicit drugs, down from 48% in 1990 to 44% in 1991,

cocaine, down from 9.4% in 1990 to 7.8% in 1991,

marijuana, down from 41% in 1990 to 37% in 1991,

heroin, down from 1.3% in 1990 to .9% in 1991 (Sullivan, 1992).

The survey also included data on drug use from a sample of 6,600 members of previous graduating classes one to 10 years after leaving high school. Follow-up data on these young adults 19 to 28 years old show decreases in annual use of any illicit drug, which decreased from 31% in 1990 to 27% in 1991. In this group, annual marijuana use declined from 26% in 1990 to 24% in 1991. Other illicit drugs showing decreases in annual use in the 1991 survey include cocaine—both crack and powdered—MDMA ("Ecstasy"), and stimulants.

Follow-up data on those young adults who are now in college showed that annual use of any illicit drug was down from 33% in 1990 to 29% in 1991, and of cocaine from 5.6% to 3.6% (Sullivan, 1992).

The United States still has the highest incidence of alcohol and drug abuse among its youth of any country in the world (Bronfenbrenner, 1986). Of the graduating class of 1987, 56% began drinking between grades 6 and 9. Recent findings (Sullivan, 1992) of a study done in 1991 of approximately 18,000 8th graders and 16,000 10th graders were that within the last 30 days

alcohol was used by 25% of 8th graders and 45% of 10th graders

cocaine was used by 0.5% of 8th graders and 0.7% of 10th graders

binge drinking—five or more drinks at one sitting—was reported by 13% of 8th graders and 23% of 10th graders.

cigarettes—44% of the 8th graders, who have a modal age of 13, have already tried cigarettes. Smoking in the past 30 days is reported by 14% of 8th graders, 21% of 10th graders, and 28% of 12th graders.

What Can Peer Programs Do? Peer programs that focus on prevention can assist schools, businesses, and communities in reducing alcohol and drug abuse. The prevention efforts can be through classroom presentations, small group efforts, support group leadership, and one-on-one helping. Peer helpers also can be used in intervention efforts. Finally, peer helpers can be used to assist others in their efforts to maintain a drug-free life.

Tobler's (1986) meta-analysis of 143 drug abuse prevention programs found that unlike programs that primarily emphasize knowledge about drugs or personal growth, "peer programs were found to show a definite superiority" in effectiveness and were especially useful with school-based populations." Clark, MacPherson, Holmes, and Jones (1986) found that peer educators were effective in teaching junior high school students skills to resist peer pressure to smoke.

Evidence shows that peer programs are one of the most effective strategies to prevent substance abuse.

Prejudice and Poverty

Many of our schools are faced with students who not only speak different languages but have a variety of other cultural differences. One high school in San Francisco has 21 different languages spoken by its students.

A Profile of Poor Children in America

Out of 100 poor children in America

Ethnic Group
    40 are white, non-Latin
    34 are Black
    22 are Latino
     5 are Asian, Pacific Islander, Native American, Alaskan
        native
Family Household
    37 live in married-couple families
    59 live in female-headed families
     4 live in male-headed families
Work
    62 live in families with at least 1 worker

17 live in families with 2 workers

22 live in families with at least 1 full-time, year-round worker

Urban/Rural

45 live in central cities

32 live in suburban areas

24 live in rural areas

Income

44 live in families with income of less than half the poverty level ($6,962 for a family of four)

Age

40 are younger than 6

11 live in families headed by persons younger than 25

(Children's Defense Fund, 1992)

Teachers are frustrated when they lack the skills to communicate with people speaking languages other than English. They experience a rising prejudice because of a lack of understanding of different cultures.

America is changing. To understand these changes, an important step is to look at the population growth and what ethnic groups seem to be changing the most.

Growth of groups within the U.S. population between 1980 and 1990 was as follows:

Black — +13.2%,
White — +15%,
Indian — +37.9%,
Asian — +107.8%,
Hispanic — +56% (Hodgkinson, 1992).

One prediction is that by the year 2010,

Washington D.C. will be 93% minorities,
New Mexico 79.5% minorities,
Texas 56.9% minorities,
California 56% minorities,
Florida 53% minorities, and
New York 52% minorities (Hodgkinson, 1992).

Schools and businesses will be made up of very different populations from today. The requirements for multicultural cooperation and integration will be enormous.

If we look at the research in reference to minorities in the United States, the picture is glum. For example, most ethnic populations (other than Native Americans) use alcohol and drugs at a lesser rate than Whites. However, as ethnic groups become more acculturated and assimilated into the dominant American culture, research has shown that their use of these substances increases (Bernard, 1991, April).

Children and youth of ethnic minority backgrounds constitute a large percentage of the youth living in poverty. According to Pallas (1989), "In 1989, the poverty rate for White children was 16.1% whereas 38.7% of Hispanic children were living in poverty households, and 46.2% of Black youngsters were living in poverty. Although Blacks and Hispanics made up one-quarter of the 1- to 17-year-old population in 1984, they represented more than one-half of the children in poverty." The research of Martin Orland found that for each year a child lives in poverty, the likelihood of falling behind his or her expected grade level increased by 2% (Reeves, 1988, p. 15). A child whose family has been mired in poverty for 10 years is 20 times more likely to do badly in school than a child who is poor for only a year.

Here is something to think about. If we could at this very moment shrink the earth's population (5.2 billion) to a village of precisely 1,000, with all the existing human ratios remaining the same, there would be

564 Asians and Oceanians,
210 Europeans,
86 Africans,
80 South Americans, and
60 North Americans (Hodgkinson, 1990).

By the year 2000, futurists predict that economic considerations will transcend political considerations because of a worldwide free trade. To be successful economically,

Americans must consider international business and relationships. Thus, the future of society rests on our ability to respect diversity and communicate with others who are different.

Another prediction is that in the next 20 years, the White population will be down by 3.8 million and the minority population will be up 4.4 million.

Research clearly demonstrates that if we are truly to address the issues of substance abuse and poverty in ethnic minority populations, we must face head-on the underlying dynamic of racism in our society. What is equally clear is that to create a society that values and nourishes its cultural diversity, we must create environments for people that are characterized by respect for differences and by high expectations of success for all children.

What Can Peer Programs Do? Peer programs emphasize respect for all people. Peer helpers are taught the skills of empathy and also how best to help others. Peer programs also focus on self-esteem.

Studies consistently have shown a significant correlation between low self-esteem and prejudice (Pine & Hilliard, 1990).

Most peer programs make an effort to have a variety of cultures and languages represented in their programs, thus offering a bridge between ethnic groups and serving as role models for others.

Sex-related Problems

The United States has the highest rate of teen pregnancy of any industrialized nation, with an estimated 50% of the 15- to 19-year-old age group being sexually active. Teenage pregnancy is a significant social problem. One organization estimates that births that occurred when the mother was a teenager cost U.S. taxpayers $21 billion in 1989 (Armstrong & Waszak, 1990). Each year more than one million young women age 19 or under become pregnant. Of the teenage pregnancies conceived in 1987, 36% ended in abortions, 14% in miscarriages, and 50% in live births (Forrest & Singh, 1990). Of great concern is that 82% of the pregnancies to teens in 1987 were unintended (Forrest & Singh, 1990). Thus, teen pregnancy is experienced as a problem by young women themselves.

Many young women are at risk of pregnancy. Although the majority of young women under age 15 have never had sexual intercourse, 27% have had intercourse at least once, and 13% are currently sexually active. Through the teenage years, the proportion of young women who have had intercourse increases significantly. Among sexually active teens, those who were younger and those with low incomes (Forrest & Singh, 1990) were less likely to use contraception.

One-fourth of all sexually active adolescents can be expected to contract a sexually transmitted disease. In addition, among teens who give birth, 46% will go on welfare within four years, and among unmarried teens, 73% will be on welfare within four years (Carnegie Council on Adolescent Development, 1989).

Statistical data on sex-related activities include the following:

- Every 31 seconds, a teenager becomes pregnant.
- Every 2 minutes a teenager gives birth.
- At present rates, 40% of today's teens will be pregnant at some point—the U.S. has the highest teen pregnancy and abortion rates in the developed world (Jones, 1985).
- At present rates, more AIDS deaths occur each year than traffic deaths.

Pregnancy is the most prevalent reason for female students (60 to 80%) and male students (40%) to drop out of school. The cost of teen pregnancy is high. For example, the state of Georgia, with the fifth highest teenage pregnancy rate in the nation, spent 50 million dollars in 1985 on AFDC, food stamps, Medicaid, and other health costs related to teenage pregnancy. The National Research Council estimates that a minimum of $6,000 to $7,000 can be saved per teenage birth if childbearing is delayed to the age of 18. The savings to Georgia in 1985 would have been approximately 35 to 39 million dollars if every teen under 18 years had postponed childbearing.

In a St. Louis, MO, county school district, a health education survey to which 312 7th graders and 317 8th graders responded found that in the 7th grade, 19% of the girls and 55% of the boys were sexually active, with 55% of sexually active boys and 35% of sexually active girls having reported more than one sexual partner. In terms of use of contraception, 48% of the boys, and 56% of the girls reported that they did. By the 8th grade, 29% of the girls and 50% of the boys were sexually active, with 67% of the boys and 49% of the girls having reported more than one sexual partner, and 72% of the boys and 67% of the girls reported using contraception (Salmon, 1992b).

Sexually Transmitted Diseases (STDs) are passed predominately from one person to another through sexual intercourse. One of the most serious forms of STDs is Acquired Immunodeficiency Syndrome (AIDS), a fatal disease caused by the human immunodeficiency virus (HIV).

Today, even though men account for 90% of reported cases, women and children represent the country's fastest growing population of newly diagnosed HIV and AIDS cases (Watstein & Laurich, 1991).

The Centers for Disease Control (CDC) in Atlanta reported that AIDS related complications collectively are now one of the five leading causes of death in women in major metropolitan areas. The total number of cases recorded in the United States, according to CDC, is 226,281, with 24,323 being women (the majority aged 25 to 44) and 3,898 being children under age 13 (from all methods of transmission, not just from mothers). According to Centers for Disease Control *Clinical Review* (1992, August), the incidence of HIV and AIDS in African-American women is 13 times greater than that in White women. American women of Hispanic descent show an incidence eight times higher than White women.

Scales (1988) indicated that there is no cure for AIDS, and in the future AIDS probably will be the number one killer of youth. Part of the reason is that so many youth are involved sexually and are not practicing "safe sex." The attitude of many young people is, "It can't happen to me."

How Can Peer Programs Help? The most powerful influence on youth is peers; therefore, a program that utilizes peers as resources as opposed to recipients of care is important to consider in prevention of youth sex-related problems.

Peer programs can and do emphasize prevention through education. Examples are seen in Teenage Health Consultants Programs. These teens prepare lessons to be taught in regular classrooms concerning AIDS prevention, pregnancy prevention, and STD prevention. Pregnancy prevention and STD prevention are most common in these presentations. Ft. Lee Schools in New Jersey focus extensively on AIDS prevention. The San Francisco Peer Resource programs also have an extensive program of AIDS prevention that is well researched. The Georgia Health Department has started community peer helping programs to help reduce pregnancy. Some peer helping programs emphasize one-on-one help for teens at risk, which can provide quick referrals. Some of the middle school programs emphasize learning to forgo sexual activity and waiting and teaching assertive skills. Girls Inc. (formally Girls Club of America) has put together a peer program to reduce pregnancy.

One special need for any adolescent is to have a positive role model, a person who not only is caring but tangibly exemplifies desired behavior.

Community programs that emphasize awareness, through one-on-one meetings between community volunteers and people from their own neighborhoods, of prevention and early referral are important.

Family Distress

As family life in the final decade of the twentieth century becomes more complex, through disruptions such as divorce, single-parent families, and blended families, there is an inevitable pressure to provide support to youth from these families. Divorce is stressful for both parents and children. Many studies suggest that loss of parent through death or divorce is the best predictor of eventual mental health referral for school-aged children. Hetherington's (1984) extensive research has documented the range of problems and difficulties created by parental divorce, separation, or both. Most recently she has found clear evidence that the time of greatest vulnerability is during early adolescence. Her research showed that well over one-half of young teenagers reacted to divorce with psychological upset so extensive as to seem pathological (Hetherington, 1984). Ironically, other recent research (Ursone, 1990) has shown that such children do not seek out school counseling services because of the perception that school counselors are already too busy with other tasks.

Unemployment has negative psychological effects on individuals, including lower self-esteem, lower general well-being and life satisfaction, depression and anxiety, and psychophysiological distress (Cohen, 1978; Farran & Margolis, 1983). Job loss often impacts children by creating feelings of insecurity and social embarrassment (being on welfare or a lunch program). Children have to cope with their new financial status, as well as coping with a parent who is feeling financial pressure and possibly lowered self-esteem.

Chronic illness and death in the family can be traumatic and stressful. Often children go through stages of emotional denial, anger, bargaining, depression, and finally acceptance before they are able to cope with a loss. The feelings may be present for months and sometimes even years after the loss. If the child does not work through appropriate stages, anxiety, depression, withdrawal, or somatic complaints may signal that the child has not adjusted to the loss.

The effect of chronic illness on family functioning has been long recognized by mental health professionals as detrimental to healthy family dynamics. A growing number of studies document potential conflicts and breakdowns that follow the onset of illness. Studies have found that more fighting and delinquency problems occur with siblings of a disabled child. Researchers have suggested that role tensions increase among family members when the parent is seriously ill. Illness of a family member often brings stress on the entire family, which results in problems in adjustment and deficiencies in coping.

Abuse has become a social disease of epidemic proportions.

- By age 18, 1 in 4 girls and 1 in 10 boys are sexually abused (*Sexuality Today Newsletter*, 1986, July 7).
- Child abuse and neglect is so rampant that from New York City to Anchorage, social workers around the country are handling two to three times the maximum number of cases for adequate care (Lawrence, 1987).

The legacy of abuse is often lifelong trauma and reduced functioning in society.

Suicide attempts and completions are on the rise in America. Suicide is the second leading cause of death among young people. Every 78 seconds an adolescent attempts suicide. Every 20 minutes an adolescent is killed in an accident (Scales, 1988). The impact on survivors is devastating. For those who attempted but did not complete suicide, the road to recovery is long.

Eating disorders represent a growing behavior and chronic problem among young people. Anorexia nervosa involves starvation, and bulimia involves binging and purging. Compulsive overeating involves binge eating. The end result is distorted thinking, depression, and medical problems such as heart problems, esophagus problems, loss of tooth enamel, and loss of calcium. Some research indicates the incidence of eating disorders is as high as 40% on some college campuses.

The preceding paragraphs contain just a few examples of how distress is created within the family.

How Can Peer Programs Help? Peer programs that focus on peers helping other peers who are under stress can obtain referrals to agencies that can help reduce the stress. Peer programs that involve training support group leaders can be helpful to families dealing with chronic illness, disease, death, divorce, and suicide. Sprinthall, Hall, and Gerler (1992) reported a successful peer program that helped middle school students cope with divorce. The Alliance for Genetic Disorders has set up training for support group leaders. Schools and communities have many models of successful peer programs that focus on preventing eating disorders and offer support for other family issues.

Loneliness

At all levels of our society, individuals face the sad state of loneliness. Often in schools, certain children are made fun of and excluded. For example, children who are overweight, shy, or disabled are often found eating in the lunchroom by themselves or playing by themselves on the playground. The end result is one of feeling hurt and angry because of lack of friends.

Middle school and high school years can be devastating for some youth because of lack of friends. At times, young people turn to gangs, substance abuse, or sexual activity to find acceptance. Some grow up without friends and as outcasts, not learning the social skills needed to get along as adults.

The homeless in our society often are looked upon as non-entities. Some of the homeless have psychiatric problems; others simply are unable to fit into society because of lack of skills or jobs. Any major metropolitan area has a group of homeless people who are shunned by others.

As longevity increases for both men and women, care for the elderly becomes critical. Many elderly people live by themselves, unable to leave their homes, and others live in nursing homes. Often family members are unable or unwilling to provide time for the elderly, and the end result is one of loneliness.

What Can Peer Programs Do? Peer programs can be developed to focus on reducing loneliness and emphasizing being a buddy to others. For example, some elementary school programs emphasize reaching out to those students who are loners on the playground. Some programs work with handicapped students. Some school programs work in homeless shelters to assist others. Some school programs work with nursing homes as well. Many church programs involved in volunteer work reach out to homeless shelters and nursing homes.

Peer programs have been developed in some governmental agencies such as the Jefferson Barracks Department of Veteran Affairs Medical Center in St. Louis and the Senior Health and Peer Counseling Center in Santa Monica. Grace Hill Neighborhood Association in the City of St. Louis is designed to help train neighbors to help neighbors find resources.

We must help communities form coalitions to develop peer programs that impact neighborhoods, families, elderly, and homeless people and to move toward prevention of loneliness. We must help these community coalitions adopt a prevention goal and all aspects of the community work toward that goal. We need to involve groups from churches, schools, child service agencies, businesses, government agencies, police, and hospitals. Each group can initiate peer programs in its own unique way.

The new peer helping paradigm is emerging in the schools and the communities. After-school programs also are being offered in churches and community agency facilities.

PEER HELPING = BRIDGE TO PREVENTION

Many societal ills face us today. We must move toward more creative ways of attacking these ills. We must help schools change to infuse peer resource programs within schools through peer helping programs, service learning, cooperative learning, peer leadership programs, conflict mediation, and peer tutoring.

We must impact our policy makers to focus more on prevention. We currently are spending 85% of our resources on cures while only 15% goes to prevention. If we look at a study of 18,000 inmates in juvenile long-term facilities, we find that 60% have used drugs regularly, one-half by age 12, 70% did not grow up with both parents, and 25% had a father in jail (Hodgkinson, 1992).

We must help develop peer helpers in the community to help relieve some family stress. Businesses and industries need to go beyond their E.A.P. programs and train volunteers to be day-to-day helpers in the workplace.

We must change our attitudes so that we utilize people as resources rather than relying on the traditional treatment model of only professionals being able to provide help. It is clear from the research on resiliency that peer helping and cooperative learning, as well as cross-age helping and mentoring, are strategies of reciprocity that work in all systems through the life span to achieve all three of the protective characteristics-caring and support, high expectations, and participation. Those foster the development of youth with social competencies, problem-solving skills, autonomy, and a sense of purpose and future (Bernard, 1992; Carbarino, 1992; Muller, 1992; Noddings, 1992; Sergiovanni, 1992; Werner & Smith, 1992; Wolin, 1993).

Professionals are needed, of course, in extreme cases. But if we truly empowered leaders in all areas of our society, we could be further along in helping those at risk and the whole of society.

Let us look at a family at risk and at how peer helping programs can impact the family members. In some instances, programs prevent future problems; in other instances, they can intervene to get help or provide support.

This family lives in the inner city of a large metropolitan area. The grandmother is living in the home and is blind. The mother, Adell, has just learned that she has developed diabetes. The father, John, has just been laid off from his job. There are three children: Angie, age 16; Steve, age 14; and Sean, age 10. Angie has just found out that she is five weeks pregnant, Steve has joined a gang that is known to deal in drugs, and Sean has a learning problem and finds it difficult to read.

Churches, business, schools, and communities all have strong peer helping programs. The local Catholic church has a trained group of volunteers who call on the elderly and help in some way. On two mornings a week, the grandmother is taken for a walk and shopping by one of the volunteers.

A local hospital has trained some volunteers to educate newly identified diabetics about the disease and to provide emotional support.

The company that laid John off has a trained group of volunteers, supervised by the EAP professional, who offer support and leads for other jobs.

Angie first confided her pregnancy to a peer helper at her high school. The peer helper took her to a local agency for an examination, information, and support. Current prevention literature indicates that if we can get mothers to get an examination within the first trimester, handicapped babies can be reduced by 25% (Hodgkinson, 1992).

Steve recently was selected to be part of a service learning project for his school. He was responsible for working with families in a homeless shelter. After spending time with others in his group, he decided to drop his gang affiliation and try to encourage gang members to help also.

Sean recently started working with a middle school student to improve his reading skills. Sean believes his tutor is his best friend now and really wants to work hard. He is optimistic about the future.

As you can see, through peer helping programs, this family at risk received help and support to cope with their stressors. The end result will be a healthier family, able to cope with life more effectively. They in turn will provide help to others. As can be seen, through service, people can become resources instead of receivers of services in society.

Join others as you create a more caring society.

> *To dream the impossible dream. . . .*
> *To fight the unbeatable foe,*
> *To bear with unbearable sorrow*
> *To run where the brave dare not go. . . .*
>
> Don Quixote
> *Man of La Mancha*

CHANGING PROFESSIONAL HELPING ROLES

No longer can professional counselors feel comfortable about their competence when their counseling activities are restricted to individual sessions or small group processes. Both philosophic and economic conditions negate the number of individual sessions and small group processes as the measure of counselor effectiveness. The philosophy that counseling skills are, in reality, human skills and need to be taught to as large a number of nonprofessionals as possible is most relevant. The relatively small number of people whom counselors can help each day is no longer an accurate measure of counselor effectiveness. The emergence of peer training, deliberate psychological education, teaching of pro-social skills, and confluent education in public and private community systems further indicates that traditional roles and functions of the counseling profession are faced with new and interesting challenges.

The emergence of nonprofessionals is the direct result of both an increasing demand for counseling services and the inability of professionally trained personnel to provide all of these services. Sensitive professional counselors, therefore, are feeling pressure from their critically perceptive colleagues to examine closely roles, functions, and philosophy of counseling as it relates to the major foci of education, religion, government, business, and community agencies.

Administrative functions often impinge upon counselors' opportunities to help greater numbers of people. Although administrative tasks are often important and necessary, they can detract from functions that relate directly to helping others. Therefore, to devise effective means to assist more people in a limited time becomes important. As a result many schools have, for example, hired crisis counselors, prevention specialists, and school-home liaisons.

Economically, the condition is the same. In a time of reduced resources, high taxes, inflation, and increasing demands on limited funds, one-to-one counseling becomes expensive and difficult to justify. Public and private support of counseling will continue to increase demands that counseling skills become available to larger groups of people.

Peer approaches have been utilized for the last 25 years. Excellent research data are available to support peer helpers' effectiveness in such helping forms as peer tutoring, peer coaching, and peer editing. For example, in the business community, peers have been active in reaching out to troubled employees. One such program is the Volunteers Group of McDonnell Douglas Corporation in St. Louis. A new wave of peer movements is occurring in churches called "peer ministry" or "youth ministry." This is the result of trying to provide services to the community.

In 1987, with the forming of the National Peer Helpers Association, a new spirit has swept the country as more than 350 attended the first conference in St. Charles, MO, and more than 550 attended in Ft. Collins, CO, in 1988. National conferences have been held also in New Orleans; Flagstaff, AZ; Seattle, WA; Chicago; and Boston. All states and several foreign countries were represented at these conferences. Attendance grows each year as people interested in peer programs come together to network and learn new ways of working with peers. To help raise the level of professional peer programs, steps have been taken:

1. the Ethics and Programmatic Standards were developed by the National Peer Helpers Association and disseminated at conferences and at workshops to guide the profession,

2. the *Peer Facilitator Quarterly,* which is the official publication of N.P.H.A., is issued regularly,

3. intensive training sessions related to peer programs were started by N.P.H.A. in 1992-93 and are offered at the annual conference and regional training meetings,

4. 20 official state associations have been formed and are dedicated to the encouragement of peer programs, and

5. the N.P.H.A. has published articles in popular magazines, with overwhelmingly positive response from both teens and adults.

Clearly, the "crystal ball" focuses upon the need to reexamine, reeducate, and retrain counselors for new and expanding roles in community systems. People in schools, churches, and other public and private agencies have pigeonholed counselors into roles that these agencies can no longer afford nor tolerate. The counselor's responsibilities include the need to identify, develop, and sell new counseling concepts to these agencies. The counselor, better than anyone else, is able to fulfill these responsibilities.

SCHOOL COUNSELING

In education, school guidance programs consist traditionally of informational and administrative guidance activities plus a varying amount of individual and/or group counseling. Although each of these activities is an important function of a good counseling program and should be maintained, the pressure to develop a more efficient and effective use of the counselor's time and skills demands that these activities cannot continue to be the major concerns of the counselor. As Ivey and Alschuler (1973) stated

> ....individual treatment, group counseling, advising, behavior therapy, values clarification, and so forth, are not valid per se; they simply are less effective than a systematic combination of several different procedures used to reach a single goal. (p. 584)

Riessman discussed at the 1987 National Peer Helpers Association Conference in St. Charles, MO, the rationale of "The New Peer Wave: Why Now?" Riessman cited such factors as what is occurring in the redesign of teaching from being teachers to being classroom managers, facilitators of learning, and planners. He also discussed the adolescent crisis. The public has become dismayed by all of the problems of adolescents. In light of the limited resources available for school counseling staffs, a better approach would be for counselors to plan, facilitate, and monitor peer counseling rather than provide all the counseling themselves, and not only for economic reasons, but because peers reach peers more effectively.

The concepts of peer training, deliberate psychological education (DPE), and other affective education concepts are relatively new to the field of education and, generally, have not been emphasized in counselor education until very recently. The assumption can be made, in light of the recent emergence of DPE, that its concepts currently do not lie in the mainstream of counselor education.

Graduate programs also tend to emphasize traditional counselor training. Testing, theories, program administration, and academic constructs still predominate in undergraduate and graduate counselor training institutions. Conversely, indications of changes are occurring and being implemented by some states: Michigan, North Carolina, Oregon, Texas, and others. Also, the training programs and ideas of Carkhuff, Ivey, Egan, Gazda, and others are being incorporated into institutions of higher education.

Many states (e.g., Missouri) are shifting to Model Guidance programs, which involve counselors in the classroom teaching skills in a wide variety of areas and force counselors to change their focus. The program was developed by the Ferguson-Florissant school counselors under the leadership of Dr. Shirley Salmon for the Department of Education in Missouri.

Some universities are establishing graduate courses in such areas as mentoring (North Carolina), conflict resolution (N.E. Missouri State University), and peer helping (Lindenwood College in St. Charles, MO) (University of Minnesota).

The multiple administrative functions assumed by counselors partially explain why counselors have been slow in meeting the changes affecting them professionally. School administrators frequently are not aware of positive outcomes from effective counseling and, as a result, assign administrative tasks on a regular basis to counselors. Counselors who accept these activities either prefer the more clearly defined tasks of administrative detail to the risks of developing effective counseling relationships, or they are unable to define a counseling role and function realistically to their administrators.

Counselors often are involved in schedule changing, report writing, and various other clerical tasks that only remotely relate to the counseling function. The prevailing climate and conditions can make it extremely difficult for professionals to change their roles. They must overcome the handicaps of administrative duties, a lack of initial training, and the difficulty in becoming retrained adequately.

Research on how to train paraprofessionals is limited, but growing. Often studies do not cite a control group. As a result the research is more summative. Few resources are available for professionals to utilize in training peers. This is beginning to change as more people are writing in the field and public funds are being given to develop media to assist in training and awareness of paraprofessionals (e.g. the State of Kentucky and National Institute of Drug Abuse).

Consequently, all indications appear to support the statement that counselors on the job have little training and/ or skills in affective education strategies. Frequent letters containing requests for information and good attendance at workshops on peer helping lead to the conclusion that counselors are becoming aware of the need for change.

Schools also have added crisis counselors whose role is to work with students experiencing crises and to find appropriate interventions for them. The crisis counselors have found that peer helping programs can be utilized to assist these troubled students in recovery and as support.

Some school systems have employed prevention specialists and wellness coordinators to focus on strategies to prevent problems from developing and reduce some at-risk behavior. Those who supervise programs have found that peer programs using service learning, health educators, and small group leaders have been effective in changing at-risk behavior.

The number and kinds of problems at all ages are endless. For example, loneliness, low self-esteem, health issues, violence, different cultures trying to communicate, and declining academic skills are just a few examples of problems that can be helped through a peer helping program. These issues cannot be addressed only by professionals; the professionals must have help—through training others.

Schools must be restructured with definite programs designed for prevention of at-risk behavior (Bernard, 1991, April). Counselors and teachers need to form a collaborative effort to develop peer helping programs. These programs must be infused into the curriculum receiving formal credit. Classrooms need to be centered around students helping students through peer editing, peer tutoring, and peer leadership. Volunteerism needs to be infused into the curriculum by making service learning a part of social studies and other formal disciplines. Students must first be trained, then given an opportunity to help, follow-up supervision, and an opportunity to discuss what they have done.

For peer programs to be effective, teachers and administrators need to be involved in the planning and the implementation. A collaborative approach is needed that involves administrators identifying the needs in the school and how peer programs might meet those needs. For example, if the school has a high incidence of dropouts, then a variety of approaches to reach out to the at-risk students need to be part of the utilization plan for the peer program. Teachers and counselors need to become partners in the program planning and implementation. For example, teachers may teach the basic skills indicated in *Peer Power, Book 1*, and the counselor may be involved in the weekly supervision meeting once the peers have started their projects. At times, team teaching is an exciting way for teachers and counselors to work together. Many schools are moving toward credit for peer programs, so the involvement of central office administrators is critical.

RELIGIOUS COUNSELING

The religious community today must address its own internal problems. Declining church attendance, the advancing age of existing members, and an increasing challenge in keeping members involved and interested in church programs are causing some clergy to look for new ways of approaching people (Olsen, 1974). Religious leadership faces three challenges in attempts to keep churches viable in the community:

1. meeting the pressure of maintaining traditional responsibilities;

2. meeting the increased demand for counseling services; and

3. meeting the increased need for a significant number of people who are competent in human relationships, communication, and other interpersonal concerns. (Olsen, 1974, p. 27)

Traditional religious responsibilities of the clergy have remained constant or have increased, and additional new demands for counseling help often have been added. This additional work load has forced clergy to find new ways to meet the responsibility of this role. In recent years, religious education has trained religious leaders in counseling techniques, increasing their interest in and capacity to assume counseling responsibilities. Even with training, however, priests, pastors, or rabbis cannot hope to meet all the needs of their members. The need has increased to the point that a national organization has been formed (American Association of Pastoral Counselors), which is helping to increase the counseling skills taught to religious leaders.

Another challenge facing religious leaders is the increasing demand by members of the congregation for help in improving their interpersonal relations skills. To meet this challenge, the base church concept is evolving. A major goal of the base church is to establish a system by which people relate more effectively with others and learn better interpersonal relationship skills and attitudes.

Since the base church concept consists of small groups of people in open, face-to-face contact characterized by warmth and intimacy, new skills and leadership training are needed. In order for the implementation of the base church concept to be successful, the leadership must have interpersonal relations skills developed to a high level of facilitation and be able to teach these same skills to members of the base church. Without effective people with these interpersonal relations skills, the base church concept will not satisfy people's needs any better than the traditional religious groups.

Olsen (1974) felt that the base church concept of small group interaction would bring to the surface the same individual "hang-ups," insecurities, frustrations, guilt, and idiosyncrasies exposed by the traditional church struggles, but it would expose them more quickly and more effectively. The combination of a small group format with a desire to know and relate to others on more than a superficial basis creates experiences within the base church that require many people to possess highly developed interpersonal skills. The small group church concept is validly related to religious concerns because members are given the opportunity to experience affective human interaction produced by effective leaders. They often report their experiences as highly meaningful in a religious sense.

Olsen (1974) also maintained that human potential experiences can be effective only if they foster growth in all participants in these experiences. He espoused the extended use of encounter groups, Gestalt concepts, psychodrama, sensory awareness, and all of the strategies employed in teaching for improved affective education. In order to meet the expanded needs of church members to develop better interpersonal relationships, religious leaders would be wise to teach others their own counseling and interpersonal skills.

Also, by establishing training programs for nonprofessionals within the church, the church leaders can make better use of lay leaders in religious education, internal leadership and outreach crisis intervention, tutorial, and other community responsibility programs with a degree of effectiveness not previously possible. Lay leaders often have the desire to improve the basic communication skills and look to their minister, priest, or rabbi for help. If the training is not provided, members can be alienated by the professionals in churches or synagogues, often feel left out, and retaliate by leaving the congregation or reducing their involvement in its activities (Olsen, 1974, p. 36).

Lukens (1983) surveyed 17 programs where systematic training was being delivered at the paraprofessional level. Varenhorst and Sparks (1988) developed a training guide for peer ministers.

A strong movement can be found in all faiths in reference to "peer ministry" and "youth helper" programs. Les Stohl of the Lutheran Church reported that more than 15,000 youths attended conferences centered around these issues. Barbara Varenhorst has done a considerable amount of work using her training model in Peer Ministry.

The *P.F.Q.* has a column devoted to Peer Ministry. Ken Haught has set up the Stephen Ministry series system to train lay ministers in the church to care for other church members under stress.

BUSINESS AND INDUSTRY

With the new fear of drug testing on the job and the loss of productivity as a result of stress and personal problems, business and industry are looking at a variety of methods for dealing with problems relating to such issues as drug and alcohol, stress, attendance, family problems, mid-life transitions and downsizing.

Many companies have established employee assistance programs (EAP). These programs sometimes provide all of the counseling for employees, or the counselor may see the employees once and then refer them to other professionals in the community. In some companies, the EAP counselors are highly trained professionals; in other companies, they are peers who have completed some helping training. Still other companies have peer helpers who work with troubled employees and bring them to the attention of the EAP counselors.

American industry is very competitive, and one way of being competitive is to keep employees emotionally healthy. This, of course, cannot be done only by professional counselors; companies and corporations must rely as well on paraprofessionals for help. One example is the use of peer assistance with flight attendants (Gant, 1992).

EAP professionals and human resource professionals can develop effective peer helping programs to help the employees cope with daily problems, such as substance abuse, loss, family problems, and work stress (Gant, 1992). By training volunteers to become resources to others, peer helpers are assisting people in their daily work lives and preventing problems from mushrooming. Peer helpers also serve as links to the professional community.

PREVENTION SPECIALISTS

Prevention specialists are emerging in the helping field to work in schools and communities. Their role is often to identify the at-risk behaviors the community wants to target and then develop programs to meet the needs of the area. For example, many prevention specialists are involved in reducing substance abuse. They often facilitate TREND activities, which are drug and alcohol abuse prevention activities in the St. Louis area, including volunteer activities, leading others on rope courses, and providing informational materials to students and employees. As Tobler (1986) indicated, the most effective prevention programs use peers. Many prevention specialists are involved in setting up programs or training peer helpers or peer professionals. Prevention specialists' role appears to be shifting from a school base to a community base.

JUVENILE JUSTICE SYSTEMS

Because a large percentage of our adult prisoners also were involved in the juvenile system, many juvenile workers are looking for programs that will be more effective and help youth. The state of Kentucky Youth Services is designing a program to train all of their paraprofessionals in group homes in helping skills. Some systems are developing programs within the institutions to have peers influence others. Fatum (1993) described a program in a prison setting for adolescents.

SELF-HELP GROUPS

Self-help groups have been shown to be very effective in helping people maintain healthier behavior and cope with stressful life events. Many of the lay leaders are now receiving training to be more effective as leaders.

OTHER COMMUNITY AGENCIES

The paraprofessional concept has received acceptance and provided impetus in community agencies that are concerned with people in trouble. Illustrations of such agencies are crisis centers, drop-in centers, and teen centers. Gartner and Riessman (1974, 253-254) identified five major reasons for the development of nonprofessional helpers:

1. the consumer previously was not served adequately by people who could understand his or her problem;

2. the poor were locked out of achieving professional skills by the usual paths;

3. nonprofessionals filled a gap between professionals and the complaining public;

4. jobs were needed that government agencies could provide; and

5. delivery of services, especially to the poor, was lacking.

As a result of these needs and conditions in the community, there was a rush to provide nonprofessional services in many counseling roles. As the need to fill the void created by an insufficient number of professionally trained counselors became apparent, attempts were made to train nonprofessional or paraprofessional staff. Traditional counselor training institutions were unable to provide adequate help. Emphasis in training has been, and still is, directed mainly toward training professionals. To date, the facilities and procedures for teaching nonprofessionals have been inadequate. Programs to train nonprofessional counselors have focused typically on academic and theoretical understanding rather than on the skills needed to facilitate client change (Brown, 1974). Because the demand for helping agencies is so great and the technology to train lay helpers so meager, the results often are frustrating, damaging, and ineffective.

The gap between the great demand for help and the deficient quality of training procedures emphasizes the need for methods and processes that can be given to staff members for training nonprofessionals in workable helping communication skills and attitudes. When training methods are available and staff members are trained adequately, the result can be a vital program of peer helpers.

Bridgeton, MO, provides an example of a teen center that struggled for several years until it was staffed by a person who had received adequate training in helping skills and additional trainer skills. The staff member proceeded to develop a program in which peers were trained on a continuing basis, and the center has functioned as a social teen center—a center where peers can help their contemporaries with problems and concerns. Programs such as this can serve as models for adolescent centers in which both social needs and interpersonal needs are met. Other community service groups such as Boy Scouts, Girl Scouts, Girls Inc. (1991), and Big Brothers-Big Sisters of America could expand their effectiveness if individuals within these organizations were to have the necessary peer counseling training and experience to meet the needs of those who seek help.

One of the problems facing the leadership in community social action groups is faced similarly by school counselors; that is, an incapacity to keep abreast of the changing human service scene. The result of this failing is that the scope of their creativity is limited to the traditionally described counselor role. The face of the country is changing, and helpers must either adapt to that change or see their impact severely diminished.

An effective way to accomplish these changes is to accept the premise that counseling skills should not be kept secret but rather should be given away. Counselors are in a most advantageous position to distribute these skills.

Peer helping, therefore, becomes an important concomitant to the educational goals not only of schools but also of other helping community agencies. The training of peers in basic communication skills can contribute greatly to improving the impact of interpersonal relationships on the entire community.

In looking for research to support the upgrading and dissemination of peer helping skills, an important procedure is to look at research that offers a variety of techniques, such as pre-help and post-help testing, comparison groups, objective and self-report, and subjective evaluation.

If you are in need of a more complete bibliography, you may want to write to

Dr. Rey Carr
Director of Peer Counseling Project
University of Victoria
Victoria, British Columbia, VBW 2Y2.
Canada

He has compiled a bibliography entitled *Peer Counseling: An Annotated and Indexed Bibliography* (1992). Order from

4452 Houlihan Court
Victoria, British Columbia, V8N 6C6
Canada

Leadership:

Empowering

through Communication

Chapter V

BRINGING YOU UP TO DATE: RECENT STUDIES IN PEER HELPING

This chapter is not meant to be a review of the peer helping literature; rather, it is to provide some evaluation examples and support for peer helping in various settings such as schools, agencies, hospitals, prisons, businesses, and various populations and settings. Some research for training will be reported on. Hopefully this chapter, along with Chapter III, "Why Peer Helping Now," will assist you as you begin to formulate your thinking about your own program and to convince others of its importance.

Evaluation of peer programs can occur in a variety of ways. Most programs provide some summative manner of what happened. This is often a description of what has happened. As a peer helping professional, an important aspect is for you to know if what you hoped would happen actually did happen. Some evaluation programs also are designed as research studies.

Some of the research techniques commonly used are pretest-posttest method, comparison group method, and self-report. The pretest-posttest method examines the same population before the treatment and after the treatment. Some of this evaluation can be long-term. The comparison group method will compare a treatment group and a control group and is said to be the best type of research. The self-report is a simple reporting of results of a questionnaire or narrative reports from helpers, helpees, or those in charge.

DESCRIPTION OF PEER HELPING PROGRAM

Decision makers need to understand that the first person to whom someone would go with a problem would be a peer or slightly older peer. This is demonstrated in research studies. Next, it is important to let the decision maker know what kind of program you have. Guilford County School System in Greensborough, NC, decided to expand their peer helping programs in 25 of their elementary schools and 15 secondary schools. In a single semester, they were able to have programs in all of their schools. The programs were either peer assistants who worked with new students or peer tutors and peer counselors who did one-on-one listening or group work and peer mediation (Bishop, 1992). A simple report was prepared consisting of X's indicating the type of programs available at the beginning and at the end of the year.

Another type of reporting is the number of students served. For example, Sachnoff (1992) reported in summary form, as shown in Figure 5.1, the number trained and number served.

San Francisco Peer Resource Programs
Student Services
1991-1992

Peer Counseling
    Peer Counselors Trained 555
    Students Counseled   1,069
    Counseling Sessions   2,379
    Students Served through
        Conflict Mediation 465

Peer Education
    Number of Presentations 444
    Students served   19,970

Peer Tutoring
    Peer Tutors Trained   654
    Tutees Served 1,519
    Tutoring Sessions 21,483

Students Trained

More than 1,000 Peer Helpers were trained to provide services for peers in 40 San Francisco Schools.

Figure 5.1. Number trained and number served in San Francisco Peer Resource Program.

The summary contained in Figure 5.1 is the minimal kind of data that needs to be collected in a program. It is important to plan so that you can collect data to provide support for your program. The following are some commonly used techniques for gathering, analyzing, and reporting data that reflect your results.

RESEARCH TECHNIQUES USED

Pretest-Posttest Method

Rapp, Dworkin, and Moss (1978) reported the effects on peer helpers of a middle school peer program. The researchers' findings indicated there was no decline in the academic performance of peer helpers, nor was there any increase in their self-concept or positive attitudes toward school. Bowman and Myrick (1980) described a peer program with students in grades 3 through 6 who were trained to be "junior counselors." All peer helpers showed positive gains in self-concept when pre- and post-evaluations were analyzed.

A peer facilitator program in a rural junior high school was reported by Garner, Martin, and Martin (1989). The program was called Peer Assistance Leaders (PALS). The program was designed to model and teach coping and communications skills. PALS were selected from seventh graders, and group members were sixth-grade volunteers. PALS completed a 13-session training program that used videotaped feedback for empowering/reinforcing behaviors. The program included exercises in helping behaviors, attending behaviors, and empathy skills. Grade point averages and behavioral classroom ratings improved for both PALS and group participants.

A peer helping program was initiated in India at the college level. The peer helpers' learned skills were evaluated with a pretest and posttest index of communication developed along the lines of Carkhuff's (1969) "standard helpee" method, a self-concept inventory by Sharma, and Carkhuff's Facilitative Interpersonal Functioning (1969) to evaluate learned skills. The peer helpers produced a significant improvement in overall counseling skills and some improvement in individual skills (Vijayalakshmi & Mythili, 1985).

Robinson, Morrow, Kigin, and Lindeman (1991) reported a high school program that stressed personal growth, acceptance of diversity, self-assessment, and microcounseling skills. They found that the peer counselors who participated in Year 1 training significantly improved their ability to recognize and produce effective counseling responses from pretest to posttest.

Thompson (1986) described implementation of a high school-level peer-group facilitator program consisting of a heterogeneous group of representatives of the student body. Seventeen group facilitators were trained to help others as effective leaders, peer group listeners, and positive role models. Measures of dogmatism and self-concept taken at the beginning and end of the five-month program suggested that the peer group facilitators tended to become less dogmatic, were more open to new ideas, and felt more adequate as persons.

Comparison Group Method

Several good studies utilizing group methods show comparison of peer helping to no peer helping.

Reardon (1991) examined the effectiveness of peer counseling on high school students who failed two or more classes in a nine-week quarter and received peer counseling, and students who failed two or more classes and did not receive peer counseling. Additionally, the effects of peer counseling on individuals of varying grades and numbers of failed courses were investigated using a pretest-posttest matched group experimental design. The results indicated a significant difference in grade point average (GPA) between those students who received peer counseling and those who did not. Nine weeks after peer counseling was terminated, the GPAs for the counseled students were still significantly higher than the GPAs of students who did not receive peer counseling. Dropouts also were examined. The findings from the researcher's study show that 2% dropped out of school from the counseled experimental group compared to 11% from the noncounseled control group. Thus, the intervention of peer counseling appears to be the significant variable for the students who stayed in school.

In another study, Sprinthall et al. (1992) evaluated ego development based on cognitive developmental concepts, particularly those of Loevinger (1976). Loevinger's theory suggests that ego- or self-awareness may proceed in a stage and sequence framework through levels of psychological differentiation and integration. It was the view of the researchers that a group of high school students who served as peer helpers could be effective in helping middle school students deal with the disruption caused by divorce in the family. It also was felt that such cross-age relationships would help reinforce responsibility and maturity in high school students.

The study included two experimental groups of high school peer counselors and one control group. The groups were assessed on a pretest-posttest basis with an 18 item version of the *Loevinger Sentence Completion Test* (Loevinger, Wessler, & Redmore, 1970), which measures ego development. The high school students also were given the *Rest Defining Issues Test* (Rest, 1986), which measures levels of principled reasoning. Middle school students were assessed on a pretest-posttest basis with the 18-item Loevinger Test and the *Nowicki-Strickland Locus of Control Scale* (Norwicki & Strickland, 1973). No comparison group was utilized for middle school students in the divorce-disruption group. High school students took a one semester course in peer helping, using Tindall's *Peer Power, Book 1: Becoming an Effective Peer Helper and Conflict Mediator* for basic peer helping skills and *Changing Family* (Ciborowski, 1984) and other video material. The second semester, the high school students met with middle school students twice a week for discussion. The high school students continued to meet with the instructors each week for reflection, discussion, and planning.

The high school students made significant gains on ego development. Characteristics of self-awareness and problem-solving ability at that level include an increase in interpersonal awareness and individuality, greater psychological causation, and the gradual internalization of standards for mature judgment.

For middle school students the development was away from self-protectiveness and seeing obedience and conformity as absolutes, and toward some individuality, a rudimentary inner life psychologically, and a greater awareness of self in relationship to others. Also, the increase in locus of control toward the self and away from other-directedness complemented the change in ego-stage level. Taken as a whole, these empirical results support the developmental goals of the program for both high school students and middle school students.

In addition to empirical data, excerpts from student journals added qualitative information about the program. High school students tended to focus their discussions, especially in the training sessions, on themselves and some of their own personal agendas. By the second semester, some broadening of perspective was taking place along with more willingness to think and feel about what middle school students were experiencing. The excerpts from journals of middle school students reveal their positive feelings about the process and some commentary about an increase in self-awareness. These themes tend to confirm the changes documented through the empirical measures.

This is a significant piece of research in that it clearly demonstrates that appropriate training and follow-up can produce help not only for the peer helper but also the helpee. The role of the school counselor is shown as increased in effectiveness by becoming a consultant rather than direct service.

The effectiveness of support group leadership led by professional staff and an experimental group led by peer-led self-help were compared in a study of two ambulatory alcoholism treatment programs. The patients were evaluated over the course of one year. Data collected with a patient status form and a clinical assessment instrument applied monthly indicate that the peer-led patients scored significantly higher on social adjustment, although retention of learning, drinking rates and utilization of A.A. were no different from the professionally led group (Galanter, Castaneda, & Salamon, 1987).

Henriksen (1991) described the implementation of a peer helping program composed of 22 Canadian ninth graders. The program, which ran for one semester, was designed to train selected students in basic helping skills and to promote students' self-confidence, communication skills, and problem-solving and decision-making abilities. Helping tasks, tutoring, and designing instructional materials also were included. Evaluation of the program included pre- and post-training surveys of the trainees and an untrained comparison group as well as surveys of parents, teaching staff, and student body. Results show that the program had a positive effect on both the helpers and the school.

In a college setting, 146 undergraduates interested in helping others were assigned to peer helping (counseling) or control groups. The peer helping group participated in a peer helper skills training program, while the control group did not. All groups were assessed on their effectiveness in peer helping and completed the *Sixteen Personality Factor Questionnaire* (16 PF) and a self-ideal disparity scale. The peer helping group improved significantly in skills. Comparisons between pretest, posttest, and follow-up tests of peer helping and control groups yielded similar results, but positive self-concept changes that were not evident at the time of posttest emerged in the follow-up testing for the counseling group. The mean score on the relation of self to ideal-self scale increased significantly, while self-ideal disparity decreased. This appears to support the fact that self-esteem does not increase simply through training. The peer helpers must be able to put their skills into action for the changes in self-esteem to take place (Vijayalakshmi, Mythili, Rao, & Krishna, 1986).

Booth (1990) reported a peer model for treating shyness in college students. He assigned 38 shy college students (ages 18 to 49) to one of two treatment groups or a waiting-list control group. Four female peer counselors trained to understand and teach basic social skills to their shy peers were assigned to the treatment groups. Results show that the trained peers influenced the level of shyness of shy students downward in a short time, using a social skills intervention model.

Bowman (1982) examined the effects of helping projects on fifth grade student helpers in nine elementary schools. No significant differences (.05) were found in the peer helpers in terms of self-concept or attitudes toward others. Significant differences (.05), however, were found in the problem-behavior students for improved classroom behavior and school attitudes.

Tindall (1978) assessed the effect of training versus nontraining on high school students' ability to function as peer facilitators in an individual setting. The control group consisted of five students at a high school working in an office; the experimental group consisted of eight students serving in a peer helper role at a high school. Two expert judges rated the experimental (trained) students significantly higher as individual helpers than the control (untrained) students on both the 15-minute taped interview (p < .007) and the written *Communication Index* (CI) (Carkhuff, 1969) (p < .002). Interrater reliability among the expert judges was found to be .76 for the taped interview and .80 for the written index.

Cooker and Cherchia (1976) conducted a study to ascertain the effects of training versus nontraining of peer leaders in a high school setting. They looked at the effect of training on the peers' ability to function as facilitators in a group setting with fellow students as participants. They also looked at the effect of communication skills training on the subject's level of facilitative communication. They selected the control and experimental groups from 60 students (28 male, 32 female) attending an Oxford, MS, high school. The participants were chosen by a faculty-student committee to be trained as group facilitators. Selection was made with the intent to represent a cross-section of the student body. The committee selected students for their leadership ability among fellow students; their ability to recognize and to influence others was seen as important in terms of leadership. Upon completion of training, each facilitator was expected to lead discussion groups of 10 to 12 fellow students randomly assigned from the remainder of the student body of 625 pupils. This was initiated to make peer groups an integrated part of local drug education programs. The intent was to give students an opportunity to participate in small group discussions in which students held the responsibility for content and direction. A 40-20 split was used so that a substantial number of trained facilitators would be available for the next school year. Those selected for the experimental treatments were assigned randomly to one of five training groups of eight students each. Each group met with a trainer for a total of eight hours, one hour a week over an eight-week period.

The CI was used, as was a 15-minute taped interview with a coached client who presented a standard situation. Both the written and taped responses were rated by two counselors familiar with the scales.

Cooker and Cherchia (1976) found a significant difference in the means of the posttest scores on the CI and interviews. The CI scores yielded a significant difference between groups, $F(1,59)=41.42$, $p < .05$; and the taped interviews, a significance at $F(1,59)=36.54$, $p < .05$. The researchers also found that in both the CI scores and the interviews the trained students in the role of group facilitator were rated significantly higher than untrained students. The expert judges' ratings were $F(1,59)=36.54$, $p < .05$; and peer ratings were $F(1,59)=6.71$, $p < .05$. This indicates that trained students functioned at higher levels in facilitating small groups than did untrained students. The real significance of this study is revealed in the finding that training peer helpers is more desirable and productive than not training them. The assumption that existing leadership skills or qualities are sufficient for adequate peer helping may thus be invalid. It appears that professional helpers need to spend some of their time disseminating their skills by training others.

Examples of other studies using comparison groups to research different counseling methods are the following: with disruptive youths (Creange, 1982; Bowman & Myrick, 1980), changes in behavior (Boan & Myrick, 1987; Lobitz, 1970; Samuels & Samuels, 1975; Vriend, 1969), and different training methods (Allbee, 1976; Gray & Tindall, 1974).

Self-report

Gumaer (1976) used the Likert-type scale in his self-report study. His findings suggested that both the peer helpers and those students with whom they worked had positive attitudes toward the peer-helper experience and believed it should be a part of every school.

Tindall (1978) reported results using the *Youth Listener Evaluation Survey*, which was given to a random sample of students, grades 10 through 12, as part of the *Guidance Evaluation Survey*. The items and data obtained are shown in Figure 5.2.

PLEASE ANSWER THE FOLLOWING

A. Have you ever heard of this program?   Yes   84%   No   16%

B. Do you think that there is a need for this program?   Yes   83%   No   17%

C. Have you ever talked with a Youth Listener about a personal concern of yours?   Yes   13%   No   87%

(IF YOU CHECKED YES, PLEASE ANSWER THE QUESTIONS BELOW)

1. How did you feel after talking to the Youth Listener?

1	2	3	4	5
Somewhat Worse		Better		Much Better
6%	4%	11%	43%	36%

2. Rate how well the Youth Listener listened.

1	2	3	4	5
Did Not Listen		Listened Halfway		Listened Well
4%	2%	6%	23%	65%

3. How would you rate the outcome of your problem after talking with the Youth Listener?

1	2	3	4	5
Things Got Worse		Nothing Changed		Things Got Better
3%	—	16%	40%	41%

4. Would you feel comfortable talking to a Youth Listener again?

Yes	No	Unsure
88%	9%	3%

Figure 5.2. Items and data obtained on survey of students in grades 10 through 12.

Varenhorst (1987) reported on a study done by Edge in which Edge randomly chose 133 students in grades 7 through 11 to respond to a questionnaire. Of this group, 80% said that they would consider friends as being likely individuals to help them with problems, while 36% indicated that they were unsure about the adequacy of the Fulton Peer Counseling Program in training students to assist others, and 47% were unsure of the methods by which they could contact a peer counselor. However, 14% indicated that they talked over a problem with a person whom they knew was a peer counselor.

Additional studies include Hamburg and Varenhorst (1972) and Hensley and Mickelson (1978).

Summary of Research

There is always room for more controlled studies. We still need much research on longitudinal work. We also need research on various training materials. Many authors have written about peer helping. Sobey (1970) wrote about lay helpers; Eisdorfer and Golann (1969) referred to the concept as the "New Professional"; Tindall and Gray developed the book *Peer Counseling* (first edition in 1978) for training peer counselors. It has been revised three times. The American School Counselors Association (See Chapter 12) has developed a position statement on peer counseling. National Peer Helpers Association has developed the Standards for Peer Helping (Chapter 12). Akita and Mooney (1982); Foster (1992); Goldstein, Reagles, and Amann (1990); Hazouri and Smith (1991); Keboyan (1992); McLaughlin and Hazouri (1992); Myrick and Bowman (1981); Myrick and Folk (1991); Myrick and Sorenson (1992); Painter (1989); Samuels and Samuels (1975); Schrumpf, Crawford, and Usadel (1991); Scott (1985); Tindall and Salmon-White (1990); Turney (1988); Varenhorst and Sparks (1988); and Waas (1991) have written books concerning peer training.

As the peer helper movement has gained momentum, more presentations on this topic appear on programs at the state and national conferences each year. March 1983 saw creation of a periodical devoted entirely to peer helper programs— *Peer Facilitator Quarterly*, which is the official publication of the National Peer Helpers Association. More than twenty states have official peer helping associations. It appears that peer helping has grown from a small beginning in the late 1960's to what is now a recognized, viable way of helping others.

TRAINING PEER HELPERS

Perhaps the most critical component in any peer helper program is training. The procedures chosen to train peer helpers can make a difference between a successful program and an unsuccessful one. Many peer programs were launched in the 1970's, but those that lacked planning and organization soon floundered. In others, however, the planners ensured success and support for their program by being more systematic in their approach, defining the training programs in detail, and carefully selecting the peer projects and tasks (Myrick & Bowman, 1981).

A growing body of research contains information to indicate that a more systematic approach to teaching helping skills will lead to more successful interventions (Allbee, 1976; Bowman & Myrick, 1980; Briskin & Anderson, 1973; Cooker & Cherchia,

1976; Foster, 1991; Kum & Gal, 1976; McCann, 1975; Sprinthall & Blum, 1980; Tindall, 1978). Gains in self-esteem, classroom behavior, and academic achievement are reported for peer helpers and their helpees in programs that have fully defined goals and objectives of training (Myrick & Bowman, 1981).

Foster (1991) conducted a study in which she was trying to examine the questions, "can students' emotional development be increased through a peer tutoring experience, and are there differences in the amount of development based on the length of training?" She conducted the research at the elementary school level. Thirty-four fifth graders were trained as peer tutors for students in kindergarten through third grade. The 34 fifth graders were divided into three randomly assigned groups for purposes of comparing different training periods. The first experimental group participated in a 20-hour, six-week tutor training experience followed by a four-week peer tutoring experience. The second experimental group participated in a 10-hour, three-week peer tutor training experience followed by a four-week peer tutoring experience. The third group, the control group, received no training at all, but the members did have the opportunity to participate in the peer tutoring experience. The length of tutoring was the same for all three groups and occurred simultaneously, which helped to focus on the training as the variable that made the significant difference in the growth rate of the different tutors.

The aim was to create a program with a developmental perspective on supportive role-theory in an attempt to increase emotional development as one means of changing behavior. Changed behavior would be demonstrated through improved role relationships, emotional reactions/actions, and moral development. Results of the study were greatly satisfying in that those students who received the longer training made the greatest gains in emotional development. The second group made the second greatest gains, and the control group gained the least. It was determined that the six weeks of training for fifth graders yielded greater emotional growth than three weeks of training. The peer tutors moved from an appearance of insecurity and anxiousness in the first week of experience to an air of calmness, understanding, and eagerness by their third week.

The results indicated that the training sessions need to last at least 30 minutes because any less time reduces opportunities for all members to participate adequately and process lessons. Fifth graders have a need for specific guidelines and expectations. Lessons need to be presented in concrete ways with a variety of strategies used to present each lesson, and time for skill practice must be provided. Routine sessions for reflection must be planned, and all activities must be supervised. Students need to have contact with their tutees at least three days a week with one day of processing with guided reflection. With this systematic structuring, successful experiences are most likely to occur.

In the past, others have compared three different training models (Allbee, 1976) demonstrating significant differences among two structured training groups and one group with no training. Another training model has been presented by Zwibelman (1977), who used basically didactic and experiential aspects in a model consisting of three distinct elements: (1) a therapeutic contact with a high-functioning trainer, (2) a highly controlled program of techniques, and (3) a group experience in which the trainee is allowed to integrate personal values into the program.

A peer counseling program instituted by Hamburg and Varenhorst (1972) consisted of training through didactic instruction and practice through role-playing. Although they found personal growth of the trained students, it was not related to the effectiveness in the training. Studies that measured the changes in the skill levels of facilitative behaviors (Gray & Tindall, 1974; Truax & Carkhuff, 1967) support the hypothesis that individuals can change their behavior through using interpersonal skills and, as a result, can improve in growth-producing behaviors.

Training also must include practice in activities that peer helpers will perform. For example, a teen telephone line was implemented in Ohio in which the majority (96%) of the phone calls dealt with common, less urgent adolescent issues, such as peer relationships, family dynamics, and the need to have someone with whom to talk. The training involved special training in telephone hot lines (Boehm, Chessare, Volko, & Sager, 1991).

Apparently, an important aspect of training peer helpers is to use a model structured in listening skills as opposed to nontraining or simply using personal growth and group counseling activities. If the goal is self-concept developmental and personal growth, perhaps the group experience should be called "group counseling" or "building self-esteem" rather than peer helping training. This is supported by Gray and Tindall (1974) and Vijayalakshmi, Mythili, Rao, and Krishna (1986). This is not to say that personal growth does not take place with peer helping training, but the weight of evidence indicates that typically peer helpers change behaviors and attitudes based on the goals of the training or group experience.

Looking at those outcomes subjectively, researchers have concluded that changes in behavior are taking place, and the probability is evident that the training of the peer counselors has influenced those changes. The subjective and objective results of the studies that have been completed to date support the conclusion that beneficial effects occur when peer helping is used.

Next, I would like to turn to studies that show how peer helpers have been used in a variety of settings and systems.

PROGRAMS IN DIFFERENT SETTINGS

Peer programs have been in schools for over 25 years. At first, they were used as adjuncts to the counseling programs and later used for prevention purposes and tutoring purposes. The author found that programs flourish at the elementary, middle, and high school levels and in higher education. They also are beginning to have an impact with specific populations such as the elderly, disabled, mentally ill, hospital patients, prisoners, veterans, parents, and business people.

College Level

By far, the largest number of studies dealing with peer helping have been conducted at the college level. Buck and Pineda (1985), Frisz and Lane (1987), Holly (1987), Locke and Zimmerman (1987), and Ware and Gold (1971) used peer group counselors to help students with academic problems. Miller (1989) described a program at Colorado State University designed to improve racial and cultural understanding.

Russel and Thompson (1987) evaluated the effectiveness of a peer helping program using comparative data from no-contact (they were not contacted by peer helpers), home, and university resident hall student groups. Results indicate a significant difference among the groups in viewing the university as a personal place and in campus involvement.

Rice (1991) tried to establish an intervention program for older-than-average college students in which peer helpers made telephone contact with students during the 2nd, 6th, and 14th weeks of the fall term. Calls addressed concerns such as registration, academic progress, and advisement. Helpers provided information, assistance, and referrals. From fall to spring, student response showed a 20% increase in retention, 29% increase in GPA, and 12% decrease in withdrawals compared to the previous year.

One college focused on trying to increase utilization of the university counseling center by minorities. Through the use of a peer helping program, minority contact increased by 350% (Mack, 1989).

Kirkley, Battaglia, Earle, and Gans (1988) discussed the development of a peer-led education group for bulimics at a major university. The experience suggests that a health education group providing a credible alternative to strict dieting and binge eating is a valuable component in campus bulimia treatment programs. Sesan (1988-89) reported a program in which peer educators were used to refer the more serious cases of eating-disordered clients to the counseling center.

The Job Corp in St. Louis also is establishing peer helping programs to work with new students to assist with conflict mediation in the dorms and to provide tutoring.

Toepfer (1991) described a summary of higher education programs in which peer helpers were utilized as resident assistants, as coordinators of orientation programs for new students, as academic advisers, and as involvers in learning skills programs, health programs, and special issues concerning women issues, cross-cultural concerns, and assistance for disabled students.

The *HELP (Higher Education Leaders/Peers)* (Roper, 1991) network was established to help support and provide assistance to colleges wanting to start peer programs. A notebook was developed for groups wanting to start programs. The notebook includes samples of model programs and articles about peer helping. The HELP network is supported by the Network of Colleges and Universities Committed to the Elimination of Drug and Alcohol Abuse, U.S. Department of Education, 55 New Jersey Ave., N.W., Washington, DC 20208-5644.

High School

Cary (1989) compared 102 ninth to twelfth graders who had received peer helping with 236 ninth to twelfth graders in two control groups to examine the impact of the peer helping program on stress and social support. An adolescent family inventory of life events and a social support instrument were administered. Analysis found significant differences between the helped group means and both control group means on the social support scales. Posttests were given to the groups five months later. Analysis found significant differences between the pretest and posttest means in the helped group on measures of stress and found a decrease in one control group on measures of social support. Thus, peer helping had a positive effect on the promotion of healthy development in the people who experienced the peer helping programs.

High school athletes were used as peer educators and role models in a four-day drug prevention seminar. The athletes presented prevention activities to junior high and elementary students. The program also served as an early intervention for the athletes themselves (Palmer, Davis, Sher, & Hicks, 1989).

Past studies have supported the effectiveness of peer helping programs at the secondary level (Diver-Stamnes, 1991; Greenwood, Terry, Arrega-Mayer, & Finney, 1992; Morey, Miller, Rosen, & Fulton, 1993). All reported significant changes in academic, social, and personal areas of student concerns. Newman (1985) discussed the use of peer counselors to reduce multicultural issues. Murphy (1975) showed the effects of peer group counseling on chronically absent sophomores on the variables of attendance, achievement, and behavior. Boan and Myrick (1987) and Samuels and Samuels (1975) showed effects of peer helping on disruptive behavior. Gray and Tindall (1974) claimed that highly significant changes occurred in levels of helping skills when participants in new programs were compared with those in control groups. They also found significant changes in the academic behaviors of their "clients." Teachers reported improved grades for peer helpers as well as increased effectiveness and maturity in class. Leadership roles increased markedly, although the increase was not tested statistically.

Creange (1982) compared the effects of individual and peer group helping on a sample of disruptive high school students. The measuring instruments were attendance, grade point average, incidence of disruptive behavior, and self-concept as measured by the *Tennessee Self-Concept Scale* (TSCS). A sample of 24 disruptive students had been selected randomly at each of four high schools for a total of 96 students; each sample was then divided into three subgroups. One group received weekly individual professional counseling; a second group received peer group counseling; and the third group, which served as the control, received the minimal help usually provided by the schools. Attendance, grade point average, incidence of disruptive behavior, and the TSCS scale were given both before and after the 10-week duration of the study.

The results of the study were that over a 10-week period, individual counseling sessions by credentialed counselors with disruptive students yielded data that indicated this type of intervention had improved the attendance of female students. Peer group helping, individual professional counseling, and routine counseling sessions with disruptive students over a 10-week period yielded data that indicated that all three of these types of intervention reduced the disruptive behavior of these students.

Neither individual counseling, nor peer group helping, nor routine counseling sessions significantly affected school achievement by disruptive students as measured by grade point average. Neither individual counseling, nor peer group counseling sessions affected significantly self-concept as measured by the TSCA. In the area of attendance, high school girls appeared to have been more receptive to particular counseling strategies than did high school boys.

Middle/Junior High School Programs

A peer helping program in a middle/junior high school needs to be structured for students of that age. Such a program took place at Pattonville Heights Junior High School, Maryland Heights, MO, where Judy Tindall was counselor and George Cavanaugh was principal from 1970 to 1975. Training for the program involved basic skills in training and advanced skill training. A description of the program and a specific evaluation of it follow.

Program Description. The first step was to inform teachers and administrators who would be affected by giving them a description of the program. Then the other steps outlined in this book were followed. The program and its outcomes are presented to illustrate a peer helping program in action.

Summary Report to the Faculty. The Communication-Leadership training program at Pattonville Heights Junior High was a productive program organized to assure complete skill training, utilization of skills learned, and comprehensive evaluation of effectiveness. In the fall of 1974, 39 ninth-grade students completed 20 sessions of training as part of the "Youth and Understanding" English course, a course designed to enhance communication and insight in young adolescents. The students were given the choice of Communication-Leadership training or regular English curriculum.

The Communication-Leadership Training Program, the term used at Pattonville Heights Junior High instead of Peer Helping Training Program, used the guidance office as the physical facility for the training sessions. A "rap room" adjacent to the guidance area provided a relaxed atmosphere in which to conduct the training sessions. The sessions' format included an introduction and explanation of each skill, followed by modeling the behavior involved in performing the skill, and then followed by practice sessions with feedback from fellow trainees. Time was allotted so that each student could practice the skill and receive feedback on his/her performance of the skill. By designing practice sessions as part of the training, each student had the opportunity to become competent in the skill and to receive helpful feedback in a non-risk situation. Conceptual and practical implementation of certain skills comprised the course in communication skills.

Each session, or at least every other session, introduced a particular skill and allowed time for practice. Rating by students of their own performance provided feedback to them as well as measuring group progress. The skills introduced included the following:

1. attending,
2. empathy,
3. summarizing,
4. questioning,
5. genuineness,
6. confrontation, and
7. problem solving.

(Note: The assertiveness skill as a separate skill has been added since the study reported here was conducted.)

Practice in leading discussion groups and learning the "Vocational Exploration Group Process" were included toward the end of the program. Audio and videotaping were utilized in the training.

Following the basic training, the leaders (peer helpers) served as "rap" leaders in seventh-grade English classes and ninth-grade Career Awareness classes.

Evaluation of communication skills leadership training included five ratings:

1. Change in the values continuum of seventh-grade students as shown by comparison of pretest and posttest results obtained from students.

2. Leaders (peer helpers) evaluated themselves after each seventh-grade discussion session and indicated skills which they used.

3. English teachers evaluated the leaders (peer helpers) in terms of similar criteria at the conclusion of the seventh-grade "rap" sessions.

4. Students (helpees) in the seventh grade made a subjective evaluation of their group leaders' skills after the completion of "rap" sessions.

5. Students (helpees) in the ninth-grade Career Awareness unit made a subjective evaluation of their group leaders' (peer counselors') skills after the completion of the Vocational Exploration Group Experience.

Seventh-grade "Rap" Groups. Following the training, the peer helpers led small "rap" groups of seventh graders in the students' English classes. Eight teachers organized class schedules to allow 30 minutes once a week during which seventh graders could participate voluntarily in discussions. Each peer helper was provided with a series of activities, primarily values games, that could be used as the basis of discussion. The leader had the prerogative of initiating the values games or spending the 30 minutes in other discussion.

About 250 students in the seventh grade participated in the program that involved the 39 peer helpers.

Change of Values Continuum of Seventh-grade Participants. A measure of effectiveness of the discussion materials and peer helper-led groups included a values continuum as a pretest and posttest for group activities. A random sample was selected of 20 students to determine changes, if any, on the Values Continuum. See Appendix A for Positive Values Continuum.

Discussion. Peer helpers leading value clarification discussion groups at the seventh-grade level were able to bring about changes in three areas. One was to affect the values of the students with whom they worked as evidenced by changes the students made in responding to pretest and posttest questionnaires designed to identify values. These changes as reported occurred in the frequency students listed "important" as opposed to "sometimes important" when responding to the values continuum exercise. A second change occurred in the way students perceived their own behavior more accurately as a result of the peer helper-led discussion groups. A third change was that students' responses moved from both extremes to the middle in terms of how students thought that others viewed their behavior or ability. When viewing the data on the three changes, the trainer concluded that the changed responses indicated a movement toward a more realistic self-evaluation, a clearer conception of one's behavior, and how that behavior was viewed by others.

Leaders' Self-evaluation of Seventh-grade "Rap" Group. The rap leaders who were required to fill out the self-evaluation form reported that they used the skills taught to varying degrees. In particular, attending, empathy, summarizing, questioning, genuineness, confrontation, and problem solving were all used frequently and relied upon by these leaders. Confrontation and problem-solving skills, both of which required more active commitment on the part of the leader, were used often but not predominantly.

In general, skills that required initiation on the part of the leader were used less frequently, and skills involving listening were used more frequently. This condition was congruent with the goal of the "rap" groups; that is, to have ninth-grade leaders serve as a sounding board. In future training, initiating skill may need more stress and practice.

Seventh-grade Teacher's Evaluation of Communication Skills. Teachers rated leaders individually upon completion of the seventh-grade "rap" sessions. The leaders' (peer helpers') use of skills as viewed by the teacher can be used in comparison to the students' own evaluations. Comparisons made in attending, empathy, genuineness, and problem-solving skills revealed two distinct notions: (1) teachers, overall, responded favorably to the "rap" leaders as did the "rap" leaders to themselves; and (2) teachers' evaluations and students' self-evaluations compared almost identically in rating and in the number of skills used. The students on self-evaluation who used these skills and rated high the number of times the skills were used were given higher ratings by the teachers. (See Appendix B for samples of evaluation forms used by students and teachers.)

Teachers' evaluations were similar to the evaluations of the peer helpers in skills used. Skills observed most often by teachers and students were empathy, attending, and genuineness. Problem-solving skill, although not rated low by the teacher, was, nevertheless, observed less frequently. This report was consistent with the self-report of the peer helpers. As a result of the two evaluations, the following conclusions were made regarding future training procedures:

1. More stress on skills of problem solving, questioning, and confrontation is needed.

2. Teachers need to reinforce students more frequently when they use these skills effectively.

3. Teachers indicated more assertion skills such as punctuality, regularity of attendance, and keeping the group on task needed additional attention in training.

Discipline Referrals for Seventh-grade Students at Pattonville Heights. A study was made of seventh-grade discipline referrals to the principal. Two comparisons were made. The first comparison was from the seventh-grade classes participating in the "rap" groups as compared to other classes. The second comparison was between student discipline referrals first and third quarters (first and third nine-week periods of the school year) when the "rap" groups were not being held, and referrals second and fourth quarters (second and fourth nine-week periods) when the "rap" groups were being held. Two conclusions were drawn from the data. One, as the year progressed, more total discipline referrals were made, but those classes in the "rap" program reduced discipline referrals to a minimum. Two, during the second quarter the discipline referrals increased in the participating classes, whereas the discipline referrals fourth quarter decreased rather markedly. One factor contributing to the results as expressed by trainers and cooperating teachers was that fourth quarter leaders were better trained. The second and fourth quarters represent times when the ninth-grade "rap" leaders led groups in the seventh-grade classrooms.

Implications. Possibly, teachers of seventh-grade classes that participated in the program did try to handle their own discipline problems, or possibly the small group experience enabled seventh graders to experience group cooperation and discussion skills. As a result, class members were able to express themselves openly with their peers, thus reducing behavior that caused discipline referrals.

Ninth-grade Student Participant Evaluation. Peer helpers also worked with the ninth graders on a career awareness group. About 250 ninth-grade students were taken through two days of the Vocational Exploration Group Experience. The class was divided into groups of five students each with a "rap" leader. The ninth-grade students answered questions more directly pertaining to the leaders. (See Appendix D for sample of complete questionnaire.) In almost all cases, the rap leaders were rated high by the ninth graders. Negative responses came only for rap leaders who were not present at all of the meetings or in groups where lack of communication with the rap leader was felt. Those rap leaders who rated themselves favorably in the seventh-grade "rap" groups on skills used also were rated favorably by the ninth-graders. Considerable agreement existed between those rap leaders who saw themselves using fewer skills and leaders whose ninth-grade groups responded with less favorable evaluations. The ratings by ninth graders were significant for two apparent reasons.

1. The manner in which the Vocational Exploration Group Experience was organized required extensive use of the peer helpers for each activity and, therefore, to complete the activity without the peer helper was impossible.

2. The ninth graders (helpees) were peers of the peer helper and, therefore, made valuable "peer assessment" of the peer helper.

Comments from Youth and Understanding Teachers (Sue Heggarty and Diane Wolf*). A peer communication ("rap" group) program has made a marked difference in the functioning of our ninth-grade English classes. Two of our classes were designed to include a peer communication leadership training program as a part of the curriculum. A distinct difference in atmosphere existed in these two leadership training classes as compared to our other nonparticipating three classes. Students in the leadership training classes seemed to have a much greater tolerance for each other, which was important because of the heterogeneous mixture of abilities. The second quarter of this semester course was designed for independent study. During independent study, the peer communication really improved the activity of these classes. Students worked together willingly helping each other.

In contrast, the other three nonparticipating classes we had this year were traditional classrooms. When asked to work in groups on projects that were to be presented, students had decidedly more trouble in reaching a consensus including

---

*Ms. Sue Haggarty and Ms. Diane Wolf were ninth-grade English teachers at Pattonville Heights Junior High, Maryland Heights, MO.

every member in the group and in making allowances for the individual differences. Antagonism existed between members of a group, and the students did not know how to resolve this problem.

A student who has experienced peer communication or leadership training usually understands the workings of a group and, generally, is more sensitive to the needs of others. Students who have had these peer communication experiences function very well in a normal classroom.

Comments from Social Awareness Teachers (Clara Clark and Barry Hapner*). In doing the career simulation, we used "rap" leaders previously trained in communication skills. These leaders were effective in several areas.

The simulation and its method of division into small groups was designed to allow participants to risk expression of their goals and to motivate them to that end. The leaders helped in providing a secure atmosphere in which to take this risk because they had personally experienced the risk. Also, the fact that the groups were peer groups and peer led enabled new ideas to be expressed and, perhaps, heard and adopted more readily. Peer pressure to try something new was much more effective than teacher pressure. Also, encouragement from the leaders was effective in helping some students open up and become expressive.

Being in six places at once is an impossibility; so six leaders, who had already experienced the simulation and were trained in communications, were probably a much better training agent than a hurried teacher. The leaders also enabled us to get a better perspective of all the group dynamics in the room. We honestly can say that we learned several things from watching these leaders in action.

Grade Point Comparison of Rap Leader Groups. The grade point averages of "rap" leaders trained during the second semester of 1974 were compared with students

---

*Ms Clara Clark and Mr. Barry Hapner were Social Studies teachers at Pattonville Heights Junior High, Maryland Heights, MO.

not included in the program. The following is a comparison of the grade point averages of "rap" leaders with 25 students selected at random. As is noted, the grades of the "rap" leaders improved, whereas the other 25 randomly selected students showed little change over the same period.

25 Rap Leaders		25 Students Selected at Random
60%	Grades Improved	28%
24%	Grades Stayed the Same	20%
16%	Grades Dropped	52%

Overall reaction to the peer leaders was favorable. The use of skills and evaluation of those skills were positive. The peer evaluation was moderately improving on the seventh-grade level and positively improving on the ninth-grade level.

For future training, communications skills that require more assertive techniques need to be stressed. A more accurate scale of evaluation also needs to be designed. The peer helper's evaluations were made in terms of the number of skills he/she used each session; an additional qualitative assessment similar to the teachers', seventh graders', and ninth graders' assessments needs to be made. Because the leader's assessment was based on his/her own count, however, this assessment may be seen as a qualitative judgment.

Volunteer Rap Group. The same "rap" leaders also formed informal rap groups made up of volunteer students from the eighth and ninth grades. They met weekly, alternating hours. The leaders were trained in group discussion skills, open-ended discussion, and specific activities (value clarification and problem solving). These groups affected approximately 250 students weekly for one semester. The results reported by the group members were positive, but the time involved in administration, hall passes, scheduling, and supervising was extensive. These peer groups served as a vehicle to reduce tension in an extremely overcrowded school.

Elementary School Helpers. Students in the ninth grade served as cadet teachers to students located at a nearby elementary school. These peer helpers were trained in tutoring and small group skills. Teachers and students felt good about the program.

Shorey (1981) conducted a study with 90 13-year-old middle school students in which she compared peer group counseling with achievement motivation counseling. The results showed that no significant difference occurred in achievement or acting out behavior, but significant increases did occur in attendance for both groups.

Sasso, Hughes, Swanson, and Novak (1987) examined the effects of three interventions delivered by three nonhandicapped (NH) fourth-grade students on the social initiation behavior of untrained peers toward a 12-year-old student with a severe handicap (mental retardation, cerebral palsy). A multiple schedule design was used to assess the effects of peer initiation, reinforcement, and prompt procedures administered by trained NH peers on the percentage of positive social interactions toward the student with handicaps by untrained NH peers. Results indicated that the prompt procedure produced the highest levels of positive initiations from untrained NH peers. Findings support the use of prompt procedures to enhance social relationships between children with severe handicaps and NH individuals.

Elementary School Programs

Elementary students have been used as special friends, tutors, discussion leaders, and peer helpers. Peer helpers can play a significant role in improving both the learning process and the learning environment. Through training and preparation, they learn how to assist both teachers and peers. They become an extended hand of teachers and counselors, enabling more students to participate actively in learning experiences so that the learning process becomes more personalized (Myrick & Bowman, 1983).

Jovick (1989) described an elementary program using conflict resolution that has changed the school's environment.

Peer helpers as young as third grade have been trained successfully for a variety of projects, all of which can be carefully planned and structured for success (Bowman & Myrick, 1980). For example, McCann (1975) developed a training program to prepare sixth graders to work individually with other students in a school drop-in center. The counseling program consisted of eight one-hour sessions that focused on listening skills, nonverbal communication, self-disclosure, reflective listening, and developing alternative courses of action when faced with a problem. The center was open to fifth-grade students twice a week during recess or lunch. Kum and Gal (1976) conducted a similar program. Briskin and Anderson (1973) developed a program to teach behavioral principles to peer helpers. Sixth-grade peer helpers were assigned to work as contingency managers for two disruptive third graders.

Solberg and Whitford (1989) urged professionals who train elementary students to recognize developmental issues both from the point of view of the individual as well as the group. They suggested roles such as being a buddy to others, tutors, and Fuzzy Helper. Foster (1991) made a point for appropriate training for elementary students—the curriculum needs to fit their developmental issues.

PREVENTION PROGRAMS

Numerous experimental studies of peer-led prevention programs show that peer leader involvement is associated with changes in risk behaviors when compared to both nonintervention controls and even teacher-led interventions (Arkin, Roemhild, Johnson, Luepker, & Murray, 1981; Botvin & Williams, 1980; Telch, Miller, Killen, Cooke, & Maccoby, 1990). Effects have been seen for up to five years (Luepker, Johnson, & Murray, 1983; Murray, Richards, Luepker, & Johnson 1987; Perry, Klepp, & Sillers, 1989). Although most of these studies were concerned with smoking, others also demonstrated effects on alcohol and other substance use (Botvin, 1986; Perry, Killen, & Slinkard, 1980; Telch et al., 1990).

Peer helping professionals need to understand that peer programs can be highly effective in intervention, essential in prevention, and can have an impact on at-risk populations (Alexander, 1990-1991; Flax, 1991; Flay, 1985; Foster, Wadden, & Brownell, 1985; Hanson & Graham, 1991; Hein, 1989; Perry et al., 1980, 1989; Perry & Grant, 1991; Perry & Kelder, 1992; Steinhausen, 1983).

Telch, Kellen, and McAlister (1982) illustrated the effectiveness of a program that utilized high school peer educators to teach junior high students the skills to resist the pressure to smoke. The students not receiving the peer education program, after 33 months, reported smoking at a level three times that of the peer education group.

Luepker, Johnson, and Murray (1983) documented the results of a three-year study of cigarette smoking among 1,081 seventh graders in three different schools. School number 1 received no special smoking prevention curriculum; school number 2 received a smoking prevention curriculum taught by adult teachers; while school number 3 received the same smoking curriculum taught by student peers of the same age. The education program taught exclusively by adults was found to be effective during the first year; however, by the end of the second year, the smoking rates were as high as those in the school receiving no intervention. In school number 3, where peer educators were involved in the teaching, lower smoking rates prevailed over the entire three-year study.

In 1984, Botvin, Baker, Renick, Filazzola, and Botvin reported a 20-session program that focused on reducing adolescent cigarette, alcohol, and marijuana use. Ten public schools were randomized to either a teacher-implemented curriculum, a "slightly older peer"-implemented curriculum, or no curriculum. Substantially lower cigarette, alcohol, and marijuana use rates occurred following the intervention for the peer education group, as compared to both the teacher-led and the no-treatment group.

Black females ages 12-19 who attended an inner-city, hospital-based adolescent clinic were invited to meet individually with trained female peer educators age 16-19 to discuss AIDS/HIV and its prevention. The conclusion was that peer education improves knowledge about HIV infection and diminishes high-risk behavior (Slap, Plotkin, Khalid, Michelman, & Forke, 1991).

The results of these studies indicate that substantial evidence is available to show that peer health education programs can be effective in schools.

Tobler (1986) conducted a meta-analysis. She located more than 240 programs that were evaluated during the period from 1972 to 1984. Of these, 98 studies, encompassing 143 different program modalities, met her criteria. The program modalities were collapsed into the following five categories:

1. **Knowledge only.** Presentation by teacher of legal, biological, and psychological effects of drug abuse-scare tactics.

2. **Affective only.** Self-esteem building, self-awareness, feelings, values clarification—experiential activities.

3. **Peer program.** Positive peer influences—peer teaching, peer counseling, helping, and facilitation; peer participation—subdivided into refusal skills (saying "No") and interpersonal and intrapersonal life skills.

4. **Knowledge plus affective.** Combination of numbers 1 and 2.

5. **Alternatives.** Activities more appealing than drug abuse.

Tobler found that peer programs were dramatically more effective than all of the other programs. She concluded from the study that (1) the knowledge-only and affective-only programs for average adolescents should be discontinued; (2) the focus should be on peer programs that emphasize refusal skills as well as communication and decision-making skills; and (3) for at-risk youths, peer programs should be supplemented with alternatives (e.g., community activities, physical activities, mastery learning, and job skills).

In 1993 Tobler updated her research and found that peer programs were more effective than originally listed in the 1986 study.

Feldman and Caplinger (1983) suggested that the power of the peer group as a socializing agent is in developing positive behaviors. The critical element in the success of the peer program approach may be the sense of connectedness (participation in meaningful activities) and involvement (assumption of responsibility) that the youths experience. Another word is "empowered."

Based upon available evidence, in the prevention field peers are effective in prevention.

Bowman (1986) discussed the value of peer facilitators in serving as student assistants, tutors, special friends, and group leaders. The selection and training of peer helpers were described. Four issues in peer helper training were considered: (1) time constraints, (2) the need for age-appropriate training curriculum, (3) the importance of a logical and systematic presentation of concepts and skills, and (4) student availability.

Avis and Bigelow (1987) described the application of a group problem-solving process to work with racial/ethnic issues. Lynn (1986) described a program in Baltimore County, MD, where the program has become a strong force for change and growth in the school system. The program provides immediate help to students in need, contributes to a spirit of positive educational involvement of the students in the school program, and helps develop leadership skills. Peterson and Peppas (1988) investigated the effects of using peer helpers to ease students in their transitions to an overseas school. Results indicate some positive changes, suggesting that students can benefit from peer interaction and peer helper training.

Sometimes, programs have specific goals in mind. For example, Keboyan (1992) utilized peer helping in AIDS prevention. Rubenstein, Panzarine, and Lanning (1990) described a peer counseling model aimed at preventing repeat pregnancy and school dropout among adolescent mothers. Six adolescent mothers were paid to be peer counselors to pregnant teens ages 15 years or younger. Williams (1986) described a peer counseling program for teenage sexual abuse victims.

Agency Programs

Like schools, community agencies have turned to nonprofessionals and paraprofessionals to meet some of the problems that face the counseling profession. Problems in agencies are different from those in schools. First, nonprofessionals may or may not be peers with those with whom they are working. Second, nonprofessionals who work for agencies often are paid for their services. In fact, they become the "New Professionals," as they were called by Eisdorfer and Golann (1969). Nonprofessionals who are not hired by the agency are volunteers who come from the community and are not responsible to the agency other than through their desire to help. These two conditions create problems different from those faced by schools, where the peer helpers are both a part of the system and served by the system.

In agencies, motivation is more often to oil a squeaking wheel than to expand and improve the services of counselors who cannot meet the needs of their clients. By training paraprofessionals, agencies are enabled to meet the needs that are voiced by the poor and minorities. In this way, agencies are not forced to deal with the problems brought about by clients who are being denied services they desire. Training of nonprofessionals thus has become the most expedient way to solve the problems that agencies may face in their effort to meet the increasing counseling loads. Agencies servicing the disabled and the mentally ill have started to use peer programs to help in a variety of ways. Krantz, Ramsland, and McClannahan (1989) evaluated the effectiveness of a male autistic peer prompter (age 16 years) in increasing the conversational language of three other male verbal autistic youth (ages 11, 13, 15 years), using sports conversation as the dependent variable. The autistic younger students increased their conversational language when an autistic peer served as prompter. These newly acquired sports conversation skills, initially displayed in dyads, generalized to group conversations, to a different classroom and teacher, and to different dyads; these skills were maintained over one month.

Mathur and Rutherford (1991) reviewed the literature to evaluate the success of peer-mediated interventions in promoting social skills of children and adolescents with behavioral disorders. Twenty-one articles employing peer-mediated interventions were analyzed on their experimental, procedural, and generalization components. Results indicate that (1) 10 peer-mediated approaches have demonstrated success in producing immediate positive treatment effects; (2) typologies of peer-mediated treatments have been identified; and (3) peer-mediated approaches, in general, have contributed to the effectiveness of generalization technology.

Specific research was done by Sasso, Hughes, Swanson, and Novak (1987) and found that the use of prompt procedures delivered by three nonhandicapped fourth-grade students does enhance social relationships between children with severe handicaps and nonhandicapped individuals.

Akridge, Farley, and Rice (1987) studied the effects of peer helper training with two samples of rehabilitation facility clients. The ages were 19 through 58, and the most frequently occurring disabilities were mild mental retardation and specific developmental disorders. Results from both samples, using different trainers, show that both groups demonstrated improved basic helping skills as measured by the *Communication and Discrimination Test* and evaluated the training experience very positively.

Cooper-White (1990) determined that peer helping is probably most effective in the initial crisis phase of working with battered women.

Support Groups

Galanter (1988), in a controlled study of *Recovery, Inc.*, which is a self-help program for people with psychiatric problems, found that 201 group leaders and 155 members who had joined Recovery between six and 20 months previously completed a demographic questionnaire, a general well-being schedule, a neurotic distress scale, and a social cohesiveness scale, and indicated their psychiatric treatment history and ideological commitment to Recovery. A decline in both symptoms and concomitant psychiatric treatment was found after those in recovery had joined the group. Scores for neurotic distress were considerably lower than those reported for the period before joining. Scores for psychological well-being of long-standing Recovery members were no different from those of community control patients. It is concluded that peer-led self-help groups have value as an adjunct to psychiatric treatment.

Cohen and Livneh (1986) reviewed the Dystonia Foundation and the self-help movement and illustrated a chapter in New England that included providing peer helping and support services; establishing educational programs concerning dystonia for the medical and lay communities; serving as advocating and liaison body for members regarding the availability of medical, legal and social services; and participating in a network of services with other dystonia chapters and the National Foundation.

The *Alliance of Genetic Support Groups* is a national coalition of genetic support groups, concerned individuals, and involved professionals. It serves as a forum where people from diverse genetic disorder groups can come together to look at common concerns, identify resources, and share both information and strategies. This group sponsored a conference that would train leaders in each of the groups to set up training for the support group leaders (Burns, 1990).

It is obvious that support groups are effective. One might consider training leaders of support groups in peer helping skills, thus empowering them with skill to be more effective.

Elderly

One of the growing areas of peer helping is with the elderly population. Research has been clear concerning the effectiveness of peer programs at this level.

Examples of these programs are reported by Burke and Hayes (1986), who described Operation Senior Security and Operation Victim Support, which are community programs in central Illinois designed to train elderly volunteers to counsel other elderly persons in self-protection methods. Participants are given a 30-hour training program and ongoing support. Responses from a survey of 24 participants (ages 60 to 90) indicate that their communication skills, knowledge of community services, and problem-solving abilities had increased.

Redburn and Juretich (1989) trained and used eight widowed, female peer self-help group leaders. Toseland, Rossiter, and Labrecque (1989) compared peer-led and professionally-led support groups for caregivers of frail older persons living in the community and showed that both types of groups were effective. Petty and Cusack (1989) described an 18-month peer helper training program completed by 18 Canadian elderly (ages 63 to 73). The model was designed not only to teach helping skills but to assist participants in taking a more active role in developing and maintaining the program. Results from a quasi-experimental design show significant increases in helping skills and in the ability to compensate for sensory losses. Informal evaluative procedures suggested additional benefits of the program to clients, participants, and professionals in the community.

It seems clear that there are many effective programs currently being used for the elderly (Alpaugh & Haney 1978; Becker & Zarit, 1978; Bratter, 1986; Petty & Cusack, 1989).

Veterans

At Jefferson Barracks in St. Louis the JBVAMC peer volunteers participated in a 12-week, two-hour twice weekly training program. The training primarily emphasized the learning of helping skills identified by Rogers, Truax, and Carkhuff. The volunteers were later supervised in helping weekly at the JBVAMC Nursing Home Care Unit (Schalzman, 1992).

Parents

Some counselors are training parents to be involved as leaders of parenting groups. Brookman (1988) described a program to provide support and information for parents of children with disabilities and/or health impairments. Parents are matched with other parents who also have a child with special needs. Kottman and Wilborn (1992) described an Adlerian Parent Study group in which the counselor trained parents to help other parents. The parents had a six-week training program for 16 volunteers. The focus of the training was on Adlerian principles, group leadership, active listening, and reflection using role-play situations, videotapes, modeling, and discussion. Two parent groups were held in each school. One group was led by the school counselor and one was led by trained parents. Discussions were based on *A Parent's Guide to Child Discipline.* The subject pool was 359 parents whose children attended eight elementary schools. Ninety parents were in parent-led groups and 81 were in counselor-led groups. The rest were in a nonattending group of 95. The participants were given a Parent Attitude Survey before and after the group meetings.

The five areas measured were confidence as a parent, causation of child's behavior, acceptance of child's behavior, understanding of the child, and trust in the child. No significant difference was found in attitude change between the parent study groups led by counselors and the parent study groups led by parents on four (confidence, acceptance, understanding, and trust) of the five subtests. On the variable of causation, a significantly higher score was obtained on the counselor-led groups. Overall, parents who had participated in the study groups had a more positive attitude toward parenting and toward their children than parents who had not participated. It is obvious that a role of the professional is to train other parents to lead parent groups. In this way, many more parents can be reached.

Hospitals

France (1989) described a peer helping program at a 300-bed long-term facility in Victoria, British Columbia. The program was implemented using training materials specifically developed for older people. The average age of the first group of trainees was 86 years.

Glanz, Marger, and Meehan (1986) utilized a program of peer educators for stroke education programs for the elderly.

McGill and Patterson (1990) described a program for training former patients to be peer helpers for hospitalized psychiatric patients. Training, operation, and evaluation were discussed. Counselors reported personal benefits from participation in the program, including increased self-confidence and heightened empathy.

Lister and Ward (1985) described a training program designed to prepare youths to offer support to peers experiencing death or terminal illness.

Slap et al. (1991) described a program in which a peer education program to discuss AIDS with adolescent females was initiated at a hospital-based adolescent clinic. Comparison of individual baseline and follow-up responses revealed improvements in the knowledge of routes by which HIV is and is not transmitted, methods of prevention, individuals at risk, and general information about AIDS.

Mogtader and Leff (1986) described a program in which a total of four male and 13 female chronically ill adolescents have spent from one to three summers working beside other adolescents as counselors to chronically ill hospitalized children. The adolescents were helped to cope with their illness while helping their peers. The program directly addressed three areas of concern and stress in the lives of chronically ill adolescents: poor body image, social isolation, and self-control.

Prisons

Peer programs have been developed to be utilized with the prison population, especially adolescents. For example, Brannon and Troyer (1991) investigated the community readjustment of 53 adolescent sex offenders and a comparison group of 57 nonsexual offenders (all ages 13 to 18 years) released from a state residential group treatment facility. All sex offenders received group intervention strategies that emphasized such characteristics as honesty, acceptance of responsibility, and problem solving. Results suggest that (1) large percentages had committed "undetected" sexual assaults, and (2) the post-release sex offenders within an agency's main campus peer group treatment program produced recidivism rates comparable with those reported among specialized treatment models.

Gordon and Arbuthot (1988) described a program that uses paraprofessionals to deliver home-based family therapy to juvenile delinquents. These paraprofessionals are trained in family therapy.

EAP Models in the Business World

Peer helpers in the workplace can be effective at prevention, intervention, and support after treatment. The airline industry has two examples of Employee Assistance Program (EAP) peer network models meeting unique needs. In the late 1970's, the *Association of Flight Attendants* in Washington, DC, faced a dilemma. Traditional EAP design seemed best to meet the needs of larger single-site work forces within more traditional, hierarchical workplace environments. By contrast, AFA members were highly mobile, worked in hundreds of locations, and had minimal supervision. The AFA's solution was to implement a peer counseling model of EAP service. Full-time flight attendants volunteered their time to promote the EAP and refer inquiring coworkers to appropriate local treatment services.

The *Canadian Airlines International* and its unions chose to provide a different model of EAP service to its work force. Full-time internal EAP counselors and a number of associates provided professional assessment, referral, and counseling service throughout CAI's system. The peer contact model uses the peer network as a collection of publicity agents in every work site, who encourage people desiring help for personal problems to access the professional EAP service provider (Gant, 1992).

Unions also have played a role in peer assistance. A union program that emphasizes training in basic helping skills, experiential learning, and self-help has been designed to provide union representatives with the skill training necessary to be peer assistants (Miller & Metz, 1991).

Molloy (1989) described the National Maritime Union project aimed at exploring the use of a worker-based peer intervention and networking strategy that was modeled from the Employee Assistance Program literature. In the first phase, 30 active seamen were interviewed who had consistently used the alcohol and drug problem intervention program. The interview served initially as a needs assessment of unmet service needs and the peer model itself. Two-thirds of the seamen called alcoholism a serious problem in the American Merchant Marine. The second phase of the project was a training dialogue in which 13 of the seamen interviewed participated. Emerging themes included the concept of intervention with emphasis on these principles: the drinking culture, boredom and stress, and constructive confrontation.

Peer helping programs have been successful in elementary schools, middle/junior high schools, high schools, colleges, and agencies. Peer helpers have been used successfully with disruptive students, high-risk students, drug and alcohol programs, health education, prevention programs, and race relationships; they have been successful leading small discussion groups, serving as special friends to new students, and helping change classroom behavior of problem students with gains in self-esteem, academic achievement, and improved attendance—through such functions as tutoring and dropout prevention; lastly, they have provided help for agencies and assistance to teachers.

Peer helping has been used successfully with agency populations, elderly, hospital patients, veterans, military programs, parenting programs, and EAP programs in business and industry. Much research is needed in the nonschool-based populations. Some programs are now being developed for the homeless at storefront drop-in centers to help the homeless with a variety of issues.

ESSENTIAL CONDITIONS FOR PEER PROGRAMS

Individuals in professional settings as well as laypersons are concluding that the concept is workable. Further development is needed and should be watched with interest. However, for the time being, training of peer helpers is worthy of helper support and effort.

When several conditions are met satisfactorily, peer helping programs can be an innovative and worthwhile dimension of the counseling profession. Based on experience and research reported in the literature, peer helping is satisfactorily meeting certain needs. However, for it to be successful, peer helping must be undertaken with specific developmental training, supervision, and evaluation procedures. In summary, the necessary conditions as reported in literature are as follows:

1.   Everyone involved in the program needs to be involved in the planning.

2.   A specific planned training program is necessary. The program format may be in the form of classes, a series of workshops, training seminars, or whatever is needed, but it must have built in an effective training component.

3.   Short encounter groups or one-time workshops of short duration are not adequate to train helpers effectively.

4.   A lengthy training program is not necessary, but it must be well structured and long enough to enable trainees to integrate the training.

5.   Individuals who have the qualities of sensitivity, warmth, and awareness of others make effective trainees.

6.   Supervision of trainees is important. This includes an ongoing follow-up program while the trainee is functioning in a peer helping role.

7.   Evaluation and research must be a part of the training and peer helping program to measure progress and isolate problems.

8.   Persons involved in the program need to be interested in the concept and the application of peer counseling.

9. Do not use the peer training and subsequent employment of nonprofessionals as aides to do the flunky work with which professionals do not want to be bothered. The peer helpers must be an integrated part of the total program with responsibilities comparable to those of the professionals.

10. The ethical aspects of the training must be taught adequately and supervised fully.

11. Peer helpers should work with their peers rather than with groups that have far different values systems.

12. Peer helpers can work successfully with support groups (AA, Weight Watchers, etc.) if properly trained.

13. The peer professional needs to be able to be a trainer, coordinator, facilitator, organizer, and evaluator.

To learn to read. . . .we read

To learn to speak. . . we speak

To learn to write. . . we write

To learn to listen. . .we listen

To learn responsibility. . .

> *we must have responsibility!*

Chapter **VI**

DEVELOPMENT OF THE PEER HELPING PROFESSIONAL

In any peer training program, the trainer becomes the vital link in changing a trainee with poorly developed skills into one with highly effective facilitative skills (Carkhuff, 1969, 1972; Egan, 1986). Several research studies led Carkhuff (1969) to reiterate that the trainee is not able to function at higher levels of effective behavior than the trainer. In essence then, the trainer needs to be a constantly effective high level helper. Not only does the trainer have a responsibility to possess, at a highly integrated level, the skills that are taught, but he/she also must demonstrate to trainees the process of integration through frequent and consistent modeling behaviors. Since human growth is a continuing dynamic process and never completed except by death, a decision to delay training others until one's own skills are maximized may prevent the initiation of any training program.

Therefore, training programs should be planned, organized, and initiated with the awareness that the success of any training program depends upon the trainer. The process of self-growth as a Peer Helping Professional supersedes the ability to organize, develop, and administer programs. The starting point in any effective training program becomes the trainer.

LEVELS OF PEER HELPING PROFESSIONAL

As the field grows and peer helping professionals are called upon to provide leadership in peer programs, the development seems to be toward a person who has specialization within the area. More and more counselor positions are advertising for people with peer helping experiences. The following are recommended levels of skill development for professionals.

Skill Development for Level I—Peer Helping Professional

Start a small program.

Train a small number of peer helpers.

Manage and supervise one project for peers.

Skill Development for Level II—Peer Helping Professional

Conduct successful programs for at least five years.

Gain support from community and supervisors.

Be utilized by helpees.

Provide appropriate training for several projects undertaken by peer helpers.

Evaluate peer programs.

Skill Development for Level III—Peer Helping Professional

Meet Level I and Level II expectations.

Enlarge program to include several opportunities for peer helpers.

Work with others in training, supervising, and administrating peer programs.

Develop and utilize needs assessment and evaluation tools to guide peer programs.

Gain financial support for programs.

Share with the larger peer helping field.

Skill Development for Level IV—Peer Helping Professional

Coordinate a large program (district wide, city wide, state wide, business wide).

Demonstrate skills in management.

Demonstrate skills in leadership.

Demonstrate skills in team building.

Demonstrate skills in organization.

Demonstrate skills in placement and training of professionals.

Demonstrate skills in forming collaborations.

Demonstrate skills in gaining financial support.

Skill Development for Level V—Peer Helping Professional

Utilize skills in training other adults who will be training other adults in peer helping.

Have a broad knowledge of the peer helping field.

Be able to consult with groups concerning peer programs.

Demonstrate knowledge of adult learning.

Facilitate an adult training group.

Evaluate and research peer programs.

Write and publish in the peer helping field.

Each of these levels of skill development will of course have certain areas of competencies such as to understand theory of peer helping, to organize programs, to train others, to utilize the peers that they train in a meaningful manner, to collaborate, to evaluate programs, to follow ethics and standards developed by the field, to develop curriculum development appropriate for the group, to build teams, to influence others, to write grants, and to develop and train others in specific topical areas such as alcohol and other drug intervention.

The training committee of the National Peer Helpers Association is trying at this point to refine and develop a Professional Development Map. The *Peer Counselling Project* at the University of Victoria (Box 3010, Victoria, British Columbia, V8W 3N4) has developed a *National Registry of Peer Counsellor Trainers: Level I, Level II, Level III.*

PROFILE OF A PEER PROFESSIONAL

A peer helping professional is someone who wears many hats. He/she must be an effective trainer, leader, and helper. What are some of the characteristics of a good helper? Ideally, these characteristics are rather comprehensive and inclusive of what many social scientists call the effective person. It is what Ivey (1971) called the "intentional person," what Carkhuff (1969) and Carkhuff and Truax (1969) called an "effectively living" person, what Maslow (1968) called a "self actualized" person, or what Jourard (1971) called a "transparent person." Egan (1986) defined helpers as "effective to the degree that their clients, through client helper interactions, are in a better position to manage their problem situations and/or develop the unused resources and opportunities of their lives more effectively." The kind of maturity that is manifested in the desire for self-growth and development is, essentially, what these authors mean. Maturity that is committed to physical, emotional, intellectual, social, and even spiritual development needs to be the peer professional's focus for self-development. The important point is for the person doing the training to exhibit and model internal strength and self-confidence along with a dedication to personal growth. Characteristics that can be identified are imperative.

Some of these characteristics of effective peer helping professionals are intellectual curiosity, physical fitness, pragmatic outlook, optimism, problem-solving skills, willingness to accept responsibilities, understanding of helpees and their needs, capacity to motivate, adaptability, confidence, ability to be a good role model, knowing self, and understanding values. As you can see, many of the same characteristics are needed for a leader, helper, and trainer. At times these terms are interchangeable.

Intellectual Curiosity

Intellectual curiosity is a vital link in the development of peer helping professionals. They need to be interested in and have respect for intellectual activities that are infused within all research, creativity, innovative process, and striving for better ways to do things. They must keep an accurate perspective on personal intellectual capacities, neither selling themselves short nor being overconfident. Along with the awareness of and respect for personal intellectual curiosity, the peer helping professional must accept and respond to effective intellectual capacities in others. This response includes the ability to distinguish between positive and effective intellectual curiosity and that quality of intelligence that is essentially nonproductive or destructive in others. Intellectual competency includes the interest and ability to act effectively.

Physical Fitness

The peer helping professional needs to be aware of the importance of physical fitness. The process of helping and training peer helpers is hard work and demands large amounts of physical and emotional energy.

A potent peer helping professional maintains good physical condition through proper diet and adequate exercise. In our society, diet and exercise are often times neither adequate nor proper. The demands of high energy levels require that specific efforts are made to develop an exercise program that is taxing and consistent. The program should include exercises that are constant and strenuous enough to develop muscle tone and high energy levels.

Pragmatic Outlook

A peer helping professional basically implements theories and concepts into action thus becoming, essentially, a pragmatic person. Because his/her responsibility will be to implement practical and specific action programs, the peer helping professional must be able to translate theoretical psychological concepts into effective processes. Few psychological theories translate easily into everyday, on-the-spot behavior suggestions that can be used as a recipe for helper action. That translation is the peer helping professional's responsibility. Not only is pragmatism required, but initiative is also needed to experiment and create new ways of teaching helping concepts and skills. Because each situation is different, a training program will face some obstacles and problems that cannot be anticipated. Therefore, the burden of solving those difficulties lies on the peer helping professional. Meeting and overcoming scheduling, administrative, logistic, and personnel problems are responsibilities that are almost impossible to unload or even share. Practicality and tenacity, then, become two tools of a successful peer training program.

Optimism

Another personal characteristic that is very helpful in a training program is the peer helping professional's optimistic outlook with regard to his/her own ability to accomplish challenging tasks. Optimism and the next characteristic to be discussed, problem-solving skills, relate closely with creativity and practicality in program implementation.

Optimism is important because in many instances peer helper and peer helper training are classed with those "newfangled" frills that generate defensiveness and caution in many peers and/or administrators. It is not an idea that generates confidence among those who think competency comes only with a Master's Degree, experience, and a paycheck. Peer helper concepts frequently require selling the concepts to others who (1) have not thought about, (2) are threatened by, or (3) can't conceive of students, lay workers, or peers being effective in helping people. These behaviors, if successful, can be very threatening to coworkers who may think that helping trainees is their prerogative. Pessimism is not intended here, but the realities of experience are that peer counseling often requires that the peer helping professional educate others and "sell" the construct to others in his/her field.

Many times resistance comes from people who are resisting without having thought about the possibility of training peer helpers. The concept acts as an irritation in their status quo existence, and the peer counseling ideas require new energies on their part to cope with the new concepts. The inertia obstructing an effort to establish a new thought pattern, idea, or concept is often the only obstacle to be overcome by the objectors. Active resistance can appear when dealing with coworkers who tend to be threatened by anything that causes them to rethink their well-ingrained, educational constructs. The coworkers are not so much opposed or antagonistic as they are simply frightened or uneasy that some dire new consequences will result from these new behaviors. Introduction to innovative concepts ignites the fear in others that the ideas will create problems that cannot be dealt with easily. The newness or change from the prescribed way of doing things requires the trainer to have a degree of self-confidence as well as confidence in peer helper objectives so that resistance is viewed as a challenge to be overcome and not as a wall blocking the path.

Problem-solving Skills

Problem-solving skills and interest in overcoming obstacles are the characteristics that support optimism and become the vehicles through which the optimism becomes justified. The skill to solve problems can be learned and can be developed as thoroughly as any of the other skills taught in the program. One of the peer professional responsibilities is to develop the attitude conducive to learning problem-solving skills, and see that the process is internalized, not irrational. No manual can teach people how to have the desire to overcome problems effectively. Technology can assist in the process but not the desire. Fortunately, the quality of optimism toward challenges usually accompanies the interest in getting problems solved.

The two qualities, optimism and problem-solving skills, are vitally important for a successful program. Without these qualities, the obstacles placed in the peer helping professional's way in a traditional, oftentimes very conservative system can generate an overwhelming sense of frustration and disappointment. When the qualities of optimism and problem solving are developed, some very exciting programs are possible. In addition, the trainer gains the awareness and he/she is not only helping others in school, church, or a community system but also that some very important skills are being taught to a widely increasing circle of people.

Dedication

Many peer helpers are dedicated strongly to being helpful to others. A peer helper program requires this kind of dedication. If helping is just a job, then one is cautioned about starting a program. If, however, a peer professional feels frustration at being the only person to meet many needs, then a peer program makes sense. A program of giving away helping skills or training others in these helping skills can become an effective way for the helper to widen his/her ability to meet the needs of others.

The kind of person with all the characteristics just presented does not exist in one body, but the characteristics are ones that can be used as guides. A peer helping professional does need to function at high levels in all of the qualities mentioned. Most of the qualities presented are found to some degree in effective, mature, and genuine people. A trainer for peer helpers has the responsibility of striving for high levels of these qualities if only to develop as a person. Effective personal qualities and competent trainer qualities generally are congruent.

Role Model

As a peer helping professional, the trainer needs to be a good role model for the peer helpers. The peer helping professional must possess high-level helping skills, and also must represent ethical and legal behavior. For example, if the trainer was working with recovering alcoholics as peer helpers, it would be important to model for them the kind of behavior that is expected of them. Another example might be the issue of confidentiality. When the trainer expects the peer helpees to keep things confidential, the trainer must also respect the ethics of the group. The trainer must be a professional and personal role model.

Understanding Helpers and Helpees

If peer helping professionals are to get the most out of their peer helpers, they must understand the peer helpers so as to motivate them and work with them. The late Bear Bryant of the University of Alabama, one of the all-time greats among college football coaches, once said, "I know my players better than they know themselves. How else could I get the best out of them?" Peer helping professionals also must understand the needs of the populations the peer helpers serve. If professionals do not understand and relate to that population, they will lose their effectiveness.

Ability to Motivate

When he/she is serving as a trainer, the peer helping professional must be able to motivate through a variety of training skills such as experiential training, making training relevant, and encouraging others to learn. The peer helping professional must be able to empower peer helpers to be effective in their roles. This motivation involves the peer helpers' ability to trust the peer professional. In other words, the trainer must follow through on what he/she says will be done and must be authentic in his/her work with others.

Adaptability, Flexibility of Approach

Even though the peer helping professional may have clear goals in mind for the program and some under-riding beliefs concerning empowering others with effective helping skills and leadership skills, the peer helping professional must remain adaptable and flexible in the approach to meet those goals and beliefs. If the funding is short in one area, the peer professional may have to look elsewhere. If a particular training approach is not working, then try to find one that will work.

Knowing Self

If peer helping professionals truly know themselves, their gifts and blind spots, they can then begin to move toward self development and asking for help from others with gifts. If peer helping professionals know themselves, they can know how to take care of themselves, how to set boundaries for themselves between them and the peer program. They know how to get their needs met in a variety of ways. The first step in helping others is knowing oneself and being authentic.

Understanding Values

In addition to personality characteristics and supplementary training strategies, understanding the role of values and the process of valuing in helping is a necessity. Values are an integral part of all helping relationships. When helping another person, the helper is faced with several ways to respond to the helpee. The helpee's experiences and value systems are the conditions that underlie the helper's understanding of what the helpee may be relating. Therefore, the responses any helper makes need to be closely related to the helpee's values or value systems.

If a peer helping professional and/or helper is unaware of the value systems that are functioning, the probability of his/her responding with implied or actual bias without being aware of that bias is increased. This lack of awareness can lead to control, manipulation, or seduction in a situation where the trainee does not understand what is happening. An awareness of personal values and the ability to identify them for others can reduce the tendency to influence others prejudicially.

Thus, learning and understanding personal values, value systems, and the process of valuing are recommended to the trainer. In this way, training will incorporate human understanding of values and their significant role in the helping process. By understanding the relativity of the concept of values, the trainer can teach and practice tolerance for a wide variety of divergent value systems. In this way, tolerance of divergent values becomes integrated into the peer helping professional's teaching.

GROUP WORK IN PEER HELPING

Situational Leadership Skills for Professionals

When the peer helper professional is working with a group of trainees, he or she needs to be concerned about the purposes of the group, what his or her own focus needs to be, and how to maintain participants' focus so as to cause certain outcomes. These three concerns can be summarized for four situations as shown in Figure 6.1, summary of peer helping professional's leadership skills in terms of four situations.

Training Situation. The purpose of the training group is for participants to learn human-relationship skills. Examples of this as presented in the NPHA Programmatic Standards are verbal and nonverbal communication skills, active listening, facilitative responding, and problem solving. Examples in *Peer Power, Book 1* are attending, empathy, questioning, genuineness, assertiveness, confrontation, problem solving, and conflict mediation.

The task of the training group is to teach peer helpers to know the skills and how to utilize them with others. Research shows that people can learn human-relationship skills. Leaders expecting their trainees to facilitate classroom-discussion groups should provide a clearly defined training program to prepare them for that experience.

The professional leader's role is to direct and guide the peer helpers and to provide a role model. The leader must be clear about the goal of this particular training time. For example, the leader may say, "Today we will practice learning to hear and restate feelings in others."

Group Work in Peer Helping

Situation	Training	Group Counseling	Personal Growth	Supervision (Planning and Implementation)
Purpose of Group	—To learn human relations skills	—To work with conscious problems —To resolve short-term issues —To prevent and remediate	—To help healthy people function better —To assist individuals in their development —To change patterns of thinking, feeling, and action	—To organize activities for P. H. —To supervise P. H. —To evaluate —To establish action plans, role-play, and simulate implementation strategies
Professional Leaders' Focus is to be...	—Director/guide —Role model	—Facilitator —Structurer of activities —One who focuses on here and now	—Director/guide —Facilitator	—Supervisor —Evaluator —Consultant —Resource person
Participants responsibilities will cause each to...	—Observe —Practice —Learn new skills	—Determine focus of group —Be growth oriented —Help participants deal with barriers of change —Learn strengths and weaknesses	—Gain self-understanding —Change behavior —Better utilize interpersonal skills —Transfer behavior learned in group to daily living	—Maintain ownership of projects —Identify skills to learn —Organize structure for learning —Put skills into action —Evaluate

Figure 6.1. Summary of peer helping professional's leadership skills in terms of four situations.

The participants' focus is to observe, to learn, and to practice new skills. One skill to practice is attending through appropriate nonverbal behavior.

Group Counseling Situations. Because any effective human relations training program raises significant personal issues in participants, and because adolescent peer leader trainees are particularly sensitive to their internal processes, sometimes the advisable procedure is to provide group counseling within the formal training or refer the peer helpers to counseling groups. The purpose of group counseling is to have everyone work with conscious problems and resolve short-term issues. The counseling group may follow stages of group development (initial, transition, working, and ending). The counseling group may be either preventive or remedial. Some of the typical goals of a counseling group are

to prevent and remediate problems;

to help participants express thoughts, feelings, and make behavior changes;

to focus on concerns determined by members;

to discuss inner resources; and

to help members deal with barriers that prevent growth.

The leader's focus may be facilitative, at times structuring activities and helping members focus on the here and now.

Participants' responsibility is to determine the focus of the group, to be growth oriented, to gain awareness of strengths and weaknesses, and to deal with personal issues and barriers to change.

Personal Growth Situations. Research indicates that peer helpers grow more interpersonally than those they help; therefore, it is important to spend some time assisting trainees in their own personal growth. Some of this growth will take place as a result of skills that helpers have learned; other growth will be directed by the peer helping professional.

The purpose of the personal growth group is to help healthy people function better; typically, it is developmentally focused and results in changes of patterns of thinking, feeling, and behaving. Some of the specific goals are the following:

to initiate developmentally appropriate activities,

to practice honest self-assessment,

to share personal issues,

to give and receive feedback,

to develop positive attitudes,

to develop skills,

to change behavior,

to set goals, and/or

to practice daily living.

The professional leader serves in the role of a director, a guide, and a facilitator.

Participants' responsibilities in personal growth groups involve a self-understanding of their orientation to issues; their needs to change, behaviorally; and their abilities to transfer behavior they learned in the group out into daily-living situations. Participants may share with the leader the areas requiring help, such as drug and alcohol problems and coping with loss. The personal growth groups typically involve some kind of self-assessment, information-giving, sharing the participants' progress, and learning of new behavior and goal setting.

Supervision Situation. Peer helpers need an opportunity to deliver services in a one-on-one setting, a small group, or a classroom group. This is considered the supervision situation, which includes planning and implementing time. This time may be used to help peer helpers decide on appropriate referral criteria, and set up action plans, role-play, and simulate implementation strategies. The purpose of the supervision group is to organize activities and to supervise and evaluate peer helpers.

The professional leader's focus is to supervise, to evaluate, and to serve as a consultant and resource person. A sample of a supervision time activity sequence is to

review the past week's activities and outcomes,

reach new skills,

refer individuals or assist peer helpers in referring helpees to a professional if necessary, and

set goals for next week.

Participants' responsibilities are to feel an ownership of projects, to develop planning skills, to organize materials, to put skills into action, and to evaluate. Figure 6.1 is a summary of the various groups utilized in peer helping.

Self-development of the Peer Helping Professional

The long list of skills, attitudes, and experiences that are prerequisites to effective training of peer helpers may seem overwhelming. The requirements included are ones of a "paragon" peer helper trainer. Thus, most of the resources for growth have been included with information about how they fit into the blueprint of trainer growth. No one person can reach absolute levels of knowledge and experience in all of these areas, but gaining some expertise in each will assist in training efforts.

A key to effective training for anyone interested in becoming a trainer of others is continued self-development. Today an individual can experience a great number of interpersonal situations designed to enhance self-awareness and growth. Many proponents of self-development call for bizarre and radical experiences as the keys to that development, but also many legitimate programs are designed to help persons experience positive self-development. Assertive training, human potential experience, Gestalt workshops, group counseling, behavior modification, deliberate psychological education, and understanding self are some of the effective and legitimate models that can assist an individual in growth as a personal trainer and a leader.

Assertive Training

Assertive training uses many of the techniques of the Carkhuff model but works toward different goals. The focus of assertive training is to develop self-confidence, inner strength, potential, and worth. Helpers who cannot assert positively their personal worth and the worth of their contribution to others are not able to train others effectively to be strong helpers. Assertive training is a continuing process and to be effective, must be fully understood and adequately practiced. If assertive behavior is not understood or behaviorally practiced, alternative behaviors can become either destructively aggressive or impotently passive. Neither of these behaviors can result in trainer or trainee effectiveness as a helper.

For additional reading on assertiveness, the following are suggested:

Alberti, R.E., & Emmons, M.L. (1986). *Your perfect right: A manual for assertiveness trainers.* San Luis Obispo, CA: Impact.

Alberti, R.E., & Emmons, M.L. (1990). *Your perfect right: A guide to assertive living* (6th ed.). San Luis Obispo, CA: Impact.

Baggs, K., & Spance, S.E. (1990, December). Effectiveness of booster session in the maintenance and enhancement of treatment gains following assertion training. *Journal of Consulting and Clinical Psychology, 58,* 845-854.

Beels, C., Hopson, B., & Scally, M. (1990). *Assertiveness: A positive process.* San Diego, CA: Pfeiffer & Co.

Bolsinger, S.A., & McMinn, M.R. (1989, October). Assertiveness training and Christian values. *Counseling and Values, 34,* 21-32.

Johnson, G., Kaufman, G., & Raphael, L. (1991). *A teacher's guide to stick up for yourself: A 10-part course in self-esteem and assertiveness for kids.* Minneapolis, MN: Free Spirit Publishers.

Behavior Modification

The scope of this *Peer Programs* book limits the discussion of the merits of behavior modification in relation to more humanistic concepts. The only point to be made is that learning theory has a central part in the training of peers to be caring, feeling, and communicating human beings. Since behavior modification is an integral part of the training process and because the goals and outcomes of the training will be in behavioral terms initially, the trainer is to do both of the following: (1) become knowledgeable of behavioral concepts and behaviors and (2) avoid setting up an artificial straw man to do battle between behaviorism and humanism. The trainer is to avoid the academic dialogue that often places humanists and behaviorists against each other and thus creates an artificial condition that detracts from the value of each.

This training format of the *Peer Power* books uses the behavior modification process to teach humanistic concepts effectively. The training model employs specific learning theory concepts to teach new skills. The better the concepts are understood, the more useful they can be in the training program development. Ample research by Carkhuff (1969, 1971, 1987a, 1987b), Carkhuff and Truax, (1969), Gazda (1973), Ivey (1971), and others supports the procedure of employing behavior modification technology to teach some very humanistic behaviors.

For further understanding of the principles of learning theory as they apply to helping skills, the following sources are suggested:

Amatea, E.S. (1989). *Brief strategic intervention for school behavior problems.* San Francisco: Jossey-Bass.

Bandura, A. (1969). *Principles of behavior modification.* New York: Holt, Rinehart & Winston.

Gutsch, K.U., & Sisemore, D.A. (1991). *How to play the relationship game: The use of psychological principles to change human behavior.* Springfield, IL: Charles Thomas.

Ivey, A. (1991). *Intentional interviewing and counseling.* North Amherst, MA: Microtraining Association.

Kaplan, J.S., & Drainville, B. (1991). *Beyond behavior modification: A cognitive-behavioral approach to behavioral management in the school* (2nd ed.). Austin, TX.

Kuehnel, J.M., & Liberman, R.P. (1986). Behavior modification. In I.L. Kutash & A. Wolf (Eds.), *Psychotherapist's casebook* (pp.240-262). San Francisco: Jossey-Bass.

Rose, S.D. (1989). *Working with adult groups: Integrating cognitive-behavioral and small group strategies.* San Francisco: Jossey-Bass.

Deliberate Psychological Education (DPE)

The idea that affective education is of significant value in any teaching behavior is in direct support of the philosophy of peer helping. Since peer helping is one segment of the DPE concept, participating in a DPE program will enhance a trainer's potential for success as a peer helping trainer. A trainer must be creative and imaginative so as to bring to human learning experiences both affective and cognitive learning. Affective education is not restricted to schools but is equally viable in religious and social agencies within the community. Consequently, peer helping professionals must be aware and knowledgeable regarding what DPE is contributing to learning today. The purpose of this manual prevents explaining fully DPE concepts and strategies, but complete information can be found in the following articles and books:

Hayes, R. (1987). Research in humanistic education. *Journal of Humanistic Education and Development, 25*(3).

Ivey, A. (1992). *Developmental therapy: Theory into practice.* North Amherst, MA: Microtraining.

Ivey, A., & Alschuler, A. (Eds.). (1973). Psychological education: A prime function of the counselor. *The Personnel and Guidance Journal, 51* (9), 286-682.

Mosher, R., & Sprinthall, N. (1971). Deliberate psychological education. *The Counseling Psychologist, 2*(4), 3-117.

Sprinthall, N.A. (1971). *Guidance for human growth.* New York: Van Nostrand, Reinhold.

Sprinthall, N.A. (1973). Special feature: Psychological education. *The School Counselor, 20*(5), 332-361.

Gelstalt Workshops

The contribution of the Gestaltist is akin to the awareness taught by Otto. However, the focus of Gestalt methodology lies even more within the framework of creating awareness in self. Gestalt uses the concept of awareness and immediacy in combination to create an intensive focus upon immediate internal feelings and experience.

Several aspects are considered in the teaching and learning value of the Gestalt methodology in the training format.

1. A peer helping professional being in touch with his/her immediate feelings and experiences as a person sharpens his/her skill in developing more effective alternatives to his/her general behavior and reactions and to those peculiar to the training role.

2. An understanding of the concepts and techniques of Gestalt therapy will enable the peer helping professional to provide the same growth-producing experiences with trainees.

As a trainer and trainees experience themselves more completely, they develop a greater variety of coping and facilitative behaviors that augment and integrate the training skills. Understanding the importance of being aware of self with regard to feelings will enable the trainer to transcend the mechanical aspects of training to an integrated understanding of human feelings and of how they affect his/her behavior.

For these reasons, a familiarity with focus and strategies of Gestalt methodology is recommended to the trainer. Familiarity could be gained solely through reading, but attendance at Gestalt workshops where the peer helping professional could tie reading and experience together is recommended as a better alternative.

Barneete, E.L. (1989). Effects of a growth group on counseling students' self-actualization. *Journal for Specialists in Group Work*, 14(4), 202-210.

Blatner, A., with Blatner, A. (1988). *Foundations of psychodrama: History, theory, and practice* (3rd ed.). New York: Springer.

Holiman, M., & Engle, D. (1989). Guidelines for training in advanced Gestalt therapy skills. *Journal for Specialists in Group Work*, 14(2), 75-83.

Schaffer, J., & Galinsky, M.M. (1989). *Models of group therapy* (2nd ed.). Englewood Cliffs, NJ: Prentice-Hall.

Understanding the Self

The need to understand yourself is very important as you approach working with individuals of different types and styles of learning. Based on the theory of C.G. Jung and developed and refined by a mother-daughter team, Isabel Myers and Katherine Briggs, the *Myers-Briggs Type Indicator* as an instrument has helped individuals understand themselves as well as others. In understanding themselves, they begin to understand their work team, family setting, and intimates.

Excellent resources are *Please Understand Me* by Kiersey and Bates (1978), and *Type Talk* by Kroger and Thuesen (1988).

The *Myers-Briggs Type Indicator* can be ordered from the Center for Applications of Psychological Type, 2720 N.W. 6th Street, Gainesville, Florida 32609. The Bates and Kiersey book, *Please Understand Me,* can be ordered from Prometheus Nemesis Books, Post Office Box 2082, Del Mar, California 92014. Also, *Gifts Differing* by Isabel Briggs Myers and Peter Myers, 1980, can be ordered from Consulting Psychology, Palo Alto, California 94306.

Icebreakers and Energizers

In any group experience, the peer helping professional needs to have resources of icebreakers and energizers that help motivate peer helpers. Purposes of an icebreaker are to introduce participants to each other in a fun and quick manner; to help reduce the feelings of anxiety many participants bring with them to the learning experience; to help participants know that a high level of involvement will be expected; and to help the peer helping professional assess the initial concerns, expectations and resources of the group.

Energizers are needed to help the group gain energy during a training session. This is important especially if the training is at a retreat setting or all-day training. The energizers and icebreakers also must fit into the goals of the training.

Some of the recommended readings are the following:

Barry, S.A. (1987) *The world's best party games.* New York, NY: Sterling Publishing Co.

Consalvo, C. (1992). *Workplay.* King of Prussia, PA: Organization Design and Development.

Foster, E. (1989). *Energizers and icebreakers.* Minneapolis, MN: Educational Media.

Foster, E. (1994). *More energizers and ice breakers.* Minneapolis, MN: Educational Media.

Jones, J., & Bearley, W. (1989). *Energizers.* King of Prussia, PA: Organization Design and Development.

Jones, K. (1992). *Icebreakers: A sourcebook of games, exercises and simulations.* San Diego, CA: Pfieffer.

Scannel, E.E., & Newstrom, J.W. (1991). *Still more games trainers play: Experiential learning exercises.* New York: McGraw-Hill.

Group Experiences

Examine the following list of group skills and trainer skills, and identify in which ones you need help and find resources to assist you either through formal coursework, reading, seminars, or watching others and getting feedback on your skills.

GROUP LEADERSHIP SKILLS	Okay	Need Help
1. Active Listening	—	—
2. Blocking	—	—
3. Clarifying	—	—
4. Confronting	—	—
5. Dealing with Modeling	—	—
6. Disclosing Oneself	—	—
7. Empathizing	—	—
8. Evaluating	—	—
9. Facilitating	—	—
10. Giving Feedback	—	—
11. Initiating	—	—
12. Interpreting	—	—
13. Modeling	—	—
14. Questioning	—	—
15. Reflecting Feelings	—	—
16. Restating	—	—
17. Setting Goals	—	—
18. Suggesting	—	—
19. Summarizing	—	—
20. Supporting	—	—
21. Terminating	—	—
22. Other Skills (list)		

	TRAINER SKILLS	Okay	Need Help
1.	I understand the goals of each skill.	——	——
2.	I understand the goals of the project.	——	——
3.	I understand the goals of each training time.	——	——
4.	I know how to organize materials for training.	——	——
5.	I can utilize flip charts and A.V. equipment.	——	——
6.	I can model behavior that I am teaching.	——	——
7.	I can give feedback to participants.	——	——
8.	I feel comfortable demonstrating helping skills.	——	——
9.	I have group-processing skills.	——	——
10.	I can balance training and group needs.	——	——
11.	I can help peer helpers put their skills into action.	——	——
12.	I know about different learning and teaching techniques.	——	——
13.	I can train utilizing different learning and teaching techniques.	——	——
14.	I can make lesson plans.	——	——
15.	I know how to evaluate training.	——	——

You might list the skills areas requiring improvement and how you plan to acquire those skills.

_____

_____

_____

_____

You may get these skills in graduate courses on group leadership, NPHA training, reading, participating in groups yourself, or seeking specific training around different group skills and theoretical groups.

Hopefully, this review of the situational group skills needed by peer helping professionals will be helpful as you plan your own professional growth as well as for those on your peer helping professional team. If you have these skills, your peer helpers not only have a skilled professional working with them, they also have a road map of how to get to where they want to go; they will know that they are successful.

Much of the training of peer helpers is conducted in groups. For the peer helping professional to be familiar with both theory and practice of group interaction will be helpful. Although the training structure is disciplined and highly focused, many instances occur whereby the understanding of group dynamics can be very helpful to the peer helping professional. For example, group discussion of training experiences is an integral part of the training design and requires that the trainer have experience in group techniques and discussion techniques. The more skills and experiences the trainer gains, the more effective training procedures will become. Group experiences are helpful to the peer helping professional in several ways. These ways include the following:

Group experiences enable the trainer to learn experientially the dynamics that make up each group experience.

Group experiences enable the trainer to gain awareness and understanding of himself/herself and of others. A significant part of most group experiences is feedback from others. This feedback often is lacking in everyday living. Learning from others how to communicate through the use of the feedback loop is a helpful part of the format used. Feedback as a teaching/learning technique and its use in groups can provide valuable experience that is of benefit to trainers when they employ the same process in training.

Group experiences provide the trainer with an awareness of both good and poor human relations behavior. Within groups (because of their intensity), human behaviors that enhance or destroy growth quickly become apparent.

Effective groups are able to create some degree of intimacy and allow risk-taking behaviors. The ability to take risks and become intimate are qualities of human relations that are necessary factors in effective helping behaviors. Groups can provide experiences that demonstrate the productive and destructive potential of risk taking and/ or intimate behaviors. By intimate behaviors, we mean those behaviors that bring two or more individuals psychologically closer. As a result of intimate behaviors, self-disclosure and trust become by-products of new relationships.

ADDITIONAL READING

Groups

Different group experiences are available today. One must decide what level of group will be helpful. Suggested reading that will expand knowledge about groups follows:

Atkinson, D.R., Morten, G., & Sue, D.W. (1989). *Counseling American minorities* (3rd ed.). Dubuque, IA: William C. Brown.

Birren, J.E., & Deutchman, D.E. (1991). *Guiding autobiography groups for older adults: Exploring the fabric of life.* Baltimore: Johns Hopkins University Press.

Blatner, A. (1988). *Acting-in: Practical applications of psychodramatic methods* (2nd ed.). New York: Springer.

Blatner, A., with Blatner, A. (1988) *Foundations of psychodrama: History, theory and practice* (3rd ed.) New York: Springer.

Brown, L.N. (1991). *Groups for growth and change.* New York: Longman.

Butler, S., & Winetram, C. (1991). *Feminist groupwork.* Newbury Park, CA: Sage.

Corey, G. (1990). *Theory and practice of group counseling* (3rd ed.) Pacific Grove, CA: Brooks/Cole.

Corey, G. (1991). *Case approach to counseling and psychotherapy* (3rd ed.) Pacific Grove, CA: Brooks/Cole.

Corey, M.S., & Corey, G. (1992). *Groups: Process and practice* (4th ed.). Pacific Grove, CA: Brooks/Cole.

Corey, G., Corey, M., Callanan, P., & Russell, J.M. (1992). *Group techniques* (3rd ed.). Pacific Grove, CA: Brooks/Cole.

Douglas, T. (1991). *A handbook of common groupwork problems.* London and New York: Routledge.

Forsyth, D.R. (1990). *Group dynamics, second edition.* Pacific Grove, CA: Brooks/Cole Publishing Co.

Gazda, G.M. (1989). *Group Counseling: A developmental approach* (4th ed.). Boston: Allyn & Bacon.

Holmes, G.R., Heckel, R.V., & Gordon, L. (1991). *Adolescent group therapy,* New York: Praeger.

Jensen, A.D., & Childberg, J.C. (1991). *Small group communication: Theory and application.* Belmont, CA: Wadsworth.

Johnson, D.W. (1990). *Reaching out: Interpersonal effectiveness and self-actualization* (4th ed.). Englewood Cliffs, NJ: Prentice-Hall.

Johnson, D.W., & Johnson, F.P. (1991). *Joining together: Group theory and group skills* (4th ed.). Englewood Cliffs, NJ: Prentice-Hall.

Morganette, R.S. (1990). *Skills for living: Group counseling activities for young adolescents*. Champaign, IL: Research Press.

Napier, R.W., & Gershenfeld, M.K. (1989). *Groups: Theory and experience* (4th ed.). Boston: Hougton Mifflin.

Nichols, K., & Jenkinson, J. (1991). *Leading a support group*. London and New York: Chapman and Hall.

Ohlsen, M.M., Horne, A.M., & Lawe, C.F. (1988). *Group counseling* (3rd ed.). New York: Holt, Rinehart & Winston.

Ohlsen, M.M., Horne, A.M., & Lawe, C.F. (1988). *Group Psychotherapy*, 38(1), 29-46.

Shaffer, J., & Galinsky, M.D. (1989). *Models of group therapy* (2nd ed.). Englewood Cliffs, NJ: Prentice-Hall.

Sue, D.W., & Sue, D. (1990). *Counseling the culturally different: Theory and practice* (2nd ed.). New York: Wiley.

Tindall, J., & Salmon, S. (1993). *Feelings: The 3 Rs—receiving, reflecting, responding*. Muncie, IN: Accelerated Development.

Williams, D. (1991). *Seven myths about small groups: How to keep from falling into common traps*. Downers Grove, IL: Inter Varsity Press.

Worchel, S., Wood, W., & Simpson, J.A. (1991). *Group process and productivity*. Newbury Park, CA: Sage.

Wubbolding, R.E. (1988). *Using reality therapy*. New York: Harper & Row (Perennial Library.)

Zander, A.F. (1991). *Groups at work* (3rd ed.). San Francisco: Jossey-Bass.

Wellness/Stress Management

Wellness/stress management experience has been advocated by several authors. The whole concept involves striving toward becoming a healthy person. Knowledge of stress management and wellness concepts and activities may assist the trainer in becoming more effective.

The following are suggested books:

Gatto, R. (1990). *Controlling stress in the workplace.* San Diego, CA: Pfieffer & Co.

Karasek, R., & Theorell, T. (1990). *Healthy work.* New York: Basic Books.

Rosen, R. (1991). *The healthy company.* Los Angeles, CA: Jeremy Tarcher.

Schriner, C. (1990). *Feel better now.* Rolling Hills, CA: Jalmar Press.

Tager, M., & Willard, S. (1992). *Transforming stress into power.* Chicago, IL: Great Performance.

Drugs and Alcohol Abuse

Much literature exists on drug and alcohol abuse. Groups such as AA and Alanon are excellent references. You also may wish to contact hospitals specializing in treating chemical abusers and receive some of their materials. Following is a list of references:

Hazelden Books, Hazelden Educational Materials, Box 176, Center City, MN 55012.

Johnson Institute, 100700 Oldson Highway, Minneapolis, MN 55441-6199.

National Council on Alcoholism, located in most major cities.

Human Potential Experience

Human potential experience as espoused by Otto (1970) and his associates will assist the trainer in developing ways to help trainees understand the dynamics of their own behaviors and feelings. The Otto source provides ways to supplement training strategies in situations where the understanding of a specific human interpersonal experience will clarify the underlying rationale for a particular training strategy or technique. Knowledge of group experiences explored by Otto can help the trainer work effectively with training problems caused by affective roadblocks to learning occurring within the trainees. Using the appropriate affective human potential experience increases the peer helping professional's chance to break through the "hang-ups" that trainees may have at a particular point in the training.

SUMMARY

The single most important attitude for the peer helping professional is to want to be involved in a program and then to be willing to take the risks that such involvement entails. The growth gained by trainers in their efforts to prepare for and initiate a program is worth almost any outcome. Once the potential trainer begins to explore skills, attitudes, and experiences of peer helping, the potential for learning and development of personal skills is great.

> *"In oneself lies the whole world and if you know how to look and how to learn then the door is there and the key is in your hand. Nobody on earth can give you either key or the door to open except yourself."*
>
> —Idda Krishnamarts

STEPS TO A SUCCESSFUL PEER HELPING PROGRAM

Questions and concerns relating to peer helping programs and where to start include ones such as the following:

"Where do I start? We have so many needs, I don't know where to begin!"

"I think peer helping is a great idea, but how do I get the administration to agree to it?"

"The alcohol problem in our community is extreme. What could peer helpers do?"

"Students are dropping out of school. Would a peer program be helpful?"

"The people at the plant seem so stressed out."

"I wish I could develop some plan to help the elderly in my community."

"Certain neighborhoods in our city don't trust the professionals, so I wonder if peer helping is a good idea?"

"What kind of training do we give peer helpers?"

"How do we find and select peer helpers?"

The development, organization, and implementation of a new program involve an extensive amount of time, energy, and commitment. Specific guiding principles and practices are critical to the success of peer helping programs. Effective programs result from systematic planning, training, supervision, and evaluation. Systematic planning involves assessing needs, developing a plan that includes commitment to the program, and defining an organizational structure with effective training, supervision, and evaluation. The evaluation is of all three: the peer helpers, the system, and the extent to which helpers have benefitted. In Figure 7.1 are listed steps involved in setting up a successful program.

STEPS TO A SUCCESSFUL PEER HELPER PROGRAM

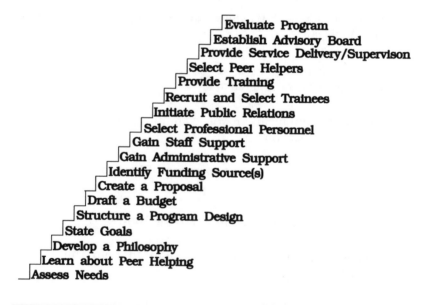

Figure 7.1. Steps to a successful peer helper program.

Step 1: ASSESS NEEDS

Professional counselors, psychologists, social workers, teachers, and religious leaders, who are responsible for the mental health of the community they serve, can improve their effectiveness by being actively involved in a systematic assessment of the psychological and helping needs of the populations they serve. This can range from an assessment of needs to a comprehensive assessment that involves testing, interviewing, and other psychological evaluation methods. Many school systems are using standardized testing to help identify student, parent, teacher, and administrative needs. One such assessment reference points out that high school students who have a problem first talk with students their own age; second, with relatives; third, with school counselors; and finally, with teachers. This kind of needs assessment, which indicates the tendency of students to consult their peers, would support the development of a peer helping program that could be helpful to students.

Another assessment strategy is interviewing students in order to determine the practicality of a peer helping program in a specific system. "Focus" groups are another form of doing needs assessments in schools, religious institutions, agencies, businesses, and industries. Teachers and administrators also have a responsibility to respond to an assessment of needs for a peer helping program. Plans to develop a peer helping program in a teen-age drop-in center require that the community needs be surveyed concerning the feasibility of such a program. If a group of peer helpers is to be employed to work with "child abuse" families, the families could be interviewed concerning their feelings about having a peer helping program that would affect them.

A form for considering needs for a peer helping program and for considering the source is provided in Form 7.1. Complete the form and recognize that you have completed the first step toward establishing a peer helping program.

ASSESSING NEEDS

Now take some time to decide what the needs are in your community and your work setting. What needs do you want the peer helpers to address? Try to indicate your source of information for each need. (Needs assessment, focus group, etc.)

IN MY COMMUNITY

Need   Information Source(s)

1. ——————————   ————————————————

2. ——————————   ————————————————

3. ——————————   ————————————————

IN MY WORK/SCHOOL SETTING

Need   Information Source(s)

1. ——————————   ————————————————

2. ——————————   ————————————————

3. ——————————   ————————————————

Form 7.1. Assessing needs, the first step toward a peer helper program.

Finally, the professional in a system could decide on a program that would be helpful in developing a more open place to attend the training sessions. The idea to emphasize is that the consumers of counseling and psychological services should be involved in determining needs. When the needs are identified, then ways of meeting those needs can be devised.

Step 2: LEARN ABOUT PEER HELPING

Before writing a proposal for a peer resource program, the literature in the field of peer helping must be examined. The person responsible for development of the program must be able to answer as many of the questions as possible that will be asked concerning peer helping. Professional literature needs to be examined in a deliberate manner. For example, ERIC (*Educational Resource Information Center*) is an important source to be contacted in a search for peer helping sources. A second resource is correspondence with people using peer helping in their programs.

A third resource, which was formed in 1987, is the *National Peer Helpers Association*. The address is P.O. Box 2684, Greenville, NC 27834. The purpose of the organization is to provide networking opportunities and support for peer helping programs. The association publishes a quarterly journal that describes programs and research throughout the country. They also hold a national conference each year. The first conference, which 350 individuals attended, was held in St. Charles, MO. The second conference, which 550 attended, was held in Ft. Collins, CO. Other conferences have been held in Seattle, New Orleans, Flagstaff, Chicago, Boston, and Portland.

The association is made up of peer helping professionals. It is one of the fastest growing associations in this country and has international membership.

Site visits to other places that have peer helping programs is a recommended procedure. The interested professional should try to spend a full day at a location to get a feel of the total responsibilities of the professional(s) in charge of the program. Observation of the training procedures, administration of the program, and innovative ideas will help to identify concepts and practices that would transfer effectively to another program.

Sachnoff (1984) reported in *High School Peer Resource Programs: A Director's Perspective* the result of a survey he conducted with directors of successful programs. These directors ranked in order of importance the different ingredients in the program. The categories and respective ranks are provided in Figure 7.2. As you start your program or refine it, you might refer to this list:

Rank of Importance	Program Category
1.	Strong program coordinator
2.	Good training
3.	Clear goals
4.	Student commitment and ownership
5.	Support from faculty
6.	Supervision
7.	Project director's contact with students
8.	Having a mixture of students
9.	Confidentiality
10.	Recruiting
11.	Students' having decision-making power
12.	Value explanation and reflection
13.	Good community resources
14.	Rewards and incentives

Figure 7.2. Rank order of importance of different ingredients in a peer helping program. Reprinted with permission from Ira S. Sachnoff (1984), *High School Peer Resource Programs: A Director's Perspective.*

During conventions of professional organizations, often programs and workshops are devoted to peer helping. Attending these meetings helps in gathering more information, gaining additional skills in operating a peer helping program, and/ or meeting other people who are involved in peer helping programs.

A person's job setting need not limit his/her learning about peer helping. An important point is to learn as much as possible about a wide variety of peer helping models in a variety of settings. For example, a crisis center counselor can learn much about training and advertising from school peer helping programs. From observations, reading, and inter-viewing, a proposal can be developed that will fit individual work settings more creatively.

A form for summarizing sources for learning about peer helping is provided (Form 7.2).

SOURCES FOR MY DEVELOPMENT

I will learn about peer helping programs from the following sources:

1. Written Material

   _____

   _____

   _____

2. Conferences and Workshops

   _____

   _____

   _____

3. Visits and Networking

   _____

   _____

   _____

4. Training

   _____

   _____

   _____

5. Other

   _____

   _____

   _____

Form 7.2. Learning about peer helping programs—sources for my development.

Step 3: DEVELOP A PHILOSOPHY

Reading and observations will compel an examination of personal feelings about a peer helping program. Investigation of peer helping will indicate that the prospective trainer needs to believe in the concepts of developmental and pragmatic helping as opposed to "crisis" helping. In other words, he/she must be sold on and be able to sell the idea of developmental helping and affective education to fellow professionals as well as to rest of the staff. An understanding of the philosophy underlying peer helping models enables the trainer to realign priorities including an understanding of oneself as a "trainer" and an increased concern for the mental health and communication skills of large numbers of people. The prospective trainer recognizes the necessity of being willing to give away his/her skills to lay people or paraprofessionals.

Try writing your philosophy and write how peer helping fits into or is allied with your philosophy. Form 7.3 is provided for you to complete this task.

> *Where there is no vision,*
>
> *the people perish*
>
> Proverb

PHILOSOPHY

On the part of the professional, the philosophy must involve an attitude of trusting others. You may want to examine your own attitudes toward involving others in decision making, involving others in program design, forming partnership with others, and allowing youth to share in organizational opportunities.

Think about your own philosophy of helping others. How does peer helping fit in? It is important that you are able to articulate this not only to yourself, but also to others. For example, "My aim is to help create a more caring community," and "I believe if you teach others effective listening skills, they will be able to be better parents, co-workers, and bosses." This helps me guide my own peer helping activities.

MY OWN PHILOSOPHY (I recognize that often my philosophy really is my own mission.)

My philosophy is ————————————————

————————————————————————————

————————————————————————————

————————————————————————————

HOW DOES PEER HELPING FIT INTO MY PHILOSOPHY?

Peer helping fits into my philosophy by ——————

————————————————————————————

————————————————————————————

————————————————————————————

Form 7.3. Summary of your philosophy and how it harmonizes with doing peer helping.

Step 4: STATE GOALS

The more specifically goals, objectives, and expected outcomes are stated, the stronger the proposal will appear to others including professional staff, co-workers, administrators, potential trainees, and funding agencies. By being as specific as possible, others are in the best position to evaluate the peer helping concept and to provide feedback relative to their interests.

Goals can be expressed in general terms and modified when additional feedback is obtained and prior to completing the proposal. Each goal will need objectives stated and as much as possible stated in behavioral objectives. When so stated, the objectives can be measured individually. Examples of a goal and an objective would be as follows:

Goal: To assist trainees in improving their attending skill. Objective: Trainees will improve their attending skill score by 10% as measured on an attending skill pre and post instrument.

Being specific regarding objectives may be difficult at this point in your planning; however, doing so will enable you to obtain feedback that will facilitate knowing how much others will support you. Also, a major point to keep in mind is that goals and objectives at this time in the planning are very much in a fluid state; thus, they can and probably will be changed with additional input.

> "Dreams are goals with wings."
>
> —Robert J. Kriegel

Form 7.4 will provide for you a place to write your goals and related objectives.

GOALS FOR MY PEER HELPING PROGRAM

For example, Goal 1 might be to train peer helpers in effective listening skills, and Goal 2 might be to reduce teen pregnancy through the peer helping projects.

Make sure that each goal relates to the need(s) as identified in Step 1, Assess Needs.

Goal 1.
    Objective A. _____

                     _____

    Objective B. _____

                     _____

Goal 2.
    Objective A. _____

                     _____

    Objective B. _____

                     _____

Goal 3.
    Objective A. _____

                     _____

    Objective B. _____

                     _____

Goal 4.
    Objective A. _____

                     _____

    Objective B. _____

                     _____

Form 7.4. Goals and objectives for the peer helping program.

Step 5. STRUCTURE A PROGRAM DESIGN

Once you have tentatively identified goals and objectives, then you can structure a program design. Here you begin to target the people who need the help, the ones who will benefit from having peer helpers work with them. Many questions need to be raised, and with tentative answers you will begin to establish boundaries.

Whom will the peer program serve? The answer to this establishes those to be included and likewise those to be excluded.

Where are they? The answer to this will be a major factor in both the peer helper training and supervision of peer helpers as they work with the target audience. Also, where they are probably will determine when the training is to be done and may help decide the facility where the training will occur.

How many people may be assisted by peer helpers? The answer here will help determine the number of peer helpers that will need to be trained and equally important the number of peer helpers to be supervised as they become practitioners of peer helping.

What are the ages of the people to be served? The answer here will help decide the desired age level of potential peer helpers to be trained.

What kind of peer helping will be offered? The answer here has two important implications for the program. First, the kind of assistance offered will determine the extent of training and the content of the training. Second, the kind of assistance offered will be determined by the level and kind of qualifications of the trainer and the supervisor once the peer helpers begin assisting others.

How many of the targeted audience will be willing to be trained and then to serve as peer helpers? Peer helping means help offered by peers. Thus, of those selected to receive the help, some of them will be the ones to receive the training and to implement their training. Their cooperation is a necessity.

What kinds of facilities will be needed and for how long? The physical requirements for training peer helpers include a minimum of a room that can be private and away from the mainstream of activities during training. Of course, the room needs to be pleasant, warm, and representative of the attitude and feelings of the group being serviced. Flexible, comfortable, and movable furniture is desirable, and adequate informal lighting is necessary.

Form 7.5 is provided to record answers to the preceding questions. With answers to those questions, you can begin to structure a program design (See Form 7.4).

STRUCTURING A PROGRAM DESIGN

Directions: Record answers to the following questions in order to give structure to the peer helping program.

1. Whom will the peer program serve? ————————————
   ————————————————————————————

2. Where are they located? ————————————————
   ————————————————————————————

3. How many people may be assisted by peer helpers once the program is in operation? ————————————
   ————————————————————————————

4. What are the ages of the people to be served? ———————
   ————————————————————————————

5. What kind of peer helping will be offered? —————————
   ————————————————————————————

6. How many of the targeted audience will be willing to be trained and then to serve as peer helpers? ———————
   ————————————————————————————

7. What kind of physical facilities will be needed? ————————
   ————————————————————————————

8. What kinds of furniture and communication (telephone, etc.) equipment will be needed? —————————————
   ————————————————————————————

Form 7.5. Questions to consider as the structure of the peer helping program is being designed.

Step 6. DRAFT A BUDGET

In developing a budget, include specific categories and costs both to the funding organization and to the supporting agency (school, church, or business). Hidden costs must be identified carefully and included in the proposal. These hidden costs include heat, transportation, telephone, physical setting, equipment, and a variety of support personnel. Listed are two examples of budget possibilities. The first (Figure 7.3) would support a small project located within the agency. The second (Figure 7.4) is typical of the budget of a large funded project.

BUDGET

Duration of Project — September 1994 through January 1995

A. Activities

1. To select peer helpers.

2. To conduct basic training for peer helpers every Tuesday and Wednesday for 1 hour for 10 weeks.

3. To assign peer helpers, once trained, to their responsibilities.

4. To provide advanced and follow-up training for 10 weeks once a week.

B. Staff

One peer helping professional
2 hrs/wk for 20 wks
2 x 20 x $28.00/hr $1,120.00

One secretary
2 hrs/wk for 20 wks
2 x 20 x $7.00/hr 280.00

Total for salaries $1,400.00

C. Materials

Video/Audio equipment, 2 hrs/wk

1 *Peer Power, Book 1, Strategies*   1 x $16.95 $ 16.95

1 *Peer Power, Book 2, Strategies*   1 x $14.95   14.95

10 *Peer Power, Book 1, Workbooks*	10 x $13.56	135.60
10 *Peer Power, Book 2, Workbooks*	10 x $11.96	119.60
4 videotapes	4 x $50.00	200.00
10 audio tapes	10 x $3.00	30.00
10 *Problem Solving* audio tapes	10 x $9.95	99.50
Total for Materials		$ 616.60
Total Cost		$2,016.60

Figure 7.3. Sample budget for a small project located within an agency.

BUDGET

Itemized Budget for — August, 1994 through July 1995

	Source of Funds	
	Funding Agency	Local Funds
A. Salaries		
Project Director (1)	$25,000.00	$10,000.00
Associate Director (2)	30,000.00	10,000.00
Adm. Assistant ½ time x 10 mos	10,000.00	-0-
Research Assistant ¼ time x 10 mos	5,000.00	-0-
Community Workers ¼ time x 10 mos	600.00	700.00
Clerical Staff		
Secretary full time x 12 mos	9,000.00	3,000.00
Grad. Assistant $350/mo x 10 mos	3,500.00	-0-
Student Clerical Workers 4.25/hr. x 3hr/wk x 36 wks	459.00	-0-
Total for Salaries	$83,559.00	$23,700.00

B. Fringe Benefits

Retirement Plan	$ 6,709.77	-0-
Hospitalization Insurance	2,000.00	-0-
Social Security (7.65%)	6,392.26	-0-
Total for Fringe Benefits	$15,102.03	-0-

C. Contractual Services

Consultants $500.00/day x 25/days	$12,500.00	-0-
Rental for Equipment	500.00	100.00
Travel for Consultants $50.00/day x 25 days (May be put in Travel section)	1,250.00	-0-
Total for Contractual Services	$14,250.00	$ 100.00

D. Travel

Domestic

200 miles x 4 cars x .28 per mile	$ 224.00	-0-

Per Diem

$50.00 (in state) x 15 days	750.00	-0-
$60.00 (out of state) x 14 days	840.00	-0-

Trips (not overnight)

(Daily rate) $25.00 x 17 days	425.00	-0-
Total for Travel	$ 2,239.00	$-0-

E. Commodities
Things that are expendable

(May need to be itemized)	-0-	$ 500.00
Total for Commodities	$-0-	$ 500.00

F. Equipment

Equipment to be purchased

(List all equipment to be purchased)	$ 5,000.00	$ 1,000.00

Total for Equipment	$5,000.00	$ 1,000.00

G. Communications

Postage	1,500.00	-0-
Telephone—long distance	2,500.00	200.00
Total for communications	$ 4,000.00	$200.00

H. Indirect Costs

(Overhead of Institution)	$ 7,841.00	$ 4,000.00
Total Cost	$131,991.03	$29,500.00

Figure 7.4.   Sample budget for a large project proposal.

Three examples of large locally supported peer helping programs are found in Palo Alto, CA (The Spark Program); New York City; and St. Louis, MO. Palo Alto has developed an extensive school-wide peer helping program. The Spark Program is the largest peer project in the country, with services at 107 high schools. Youth Emergency Service is a crisis center for runaways in St. Louis, MO. Ferguson-Florissant School District of Missouri has peer helping programs in all its schools serving a variety of needs.

Spark is a good example of how peer helping grew out of the need for teens to share and work out common problems. In 1971 a group of New York educators (funded by the *State Department of Drug and Substance Abuse Services*) created a drug-prevention program because heroin addiction was then epidemic. They learned that teens got the message best when sharing each others' life stories. So Spark set up "rap groups" under the direction of adult counselors so that the counselors might start training the students to do some of the things that the counselors do, always under supervision.

On Form 7.6 is provided space for you to record basic information related to the budget. These figures may be tentative and may need to be revised as more information is collected. By having a tentative budget you will be better prepared to talk with funding sources.

PEER HELPING BUDGET

Source	Dollars
Personnel (List Positions)	
_____	_____
_____	_____
_____	_____
Facilities (List)	
_____	_____
_____	_____
_____	_____
Equipment	
_____	_____
_____	_____
_____	_____
Materials	
Books	
_____	_____
_____	_____
_____	_____
Audiovisual	
_____	_____
_____	_____
_____	_____
Other	
_____	_____
_____	_____
_____	_____

continued

Training

Professionals

_____   _____

_____   _____

_____   _____

Peer Helpers

_____   _____

_____   _____

_____   _____

Travel

_____   _____

_____   _____

_____   _____

Communication

_____   _____

_____   _____

_____   _____

Evaluation

_____   _____

_____   _____

_____   _____

Form 7.6. Form on which to create a budget for the local peer helping program.

Step 7.   CREATE A PROPOSAL

In writing the proposal, keep in mind needs, attitudes, and values that are supported by the local community. For example, the title of a proposal might be "Youth Listener Program" rather than Peers Helping, depending upon prevailing attitudes in the community to be served.

Write your proposal so that it can be shared with others. You and the proposal will need to be flexible and the proposal modified as new information is obtained.

The extent of a proposal depends on the scope of a program and the amount of financing required to operate it. The proposal could be a few pages written to a supervisor describing a small scale program operated by one person, or it could be a comprehensive grant proposal requesting state or federal funding.

The smallest proposal can be a conversation with an administrative superior. Even with regard to a concept of small scope, one must be well organized. The organizational process must include for an effective proposal an extensive understanding of the concept of peer helping. Its assets and liabilities also should be included. The proposal needs to include a feasible plan and procedure for implementing the ideas of peer helping within a specific system. A general idea of the costs, both in time and money, is vital to selling a program. In addition, as much support as possible needs to be gained from individuals who will be benefitted by the program.

Often a program can be developed within the building itself, such as in a school, church, or industrial plant, but many times it cannot. Additional community, governmental agency, or other outside support is sometimes needed. Outside support usually is of a financial nature, and when finances are involved, a program enters the competition with all the other financial obligations of the supporting group. When a program goes outside of the school, church, or local group for aid, an extensive proposal often is needed and always is helpful.

In developing an extended proposal, specific guidelines are worth following. Each funding source, whether local, private, state, or federal, follows specific guidelines in choosing the programs it will endorse. Guidelines are usually published by the funding agency.

Step 8. IDENTIFY FUNDING SOURCE(S)

The size of your peer helping program may determine whether or not funding will be secured from local sources only or local plus another funding source—private, business and industrial, community, state, or federal. Therefore, Step 6, Draft a Budget, and Step 7, Create a Proposal, are essential steps before identifying funding sources.

To identify the agency or agencies that might lend support, contact the person in the local area whose responsibility it is to secure grants and funding. Also, the local library can provide information regarding both governmental and private funding agencies. Other sources are state and federal governments that have offices where information about funding for specific groups can be obtained. A letter or telephone call requesting this information can direct an applicant to the right source.

After determining which agencies are supporting projects of this nature, the prospective trainer *may need to revise the proposal according to the agencies' guidelines.* In addition, he/she should request assistance from the funding agency in offering constructive criticism for the proposal. When writing an agency to request guidelines, no obscurity should occur in the trainer's statements about the program he/she would like to develop. Many granting agencies will help in the writing of the proposal if they feel that the applicant has a sound, viable idea. The idea should include a clear-cut need, a rationale, and a plan for meeting that need, all described in general terms when the funding agency is contacted.

Before submitting a proposal, *work with people who have had experience developing and funding a project.* If a person has contacts with people responsible for funding, get their feedback on a proposal before final submission.

Step 9. GAIN ADMINISTRATIVE SUPPORT

Administrative support can be gained in many ways. Inviting a supervisor to read short articles, attend programs, visit peer helping projects or attend meetings on peer helping will increase the probability of administrative understanding and support for the ideas the trainer will be presenting. "Kaffee klatsch" diplomacy is another method of laying supportive groundwork with administrators prior to submitting a formal proposal. These informal get-togethers reveal areas of opposition, dissonance, confusion, or support that enable one to submit a proposal that accounts for possible administrative areas of objection or confusion.

By anticipating administrative and staff objections or problems, a trainer is in a better position to respond to objections, to clarify confused areas, and generally to meet the needs of supporting personnel. Gaining administrative support by meeting their needs as well as possible increases a program's chance of gaining outside rapport.

Step 10. GAIN STAFF SUPPORT

Successful programs require the support of staff as well as administration. In attempting to develop new programs, concepts, ideas, and gaining consensus from the group with whom the trainer will work is extremely difficult. To set consensus as a goal before initiating a peer helping program would be a mistake. A more effective way to begin a program is to identify those staff members who can be depended upon for support and interest. If a trainer seeks people who are sympathetic to the goals and attitudes of his/her program, positive reinforcement will occur in the program development. A greater chance of success is assured if the trainer works with one or two people who support his/her program than if the trainer must convince ten skeptics of the value of a program before it has an opportunity to sell itself. A successful program staffed by a small group of dedicated persons will more likely gain a wider support base from other staff members than any other program.

To get the maximum support possible, trainers must involve those who are interested in all stages of program development. This involvement includes soliciting ideas, proposal writing, program development, publicity, logistics, and all other aspects of the total project. In this way, supporting personnel have a vested interest in the success of the program. Other staff members who may not have time for program development or implementation still deserve to be kept informed on the progress and procedures of the program. Figure 7.5 is an example of a published information sheet given to staff members.

YOUTH LISTENER PROGRAM

Goals

1. To train youth listeners in communication skills.

2. To teach youth listeners in skills in career awareness.

3. To provide students with an opportunity to talk with other peers that have been trained in listening skills.

4. To help students looking for career information.

5. To help students with academic problems.

6. To assist new students with academic problems.

7. To assist youth listeners in personal growth.

Selection

1. Students volunteer to be youth listeners through cadet teaching.

2. If the counselor in charge of training thinks the student will not be effective, the student is asked to drop.

3. Possess 3.0 grade point average for cadet teaching.

Training

1. Basic training—40 hours, which include attending, empathy, open-ended questions, genuineness, confrontation, problem solving, conflict mediator, confidentiality, peer helping roles, referral sources, career center, and awareness activities.

2. Advance training—weekly meetings either individually or in groups, to set goals, evaluate programs, and obtain further guidance and scheduling.

Figure 7.5. Example of an information sheet given to staff members regarding Youth Listener Program.

Form 7.7 contains space to list activities you will do to obtain administrative and staff support. List as many different activities as you believe will be necessary and effective.

GAINING SUPPORT

Gaining Administrative Support
Overall Plan

_____

_____

_____

Specific Activities (what, where, when, materials needed, etc.)

1. _____

   _____

2. _____

   _____

Gaining Staff Support
Major Personnel to Target

_____

_____

_____

Specific Activities (what, where, when materials needed, etc.)

1. _____

   _____

2. _____

   _____

Form 7.7. Tentative plans for gaining administrative and staff support.

Step 11. SELECT PROFESSIONAL PERSONNEL

By reading this book, you will gain an idea as to what professional personnel you will need for your peer programs. At the same time, you must still focus on the concept of the TEAM, or chances of continued success may rapidly slip away. Identify key personnel in the program, help them understand their relationship to the program, involve them in the training, and this will add the strength and energy that the program will need to assist with long-term service to the trainees and the community they service. Peer helping is not a maverick program; it cannot operate by the efforts of one person, even when those efforts are unselfish and heartfelt. The chances for the success and long life of a peer helping program are directly proportional to the number of people who are involved in and feel ownership of that program.

Form 7.8 is provided so that you can identify functions needed by professional personnel. Once having done so, you identify the person or persons and their current skills. In some instances additional skills may be needed. If so, you will need to consider how, when, and where those skills may be obtained.

PERSONNEL NEEDS

Who	Function/Activity	Current Skill	Needed Skill

PEER PROFESSIONAL

	Planning		
	Recruitment		
	Selection		
	Training		
	Group Leadership		
	Supervision		
	Evaluation		
	Other		

PEER PROFESSIONAL COORDINATOR

| | | | |

ADMINISTRATOR/MANAGER

| | | | |

ADVISORY COMMITTEE

Form 7.8. Identification of personnel needs.

Step 12. INITIATE PUBLIC RELATIONS

An often neglected but vital part of any program development is gaining and maintaining strong community support systems. Support from the community leadership and population is a necessity for programs that serve agencies and churches as well as those that serve schools. Several methods can be used so that community groups can be involved in or be made aware of peer helping projects.

One method is to organize an advisory committee composed of key community leaders who will lend a solid base of support for the program. An advisory board may serve as a consulting group, as a reaction group for ideas, or as assistants in program development. Persons chosen for the advisory board do not have to be trained or experienced in affective education, but they need to have attitudes, experiences, and philosophies that would enable them to understand the concepts of peer helping. Other groups that can be employed for help include student groups and political system groups (e.g., school boards, church boards, federal agencies, and city councils).

Letters and visits to other social service agencies also will help gain acceptance of the program from other professionals in the area. Examples of groups that can be contacted are crisis centers, social welfare agencies, YMCAs, YWCAs, professional helping organizations, and private agencies. If these groups are made aware of the peer helping program, they can lend support, training, and public relations for development.

Graphic materials are an important adjunct to community support groups and need to be developed regardless of what other activities are instituted. Through the use of brochures, awards to peer helpers, thank-you letters, posters, business cards, and other graphic presentations, the scope of the program can be publicized to the individuals and groups.

Newspaper publicity, staff bulletins, spot radio announcements, and radio interviews are additional ways in which a program can be presented for public knowledge and support. Publicity is necessary during all stages of development but is vital when the program is operational. Speaking at community service groups, using slide presentations, videotapes if available, demonstrations, and audience participation experiences all work to increase the scope of public knowledge about a peer helping program.

Form 7.9 is provided for you to list potential public relations activities. To assure continuity and wide coverage, the public relations activities will require a planned program with dates, personnel, purpose, and material identified.

PUBLIC RELATIONS ACTIVITIES

1. Public Relations Plan

    Publicity (Where, When, What)

    _____

    Brochures (Kind, Theme, Audiences)

    _____

    Presentations (Who, What, Where, When, Purposes)

    _____

2. Recognition

    Professionals _____

    Peer Helpers _____

3. Professional Involvement

    National _____

    State _____

4. Writing for Profession (P.F.Q., professional association)

    _____

    _____

Form 7.9. Identification of potential public relations activities.

Step 13. RECRUIT AND SELECT TRAINEES

People to be trained can be secured in a number of ways. The alternatives described in this book are by no means complete or exhaustive. In the schools, special courses can be small units within a standard course. Students in study hall can be participants for training sessions, or training groups can be started with students from several classes at once.

In using special courses, students can apply for entrance through application or interview. The purpose of the interview is to inform potential trainees of the nature and demands of the training and responsibilities of peer helping. In addition, the trainer is able to interact initially with the participants and form a subjective opinion concerning each applicant. The courses should have special titles such as "The Art of Helping," "Communications Training," "Leadership Training," or other descriptive titles. These special courses can be a short workshop type or longer semester courses depending upon the school's scheduling flexibility.

On the other hand, the trainer may want to work through standard courses such as English, social studies, or psychology. The training procedure that is most effective with this model is co-teaching. The term co-teaching means placing two instructors in a class with different roles. In this process, students are able to select either the peer helping training or participation in the regular class activities. Each instructor would work with one group. Additional space is required by the co-teaching procedure, and that situation could be a problem if physical facilities are overcrowded. When selecting a co-teacher with whom to work, choose a person who is supportive of the peer helping concept and possesses a flexible personality.

Regular attendance is a greater problem when students are taken from study halls or other classes. These alternatives have enough disadvantages to warrant being in a low priority for selection at training times.

Finding trainees in community agencies, such as crisis centers and churches, is more difficult than in schools. Schools are fortunate enough to have a captive pool of people, while agencies or churches must rely on outside community resources. With agencies, trainees must commit time and effort to attend training sessions, which require time in addition to their regular tasks. Because this limits the population, agency trainers need to be creative in devising advertising and selling techniques. Newspaper articles, word of mouth, and speeches at community groups are all effective ways to advertise for potential peer helping trainees. With churches or community agencies, establishment of an advisory board is very important. In addition to the previously listed responsibilities, a board can be very helpful in implementing advertising procedures in a peer helping program. Another source to consider is to contact business and industry to ask them to announce/advertise in their newsletters.

Informational meetings for people interested in peer helping training are a necessary step in program development before the start of training. In this meeting, the trainer has an opportunity to

1. establish training session times by taking into account the needs of the trainees, which is more effective than an arbitrary predetermined schedule,

2. give a brief description and demonstration of the proposed training experience,

3. explain the peer helping responsibilities, and

4. meet with parents or spouses to explain programs.

If trainees are under 16 years of age, inviting parents or guardians to attend the informational meeting is wise.

One of the prevailing questions is, "Who is to be trained?" The answer that deserves serious consideration is that any person interested in receiving peer helping training deserves the opportunity to be trained. Receiving the training does not assure being selected as a peer helper. Communications training that utilizes humanistic concepts and structured models for training procedures can be beneficial to everyone. Whether a person uses the skills in peer helping activities or not, the experiences gained will be useful. Carkhuff (1969) has supported this opinion in his research and field experience, and other research has supported the fact that people experience positive behavior changes as the result of interpersonal communications training (Gray & Tindall, 1974). Salespersons, students, parents, teachers, businesspersons, prison guards, agency clients, and people in a wide range of human activities are using the skills they have learned. Therefore, training can be meaningful and helpful for all people interested. The limiting factors will be adequate funds, staff, and physical facilities.

If staff and/or funds are limited, several methods are available for obtaining information about individuals prior to selection. The methods may include one or more of the following:

1. interview method,

2. formal application,

3. pretesting, and/or

4. staff or peer referrals.

The **interview** selection process consists of a pretraining interview, the object of which is to assist the trainer in selection of potential participants. The criterion for selection is one that the trainer will develop. Research (Scott & Warner, 1974) has shown that one criterion for selection is about as good as another. Several students in Scott and Warner's literature search show that people who generate warmth and attentive behaviors, whatever warmth is, usually are more effective as the result of their training.

Formal application is another screening device that can identify superficial information in addition to the applicant's willingness to commit his/her time to the training and his/her attitude toward helping people. (See Appendices I, J.)

By using a communication exercise as a pretest, the trainer is able to get a feel for the readiness and skill level of the people applying for the program. A communication exercise pretest is included in *Peer Power Book 1*, Exercise 1.1. However, the trainer is encouraged to develop his/her own pretest to fit situations relevant to the population.

Often institutions will have a sociogram in which they ask students, employees, teachers, administrators, and supervisors who they think are good helpers—those persons who seem to be good listeners and are interested in helping them are frequent answers. From this list, potential helpers can be asked to apply (see Appendix G).

Other staff members and peers are often in a position to refer people to the trainer as trainees. These sources are not available as frequently as others but are very valuable resources. Referrals from other staff members should be encouraged as a matter of good public relations. Also, their awareness of trainees with a good potential is often helpful.

One must avoid making the entry into a training program difficult or complicated or both. The purpose is to train many people rather than only a few. Adolescents, especially, will tend to shy away from any program that runs the risk of making applicants to a program appear ineffective, stupid, or uncomfortable. A complicated or strict entrance requirement easily could defeat an otherwise good program. Teenagers and lay adults who are volunteering their service often are not willing to complete stringent screening devices.

Form 7.10 contains space for you to consider major components in the recruitment and initial selection of peer helpers to train.

PEER HELPING RECRUITMENT AND SELECTION

1. How will potential peer helpers be informed of the possibility of training? ————————————

   ————————————————————

2. Who will be recruited? ————————————

   ————————————————————

3. When will recruitment take place? ————————

   ————————————————————

4. Where will recruitment take place? ————————

   ————————————————————

5. How many will be recruited? ————————————

   ————————————————————

6. What method(s) will be used to obtain information about individuals? ————————————————

   ————————————————————

7. Who will conduct the selection procedure? ————————

   ————————————————————

8. Will all who apply be trained? If not, who will decide who is selected? ————————————————

Form 7.10. Items to consider in recruitment and initial selection of peer helpers to train.

Step 14. PROVIDE TRAINING

Your peer helping training needs to be designed to fit the age of your trainees and the ability level of your trainees. You also will want to consider the kinds of projects you will be undertaking. For example, if you are going to undertake a tutoring and classroom presentation project, you may want to first take your trainees through *Peer Power, Book 1* and then *Peer Power, Book 2* on Tutoring and Small Group Skills and Classroom Presentation. You will need to plan your curriculum to fit your time line.

Training of peer helpers comes in two phases. The first phase is the basic training that is needed by all peer helpers. The second phase is when they are applying their skills and implementing their projects. Then applied training needs to take place. Some of the components for beginning training are as follows:

What is Peer Helping?—Help participants understand the concept

Introduction to the Program—What is this program all about—try to get ownership

Look at Helping—Help participants understand helping and what this means

Attending Skills—Skill around nonverbal behavior

Communication Stoppers—Understand what stops communication

Empathy—Skills around listening for feelings and meaning of message

Summarizing—Skills around listening for total message and giving feedback

Questioning—Skills for open-ended questions and closed questions

Genuineness—Being open about self and explaining self

Assertive Skills—Skills concerning explaining self and asking for what you want

Confrontation Skills—Skills in how to change behavior in others

Problem-solving Skills—Skills in helping others solve issues

Conflict Resolution—Skills in helping others solve conflicts

Code of Ethics—Developing a code of ethics for the local program

Personal Growth—Trainees will learn about self and areas of growth

Putting Peer Helping into Action—System for implementation

Form 7.11 contains space for you to identify major components of your curriculum plan. Be sure to consider the time needed and the number of sessions for each topic.

Step 15. SELECT PEER HELPERS

Even though training may benefit and ideally should be available to everyone, all interested people do not make effective peer helpers. Therefore, one of the professional trainers' responsibilities is to make the final selection of peer helpers. The trainer is to assume this responsibility for two very important reasons: (1) public apprehension is reduced concerning possible peer helpers' inappropriate behaviors if their selection is made by a responsible professional, and (2) ultimate responsibility for peer helping rests solely with the trainer. Effectiveness of the program depends upon well-trained and well-selected participants. Trainers cannot absolve their responsibility to the population their trainees will service by avoiding the decisions of selection.

BASIC PEER HELPING PROGRAM CURRICULUM PLAN

Setting ————————————————————————————

Age Level of People to be Served ————————————————

Professional(s) ——————————————————————

Trainer(s) ————————————————————————

Others ——————————————————————————

Basic Training	Time Needed	Lessons

What is Helping?

Introduction?

Confidentiality

Look at helping

Understanding Program

Core Skills	Time Needed	# of Sessions

Attending

Empathy

Summarizing

Questioning

Genuineness

Assertiveness

Confrontation

Problem Solving

Conflict Resolution

Other(s)

Additional Skills	Time Needed	# of Sessions

Supervision of Peer Helpers ————————————————

————————————————————————————————

————————————————————————————————

Form 7.11. Identifying major components of a curriculum plan.

Trainer, peer, self, and staff evaluations of trainees, in addition to posttesting, are methods of final selection. Effective selection is improved if as many procedures as feasible are used before final selection is made.

Qualities of subjective humanistic conditions in trainees often are the major selection criteria. The characteristics of warmth, interest, acceptance of others, tolerance of divergent value systems, and high energy level are qualities that weigh heavily in the selection process. These humanistic qualities are as important for the trainees to possess as are the skills they will be learning in training.

The characteristics of the population to be served are very important for the trainer to know. The importance of the characteristics in the helping process was clarified by Kohlberg (1971, p. 13) when he stated, " ...that development is not effective in relating to people whose moral development is widely varied from theirs." Because of this condition, the trainer must be cognizant of any wide variation between peer helpers' value systems and the value systems of the people whom they serve. For example, upper socioeconomic class trainees will be ineffective, generally, with ghetto residents.

Evaluation of trainees by their peers and other staff members can augment the trainer's evaluation criteria. Evaluation input by other staff members and the trainees' contemporaries must be tempered by the fact that their information regarding trainee's behaviors and/or attitudes may be limited. For evaluation purposes, the same communication exercise in *Peer Power, Book 1* that was used as a pretest can function as a posttest.

Trainees undergo self-evaluation during the training process, and as a result, some decide not to become peer helpers. A trainee's self-appraisal usually is consistent with the trainer's appraisal. This kind of self-evaluation should be encouraged throughout the training process and can become one valid criterion for final selection.

Additional training or working with more competent peer helpers is a suggested procedure for those people who are considered marginal or ineffective in their helping skills. Some institutions meet with individuals and send letters saying that they have not been accepted into the peer helping projects.

The trainer may make the decision on how to use the peer helpers. For example, those peer helpers with good group skills will be "small group" leaders. Those with good one-on-one listening skills may work with at-risk youths. Business and industry may want to use recovering alcoholics trained as peer helpers to reach out to substance abusers. To use peer helpers in projects when they do not have the skills is a disservice to the peer helper as well as the peer helpees.

The final decision to retain or drop a trainee who cannot function effectively is the responsibility of the trainer. To drop a person from the program after all efforts to raise skill levels have been tried often is a difficult task. However, the trainer has the responsibility to do so because an ineffective person can affect others negatively in helping situations (Carkhuff, 1969).

Start one or more new basic training groups when the first group completes its training and moves to advanced training sessions. Attrition through various conditions will deplete the ranks of peer helpers unless new training groups can fill in for those who have dropped out for any reason.

Form 7.12 is provided for you to record responses to typically considered items when deciding how peer helpers will be selected.

Form 7.13 is an informal contract to have peer helpers sign. Doing so often will enable peer helpers to consider their role with the importance that it has. You may want to produce a form for your local use and perhaps spell out in more detail what the peer helpers role is.

SELECTION OF PEER HELPERS

1. What criteria will be used in selection of peer helpers to assist with the peer resource program?

   _____

   _____

2. When will the selection be done (ongoing during training or after completion of initial training)?

   _____

   _____

3. How many peer helpers are needed?

   _____

   _____

4. How will trainees be notified as to their selection or not?

   _____

   _____

5. Will trainees be selected with limitations on the kind of peer helping they will do (e.g., small group work, one-on-one helping, conflict resolution, etc.)?

   _____

   _____

6. How will the peer helper selection process be evaluated?

   _____

   _____

Form 7.12.   Items to consider in the selection of peer helpers.

```
┌─────────────────────────────────────────────────────────┐
│                    PEER HELPER ROLE                       │
│                                                           │
│  I agree to be a helper to  ────────────────────────────  │
│                                                           │
│  I agree to learn about starting a peer helping program   │
│                                                           │
│  ─────────────────────────────────────────────────────   │
│                                                           │
│  by                                                       │
│                                                           │
│  ─────────────────────────────────────────────────────   │
│                                                           │
│                                                           │
│            I want a Caring, Competent Community           │
└─────────────────────────────────────────────────────────┘
```

Form 7.13. Informal contract for peer helpers to sign as they are selected as peer helpers.

Step 16. PROVIDE SERVICE DELIVERY/SUPERVISION

Peer helpers also need to be monitored as they are providing service delivery to various programs. This is the supervision section of the program. Someone needs to meet with the peer helpers on a regular basis to monitor progress and help solve problems. This could be done with regular meetings or a regular class for credit. Someone also needs to be available for ongoing support. An example of where professional support was needed was in a college program that had resident hall peer helpers without professional support. One of the peer helpers went to a dorm room to try to prevent a suicide. The peer helper called local mental health professionals and the student was sent to the emergency ward of a hospital. The peer helper did the right thing but felt very alone.

Peer helpers have been effective with a widely diversified group of people, from working with indigent welfare recipients, to working as elementary school tutors. The number of ways that peer helpers can serve has not yet reached a limit. One thing that research has shown is that peer helper programs are most effective when peers and professionals are responsible for helping functions as conjoint workers. Using nonprofessionals for undesirable tasks has proven to be both unethical and ultimately destructive to the program.

Nonprofessionals can be used many ways to help other individuals. These uses include the ones shown in Figure 7.6. This list is not exhaustive but identifies some ways in which peers can help various populations in different settings.

Functioning As	Setting
Rap leaders	Crisis centers
Tutors	Teen centers, schools, adult learning centers
Outreach personnel	Schools
Discussion leaders	Veterans centers
Political leaders	Welfare offices
Peer ministers and youth ministers	Church groups
Individual counselors	Other organized groups
New student orientators	Schools
Leaders	Support groups
Special friends	Elementary schools

Figure 7.6. Illustrative ways that nonprofessionals are used to help other individuals and within what settings.

To provide service delivery will require attention to four very important ongoing activities:

1. assignment of peer helpers to specific functions and/or people/groups,

2. training during the implementation to assure that peer helpers have the specialized skills needed to deliver the services required,

3. professional supervision of peer helper activities, and

4. identifcation of support professionals for peer helpers.

Implementation of programs may be seen in a variety of ways. For example, if the peer helping program is to be involved in tutoring, then training in learning styles and tutoring is important. If the peer helpers are to do one-on-one peer helping, then training in one-on-one listening is important. Examples of training in the implementation part are as follows:

Skills in Classroom Presentation

Skills in Small Group Helping

Awareness of Self and Others
    •Eating Disorders
    •Drugs and Alcohol Abuse
    •Wellness
    •Loss
    •Sexuality
    •Suicide Prevention

Tutoring

Conflict Mediation

Leadership Training

Other Special Topics as decided

Ongoing professional supervision is essential. Without it, the peer helper program will fail. Through supervision, peer helpers can improve their skills. The helpers will obtain feedback as to what they are doing and how those activities are meeting needs. The supervisor must have time and a physical space to interact with helpers, often on an individual basis and at other times in a group. In many cases, the professional supervisor will be the initial support professional also. However, other support personnel will need to be identified and listed according to the support each can supply and under what conditions.

Form 7.14 contains space to record your considerations of peer helping service implementation.

Service Delivery

1. What services will the peer helper perform?
   a. Tutoring
   b. Peer Mediation
   c. Classroom Discussion Leader, e.g., Group/Health Issues
   d. Orientation of New Students
   e. Peer Listening
   f. Community Service
   g. Other _____

2. Where will service be delivered? _____

   _____

3. Who will supervise? _____

   _____

4. When will service be performed?

   a. During formal class

   b. Other _____

Form 7.14. Items to consider as peer helping service is being implemented.

The program implementation model (Figure 7.7), as suggested by the *Standards of the National Peer Helpers Association*, might be a graphic for you to put on your wall to remind yourself of the areas needed in beginning a program. You may want to develop your own graphic for your peer helper program. Figure 7.8 is an example of one as developed by Ferguson-Florissant School District.

Program Implementation Model

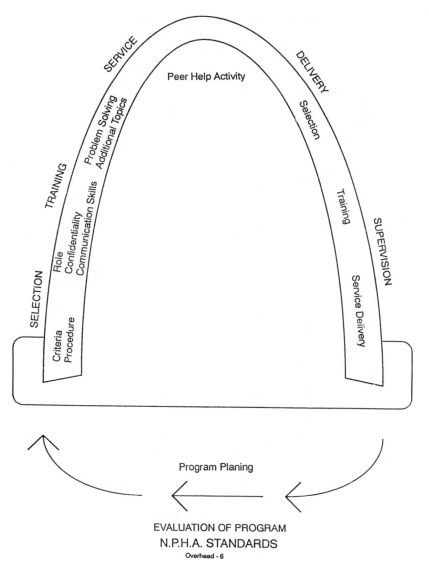

Peer Help Activity

SERVICE

DELIVERY

SELECTION

TRAINING

Problem Solving
Additional Topics

Role
Confidentiality
Communication Skills

Criteria
Procedure

Selection

Training

SUPERVISION

Service Delivery

Program Planing

EVALUATION OF PROGRAM
N.P.H.A. STANDARDS

Overhead - 6

Figure 7.7. Program implementation model as suggested by the *Standards of the National Peer Helpers Association.*

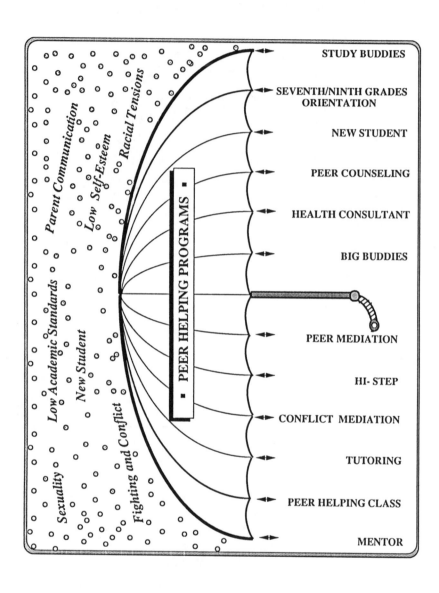

Figure 7.8. Graphic representation by Ferguson-Florissant School District of its peer helping programs.

The *National Peer Helpers Association* has designed some questions to ask yourself before starting a peer program. These questions are found in the "Dear Friends" letter.

1. What is the program mission?

2. With whom do I need to discuss my ideas—students, counselors, administrators?

3. Will they be likely to respond positively to this approach?

4. What are the needs of the target population?

5. How much time and energy do I need to expend?

6. How extensive should the program be?

7. Who will staff the program?

8. What criteria do I want to establish for program participants?

9. How will I recruit and screen the participants?

10. What is my training orientation and what are the required activities, time commitment, and appropriate training resources?

11. What are the space requirements and does the host setting have them?

12. What strength and professional skills do I offer the program?

13. How much lead time do I need for planning?

14. How will I form an advisory board and who will be asked to serve in that capacity?

15. How much money will I have? (do I have?) (want?) (need?)

Step 17. ESTABLISH AN ADVISORY BOARD

An advisory board consisting of lay members from the group to be served as well as peer helpers and professionals can be very vital to the program. Board members can supply feedback on what is occurring, the effectiveness, and what is needed. They also can review proposed changes and provide input on how well those changes may be accepted.

The advisory board need not be large in number of members but does need to be a cross-section of those who receive the service (members of the target audience), provide the service (peer helpers), supervise the service (professional supervisors of peer helpers), and administer the program. Selection of those members will depend upon your local situation.

Step 18. EVALUATE THE PROGRAM

An evaluation system needs to be designed to change the program and give feedback to the trainer. Suggested evaluation includes evaluating the skills learned by the peer helpers, evaluating projects that helpers undertake, and evaluating those who receive the services of helpers. Evaluation of the entire program is important.

Should the time and resources be available, good research would assist in this growing field. Suggested designs might be provided by the *National Peer Helpers Association* or the schools of education and psychology of the local universities and colleges.

Form 7.14 contains items to consider when doing an evaluation. Be sure that evaluation is directly related to goals and objectives as stated in the proposal. To determine change, if any, will require measurement at the start as well as at a later time.

EVALUATION

1. What will be evaluated?

Activity	Means/Instrument	Date of Collection
Planning	————————	————————
Staff Selection	————————	————————
Selection of trainees	————————	————————
Training	————————	————————
Service delivery	————————	————————
Supervision	————————	————————
Other	————————	————————
	————————	————————
	————————	————————

2. Who will be responsible for data collection?

———————— ————————

3. How will collected data be utilized?

———————— ————————

4. Who will receive data and/or evaluation outcome?

Funding source	————————	————————
Target audience	————————	————————
Peer helpers	————————	————————
Trainers	————————	————————
Supervisors	————————	————————
Administrators	————————	————————
Advisory Board	————————	————————

Form 7.15. Items to consider when doing evaluation.

> *"You can't get to second base*
> *with one foot on first base."*
>
> *Baxter*

Chapter

TRAINING MODEL AND PROCEDURES

The rationale for a disciplined form of training is derived from the initial concepts developed by micro-teaching and micro-counseling (Ivey, 1971) and the research in training helpers by Truax and Carkhuff (Truax & Carkhuff, 1967; Carkhuff, 1969, 1987a, 1987b). The use of a training structure based on these two models provides a relatively precise framework for behavioral skills and allows for the intensive practice required to learn skills thoroughly.

Training procedures that initially deal with small isolated segments of a skill are more effective in skill building outcomes when segments are taught specifically and practiced until mastered. In this way, an increase occurs in the probability of the skills becoming used, integrated, and implemented quickly and effectively by the trainee.

The training procedure in *Peer Power, Book 1* and *Book 2* are not meant to be a recipe that will produce highly competent helping persons. Instead, in the design is described a focused process that forms a skeletal foundation for training upon which an individual trainer or helper is able to combine his/her own individual thoughts, ideas, and personality characteristics. No design is a best fit for all trainees, systems, or facilities, but this one can be modified to fit individual circumstances without losing its training qualities or characteristics.

Learning Pyramid

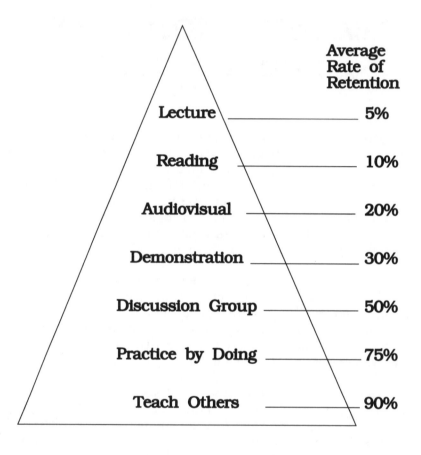

Average
Rate of
Retention

Lecture ——————————— 5%

Reading ——————————— 10%

Audiovisual ——————————— 20%

Demonstration ——————————— 30%

Discussion Group ——————————— 50%

Practice by Doing ——————————— 75%

Teach Others ——————————— 90%

Figure 8.1. Relation of retention of learning to involvement of the learner. Reproduced with permission from National Training Laboratories, Bethel, ME.

LEARNING PYRAMID

The training procedure for *Peer Power, Book 1* and *Peer Power, Book 2* was derived from the Learning Pyramid developed by *National Training Laboratories* (See Diagram, Figure 8.1) in which the amount of retention depends on the involvement of the learner. As you can deduct by review of Figure 8.1, the actual services delivered by the peer helper places learning in the 90% level.

SKILL-BUILDING PATTERN

To increase effectiveness, the trainer is to follow six essential behaviors with each training module. These behaviors are as follows:

1. explanation of and need for skills,
2. modeling of skill to be taught,
3. practicing of skill,
4. feedback to trainees from raters,
5. homework and discussion of experiences of doing and rating, and
6. preparation for next behavior.

The pattern for skill building is graphically displayed in Figure 8.2. The steps consist of three processes: "tell," by the trainer, "show," by the trainer, and "do," by the trainees. For effective training, the pattern for skill building should be consistent throughout the training program.

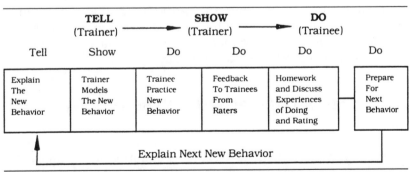

Figure 8.2. Skill-building pattern for training modules.

PERCENT OF INFORMATION RETAINED		
	After 3 Hours	After 3 Days
TELL ONLY	70%	10%
SHOW ONLY	72%	20%
SHOW AND TELL	85%	65%

Approximately 70% of Western Culture is
a Visual Learning Culture

—Geri McArdle (1993)

EXPLANATION OF AND NEED FOR SKILLS

Explaining the skill is essential in the teaching procedure. The explanation provides motivational incentives necessary to turn trainees, intellectually and emotionally, toward their new learning. The trainer cannot expect a commitment from the trainees to learn new behaviors unless they are able to see the personal benefits of those behaviors.

In other words, show by way of information or demonstrate experimentally how the new behaviors will be directly or indirectly helpful to each trainee. With younger trainees, an effective method is to have them experience the skills that they will be learning in relationship to their world in order that each skill be meaningful. Adults, on the other hand, can be motivated by a combination of research citations and personal experiences. Modeling and explanation behaviors are essential in introducing each training module.

MODELING OF SKILL TO BE TAUGHT

Learning theorists have identified that modeling is an effective way to teach. In teaching communication skills, the use of frequent modeling by the trainer is "the" most effective single teaching procedure that can be used.

To ask a trainee, whether child or adult, to take public risks with new behaviors is a frightening idea. Therefore, the trainer is to take the initial risks when presenting the new behavior for two reasons:

1. The modeling gives the trainee some visual experiences in behaviors that he/she will be asked to imitate, thus making it easier to mimic or parody others when practicing previously unknown experiences.

2. Carkhuff (1969, 1987a, 1987b) and associates have shown in their research that a trainee cannot be more effective than the trainer. Therefore, trainers must be able to function at higher levels of effectiveness than trainees in order for them to improve their skills.

Trainer modeling of desired behaviors can be done through the use of techniques such as demonstrations, role-playing, or playing of videotapes made of the desired behavior. The modeling is most effective if done immediately after introducing the skill to the trainees. Combining an explanation of the skill to be learned with the immediate modeling of the behavior is a very potent teaching method. The trainer is to teach the skill and immediately model it so that a visual demonstration is available for the trainees to mime in their attempts in trying new behavior. Trainers can demonstrate poor skills to assist trainees in discrimination, but the modeling behavior must include the effective skills so as to reinforce them.

Trainer modeling of the skills to be taught not only provides trainees with a visual design but also demonstrates the impact of the skill directly. Trainees may read about a skill and hear about a skill, but demonstrating is the most effective way to convey the skill to be learned. Discussion should follow each demonstration.

PRACTICING OF SKILL

Practicing the skills is crucial in order to integrate the new behavior into present listening and communication style. Because the skills are broken into such small segments of new behaviors, their initial impact when practiced is often found to be mechanical and awkward. Practice is the key to making the skill integrated and smooth. In the training sessions, practice allows for immediate feedback and can assist trainees in being able to modify their initial attempts at various skills. In addition, trainees should practice the skills outside of the sessions. Only through constant use of the skills will they replace the old skills that have become habitual. With practice, the mechanical aspects will become extinguished, and as more skills are added and integrated, the new behaviors become useful in interpersonal relations. The mechanical aids of video and audio tapes provide feedback that is efficient in helping trainees become more aware of their own skill development.

The use of videotape equipment is extremely helpful in the training process. At least two ways exist to use video equipment. One way is to develop modeling tapes for each skill that the trainer is teaching. The videotape modeling is sometimes better than the on-the-spot demonstration of the skill. For example, you may not want to develop tapes that show low, medium, and high levels of attending behavior. For best results, use a skilled counselor in the modeling tapes for skill building. You may want to use peers with the stimulus tapes used in the module for genuineness in *Peer Power, Book 1*. A videotape of communication skills currently is being developed for adults working with youth.

A second way of using videotape equipment is to tape the participants as they practice the skills and then play back the tape for review. This form of learning is extremely helpful to the participant. Audio taping also is very helpful.

Throughout the trainee exercises, the group size and number of trainers will change from module to module. The reason for this variance is that some modules involve more skill building than others.

FEEDBACK TO TRAINEES FROM RATER

An important aspect in the design of the learning process is for the trainee to be able to discriminate between effective and ineffective or destructive communication skills.

Discrimination of facilitative behaviors precedes the trainee's ability to communicate those behaviors. By rating others' communication skills while in training, trainees learn the difference between effective and ineffective communication in practice as well as in theory. Practice during training can be provided by having trainees identify positive and negative skills and the rationale in each others' audio or videotapes made during practice.

By requiring trainees to rate the behaviors of other trainees, they are taught to discriminate and to communicate the reasons for their ratings to the person being observed, thereby increasing their ability to understand the differences in behaviors and skills and also to learn to articulate the feedback. Knowing the difference between various communication patterns enables trainees to monitor their own behavior when they are required to practice the skills. The usual procedure for rating and discrimination skill training is to form groups of three to five members. One person functions as the helper and one as the helpee. The others in the group function as raters. Each person in the group is required to participate by assuming the role of helper, helpee, and rater within the practice session. The rating and feedback process is an integral part of each skill practice session, and training is of little value without it.

After teaching, modeling, and having the trainees practice a new skill, the trainer is to take time to have the trainees discuss their experiences within the group. The discussion after the teaching and training is vital because discussion provides a significant feedback to the trainer as to how well the skill is being perceived intellectually and emotionally. Discussion topics often provide an opportunity for the trainer to do further teaching, to check out how the ideas are being integrated by trainees, and to respond to questions necessary to clarify misunderstandings.

HOMEWORK AND DISCUSSION OF EXPERIENCES OF DOING AND RATING

Assigning homework will be a carryover activity in learning the new skills. The trainees will be asked to integrate the skill further by practicing each skill away from the training sessions and, in some instances, by completing written assignments such as diaries or observation sheets. It is important to have the trainee identify how he/she will practice the skill.

When the trainer evaluates the session after each training session, an evaluation can be made on five of the six skill-building behaviors—explanation of skill, modeling, practicing, feedback, homework and discussion—to determine which section was weak or strong. If a session has not gone well, one of these five behaviors has been omitted or poorly presented.

PREPARATION FOR NEXT BEHAVIOR

Following the session evaluations, which included individual skill evaluation, the trainees prepare for the next behavior. At this point, trainees receive the explanation of the new behavior. The explanation of the new behavior will be the beginning of the teaching module again.

FORMAT FOR TRAINING PROGRAM

Each module is presented in a uniform manner to facilitate peer professional understanding. Each module, when presented, follows the same informational structure. In this way, the trainer will be able to structure each training session. The structure is as follows:

1. module title,
2. definition of the skill to be taught,
3. behavior goals,
4. appropriate population,
5. group size,
6. approximate time required,
7. physical setting and materials required,
8. procedures,
9. evaluation process, and
10. measuring outcomes.

Stating the goals in behavioral terms aids in the evaluation process for each skill. This practice is helpful for the trainer to use in explaining the training process to others.

Group size is an important determinant of the rate of learning and the style of teaching. For example, if a trainer has two or three co-trainers, the time required for the learning process is cut almost in half. If twelve or more trainees are in the training group, two trainers are important when the group moves into the practice pattern. Also, if videotape equipment is used for modeling or for feedback for trainees, two trainers will increase the efficiency of the training.

In each phase of the training is listed an ideal physical setting and a list of materials needed, such as trainee exercises and audiovisual equipment. Training is facilitated effectively if the trainer is organized concerning material and does not waste time setting up video equipment or audio tape equipment. Training is more effective if tape recorders and videotape are available for the trainees and trainers to use.

The time required for each skill will vary, depending on the number of people being trained. The exercises are based on training up to twelve trainees in a group. If a disciplined structure is maintained, the procedures will take the amount of time suggested.

The step-by-step procedures for each skill are described fully. Alternate procedures for different ages and different groups are pointed out. The order of procedures has been field-tested many times, and variations have been attempted. The order presented in *Peer Power, Book 1* is the one that has been found to be most effective. This procedure obviously is not the only procedure that can be used for training groups, but it is a workable plan that has been successful many times.

The evaluation process can be used with the trainees or the trainers. The evaluation method may take the form of narrative comments, observations, and completion of rating sheets. All of the different methods of evaluation will be used—trainer, self, rater.

The outcomes of each step will be discussed. These outcomes may be in the form of changes in the trainee, the trainee's environment, or an institutional change.

Throughout the trainer's manual (*Peer Power, Book 1, Strategies for the Professional Leader*), space is available for the trainer to write comments, evaluate personal training skill, and make notes of effective ways of teaching. The intent is for the trainer to add personal creative teaching methods and counseling techniques to strengthen the training format.

Each trainer has different needs concerning the training processes. By keeping notes, a trainer will be better able to enter into meaningful dialogue with other trainers relating to communications, skill training, and peer helper training. Through this dialogue, all can gain skills. Hopefully each trainer will record his/her unique ways of training and arrive at evaluation procedures meaningful for the techniques applied.

> *Teach people to fish,*
>
> *They can feed themselves for a lifetime.*

UTILIZATION OF PEER HELPERS AND ADVANCED TRAINING

Utilization of peer helpers is the next vital step in developing an effective peer helping program. The peer professional needs to assist peer helpers in finding ways to put their newly developed skills to work. The term peer helpers is an overall term that takes on new titles depending upon local projects. Some examples are Youth Listeners, Health Consultants, RAPP, P.A.L., Conflict Managers, Peer Advisors, Mentors, Peer Assistants, Volunteers, and T.I.P. (Teen Involvement Program). The title of the peer helpers should be decided upon by the local group and represent what the peers actually "do." What are their roles? What projects can they develop based on their skills? What kind of additional training do they need to accomplish their roles by providing service to others? In Figure 9.1 are listed services frequently performed by peer helpers.

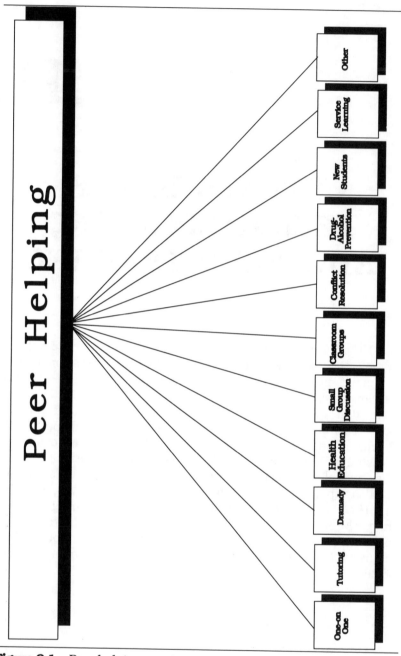

Figure 9.1 Peer helping services.

Several procedures can be followed to aid peer helpers in locating helpees. One procedure would be for the peer professional to recruit, organize, and establish groups who could benefit from peer helping. The peer professional could have projects in mind to target such as a nursing home, disabled students, elementary children, or classroom presentations. A second procedure would be for the peer professional to offer a special training program for peer helpers on how to recruit groups that the peer helpers could help. A combination of the two procedures could prove most beneficial for continued involvement of peer helping over extended periods of time.

A third procedure is to utilize the peer helping group to brainstorm possible projects. This enables the peer helpers to have ownership of these projects, which brings a certain amount of empowerment to the trainees. Much research is available to support the "ownership" concept. It is obvious that peer helpers will be more motivated if they own the projects.

The involvement of peer helpers can provide an important component in the training of future peer helpers. Enabling others to observe what is and can be done by peer helpers is an excellent means of recruitment for future training programs.

In thinking about how to utilize the peers, many issues need to be resolved!

1. Who will receive the peer helping assistance?

   (Who is the target population?)

   e.g., 9th grade health education classes

2. What is the outcome of the assistance?

   (What are the goals?)

   e.g., Students in the health classes will have an awareness of the consequences of substance abuse.

3. What is the plan?

    e.g., From October through December, peer helpers will present to the health classes the exercises from *Peer Power, Book 2, Workbook,* Module XIV—Drugs and Alcohol Abuse: Intervention and Prevention.

4. What will the peer helpers do?

    e.g., They will serve as health educators doing classroom presentations.

5. What skills do they need?

    e.g., *Peer Power, Book 1, Workbook* and *Peer Power, Book 2, Workbook*—Module XIV and XX (Leading Classroom Groups)

6. What procedures do they follow? The following is an example:
    a. Basic Training
        (1) Attending
        (2) Empathy
        (3) Assertiveness
        (4) Genuineness
        (5) Confrontation
        (6) Questioning
        (7) Problem solving
        (8) Conflict resolution
        (9) Ethics
        (10) Setting up a program

    b. Advanced Training
        (1) Drugs and alcohol—Module XIV
        (2) Leading Classroom Groups—Module XX

    c. Supervision

        d.   Evaluation

             (1)   Teachers

             (2)   Peer helpers

             (3)   Students in health classes

             (4)   Environmental—reduction in substance abuse

7.   What is the time line?

        e.g., *Book 1*—September - January

        Book 2—January - June

        Classroom Presentation—March - April

        Evaluation—January

        Evaluation—May

8.   What other support do I need?

        e.g., Administration approval for formal class

                Health teachers

                Staff support

9.   What are the logistics?

        e.g., Permission to get out of class

                Materials for presentation

10.   How will you assist others?

11.   Evaluation

        e.g., Questions on drug use

                Questions on drug use in the future

Peer helpers can serve in a variety of ways. In the following Figure 9.2 is an illustration of how one school district is utilizing their peers.

FERGUSON-FLORISSANT PEER HELPING 1992-93

AIRPORT P.R.O. Book Buddies Peer Mediators Study Buddies Conflict Resolution	**HALLS FERRY** Student Council Peace Table	**BERKELEY MIDDLE** Berkeley Middle Squad Conflict Mediation
BERMUDA Studys Buddies Job Program Rainbows CHAMPS Program Safety Patrol Conflict Resolution	**HOLMAN** Peer Helps Peer Counselor Trainees Images Classroom Assistance Peer Tutors	**CROSS KEYS MIDDLE** SAFE Conflict Mediation Students Against Fighting Enemies
CENTRAL Peer Tutoring	**LEE HAMILTON** Peer Tutoring Rainbows	**FERGUSON MIDDLE** RAPP Conflict Mediation Friendly Peersuasion
COMBS Peace Corps Conflict Resolution Safety Patrol	**PARKER ROAD** Peer Tutoring Pro Social Skills Informal Applications	**BERKELEY SENIOR** TAHC Hi Step Peer Helping Class
COMMONS LANE H.E.L.P. Peer Tutoring Safety Patrol Student Council Helping Projects	**ROBINWOOD** Student Council Helping Projects Study Buddies	**McCLUER** Teenage Health Consultant 30 Days of Fitness Peer Mentors Peer Counseling Student Mediation Hi Step National Honor Society
COOL VALLEY PATROL: Conflict Mediation New Student Orientation Tutoring	**WALNUT GROVE** Conflict Mediation Student Council Projects	**McCLUER NORTH** Minority Scholars T.A.H.C. Big Brothers/Big Sisters Hi Step Peer Helping Gate-Keepers New Student Buddies Student Relations Committee
DUCHESNE Conflict Mediation	**WEDGWOOD** PRLP Pals Classroom Guidance Assistance	**GRIFFITH** Peer Helpers Assigned Buddies

Figure 9.2.   Peer helper program as operated by Ferguson-Florissant School District.

Peer helpers can be "rap" group leaders, tutors, volunteers, personnel assistants, classroom leaders, etc. The list below is not exhaustive but is provided to get you thinking about possibilities.

SERVICE LEARNING

Volunteer activities are of various types, such as service learning, mentoring, community service, and community-based learning. These involve designing a service project, implementing the project, and finally processing the project. The processing time gives the volunteers time to evaluate what happened, how it affected them, what they learned, and what kind of impact it had on them.

One-on-one Helping

Research has supported the concept of one-on-one helping. This is done sometimes formally through identifying at-risk youth, new students or newcomers to a group or community, disabled people, lonely students, or other persons. Informal helping is done at any time with friends, co-workers, and families.

Conflict Resolution

In many institutions, conflicts between individuals and groups can be distracting from the task at hand (learning, working); therefore, many of the skills learned in basic training can be used to resolve conflicts. For example, two friends are having a disagreement. A peer helper could help reduce the conflict through active listening and summarization and problem-solving skills. Members of a group representing two different cultures or minorities could be in conflict over an issue. The peer helper could use small group skills, genuineness, and problem-solving skills to help resolve the conflict.

Cultural Differences

Often groups such as schools, community agencies, and religious institutions have students from minority groups or different cultures. There are often huge differences in the experiences of these two groups. Peer helpers can serve as friends, tutors, and rap leaders to help reduce these differences and help others of different minority groups feel good about themselves.

Rap Group Leaders

Groups can be recruited as helpers from people who have shown an interest in discussing problems with others. The peer professional can either organize the group and assign one or two peer helpers to work with the group, or the trainer can suggest that each trainee develop his/her own group from among friends, acquaintances, or individuals with a common concern. If peer helpers choose their groups, the peer professional needs to be aware of the composition of the group and meeting varied schedules. Without this trainer awareness and control, rap groups can lose their focus and become social groups. The peer professional needs to interview the rap group members before starting the meetings. The interview should include discussing goals, rules of the group, and members' commitment to participate as fully as possible in the group meetings.

Tutors

Peer helpers can be used effectively as tutors, functioning primarily in training programs within schools or other settings. Adult learning centers are possible settings for peer tutors. Peer helpers and the trainer are involved in planning and developing the program. In this way, tutoring has a strong chance of being supported by teachers as well as by trainees who will function as tutors.

Students tutoring students is a valuable learning experience. Students receive the help benefit and the tutors get an opportunity to practice concepts and skills. Tutoring others enables students to become more personally involved in the learning process, to accept more responsibility, and to find more meaningfulness in school.

Tutoring requires additional training of peer helpers to enable them to go into classes. This training will be explained later in the chapter under "Advanced Training Model."

Tutoring programs using peer helpers are used widely in the school at Hillsborough County, FL. According to Myrick and Bowman (1981), these programs are very successful because teachers believe that the trained peer helpers are more successful than are untrained students.

Discussion Leaders

Using peer helpers as discussion leaders is effective in schools, religious institutions, business and industry, and agencies such as Scouts, YMCA, and YWCA. Discussion leaders function as facilitators when working with a wide variety of discussion topics. The person in charge can use peer helpers in classrooms, problem-solving meetings, group training programs, camping programs, and other group settings. Peer helpers can relate to many topics. Individual procedures can be adapted to fit specific needs and facilities.

Persons of all ages, including children, can heighten student participation and involvement in the learning process when trained as small-group leaders. When a class is divided into small circle groups, each led by a trained peer helper, discussion become more stimulating and personalized.

Leading Class Discussions

Another method of using peer helpers is to train them with guidance materials so that a large class can be divided into small discussion groups with a student leader in each. Health educators are used to present prevention information such as drug and alcohol, eating disorders, smoking, and sex-related problems.

Peer Convention

Each year, all peer helpers in Hillsborough County, FL, participate in a special day of projects at a regional peer helper conference. Caning (1983) wrote that *Project Promise* in Baltimore, MD, holds an annual meeting with grade school through high school peer counselors.

Support Groups

Peer helpers have been extremely helpful in leading support groups such as AA, Alanon, Weight Watchers, and Narcotics Anonymous. Most of the leaders have not been specifically trained, but this is slowly changing so that the support group experience can be more effective.

Career Center

Some schools are having students assist others in looking for information in the career centers. Bowman and Rotter (1983) reported that some peer helpers have been trained to aid students with computer assisted instructions, career information, and cataloging information in schools' microcomputers.

Staff Trainers

Peer helpers have been used to train volunteers to augment the professional staff for a crisis telephone or drop-in center. With proper supervision by professional staff members, peers can effectively teach basic communication skills to volunteers. "Hotline" volunteers do not require a high degree of sophistication in communication skill development, and effective trainees often can be used with success as trainers in these situations. Supervision of peer helpers as trainers is imperative, however, and might be accomplished through the cooperation of the peer trainer and the crisis center personnel.

E.A.P. Volunteers

Peer Helpers can help refer workers to professionals and provide support for others.

Mentoring

Mentors can act as moderators, guides and inspirations to assist young people in managing life experiences. Examples of mentoring programs are as follows:

Rosenroll D., Saunders, G., & Carr R., (1993)., *The Canadian stay-in-school mentor strategy.* Victoria, BC: Peer Systems Consulting Group.

Waters, J.L., Feemas, M.E., & Remstrou, D. (1990). *Volunteer coordinators' handbook: Volunter mentor training program.* Tulsa, OK: National Resource Center for Youth Service.

Hamilton, S.F., & Hamilton, M.A. (1992 March). Mentoring programs: Promise and paradox. *Phi Delta Kappan, 73*(7) 546-650.

Mentoring Training Convention Curriculum. (1991). Alexandria, VA: United Way of America.

Murray, M., & Owens, M. (1991). *Beyond the myths and magic of mentoring.* San Francisco: Jossey-Bass.

ADVANCED TRAINING OVERVIEW

As peer helpers assume their helping responsibilities, they begin to confront some real and practical problems in their relationships that develop as a result of their helping behaviors. For this reason, regular meetings need to be held with the peer helpers after their basic training has been completed. These meetings can serve several functions. They can be used as a sounding board for problems encountered by the peer helper relationships. Advanced training is often required as the problems develop and meetings form a natural time and setting to implement several advance training techniques, attitudes, and strategies. Another function the meetings serve is that they enable the trainer to maintain surveillance over the peer helping activities that are ongoing. Housekeeping and administrative concerns are another reason for holding regular meetings.

This time can be divided into two separate periods. One is for the peer helpers to share information about their activities and themselves, set personal and program goals, and deal with problems. The second involves training in specific areas (*Peer Power, Book 2, Workbook*) with which peer helpers may deal. Time needs to be spent on self-understanding, sharing with peers, and problem-solving personal issues.

Advanced Training Model

Using regular meetings as advanced training sessions forms an effective segment in a developing peer helping program. The major purpose is to provide a forum for peer helpers who now are applying what they have learned in training.

The following model for advanced training has been constructed to keep the program vital and ongoing with time for exchange, discussion, and specific additional training.

Exchange Time

An exchange time allows the trainer to be aware of what has been happening with the new peer helpers. To have the peer helpers fill out a "Flow Sheet for Peer Helper Contact" in *Peer Power, Book 1, Workbook* (p. 322), is desirable. The purpose of the flow sheet is to assist the peer helper in focusing on his/her behavior and skill development in the peer helping sessions. The exchange time needs to be a free interchange between trainer and peer helpers as to the effectiveness of the skills and behaviors used in the peer helping sessions. See the "Supervision Situation" section in Chapter VI.

Discussion Time

A discussion of special problems and/or successes experienced by the peer helper is needed in the advanced training meetings. The group discussion allows peer helpers the opportunity to air concerns and receive feedback from the peer professional and other peer helpers. For example, a peer helper may encounter difficulties in leading a group discussion or a rap session. The reasons could be varied, but with feedback from the peer professional and others, additional resources become available for experimentation. Role-playing the situation with various people taking different parts is a way of lending insight into alternative ways of dealing with the problem. In addition, the leader can get a periodic check on each trainee's skill development and competencies in working as a helper.

Specific Advanced Training Skills

Time needs to be scheduled for specific advanced training skills including topics such as the following (these topics are covered in *Peer Power, Book 2)*:

1. group discussion techniques,

2. value clarification skills,

3. self-awareness experiences,

4. psychological theories and philosophies,

5. tutoring techniques and skills,

6. referral skills,

7. awareness of other peer helping programs,

8. drug and alcohol abuse: intervention and prevention training,

9. wellness/stress management,

10. enhancing self-esteem,

11. leadership training,

12. goal setting,

13. facilitating small group discussion,

14. classroom presentations,

15. suicide prevention,

16. eating disorders,

17. coping with loss,

18. understanding self and others,

19. helping self and others through sharing, and

20. ethical considerations in peer helping.

Group Discussion Techniques. To function effectively as group discussion leaders, peer helpers will need to understand and experience group discussion techniques. Group discussion techniques include observation, awareness of nonverbal behavior and individual verbal behaviors, ability to keep the discussion moving through communication skills, group management, beginning a group, and handling conflicts. These group discussion techniques employ the peer training skills very heavily but require a different focus and direction. When teaching discussion skills to advanced peer professionals, helpers need to be flexible in their structure in order to model the kinds of flexible behaviors trainees will need to provide to others when they lead their own discussion groups.

Value Clarification Skills. Value clarification strategies may be used as group discussion topics in the advanced training sessions. Each week peer helpers may prepare a different value clarification experience to use with the group in which they serve as helpers and to practice during the advanced training session. Especially useful for teenagers and young adults, value clarification experience gives the group discussion leader an activity to use in a given week. Also, the experience provides an activity by which participants can look at themselves and their beliefs in relationship to others and their beliefs. Such activities can be developed by the peer professional to fit needs of the group.

Self-awareness Experiences. Peer helpers need to spend some time attempting to understand themselves either through self-awareness experiences, human potential seminars, or discussions with others. In order to help others, peer helpers must understand themselves and work continuously toward being psychologically healthy persons.

Psychological Theories and Philosophies. Different kinds of training are needed to meet both the demands of various kinds of people and situations in which peer helpers find themselves. A peer professional may need to spend time teaching different psychological frameworks to enable peer helpers to gain a better understanding of human behavior. For example, peer helpers helping children in a tutorial program would find the concepts of Jung, Adler, or Transactional Analysis helpful in understanding the behavior of their students. If the peer helpers are working in a crisis center, an understanding of the theoretical helping process as developed by Rogers (1980), Maslow (1968), and Combs (1974) will aid in understanding the role and function of a counselor.

Tutoring Techniques and Skills. Tutoring requires some additional information and strategies to be successful. At least four additional concepts need to be included in advanced training experiences when peer helpers are going to use their skills as tutors. They are as follows:

1. How to conduct oneself in a classroom as a tutor.

2. How to work with teachers (using newly learned skills).

3. What kinds of tutoring procedures can be developed and followed.

4. How interpersonal helping skills can be used in a tutoring situation.

Referral Skills. Referral skills are vital to the success of a peer helping program. Different limits on the peer helper need to be discussed at this time and appropriate referrals made. For example, in most peer helping programs, life-threatening issues (e.g., suicide) must be referred immediately to the supervisor. Each local program needs to develop guidelines for which kinds of issues need to be referred. The list will be governed by life-threatening issues, local laws, and institutional rules.

Information relating to referral skills is not a training technique as such, but the information needs to be included if an advance training program is to be complete. Advanced training time must be spent in exposing peer helpers to the variety of psychological, vocational, and educational sources of help that are available to them.

The assurance of being able to refer difficult problems to professionals is an important aspect of any peer helping program. The community has more confidence in a peer helping program if a strong referral and professional support system is operating within the program. Therefore, the development of a directory of referral sources is crucial for any peer helping program. The referral source list may range from a simple card with a listing of phone numbers to an extensive list of professional agencies and personnel for types of human problems. Crisis clients may need direct medical referral. The more contact peer helpers can have with referral agencies, the more smoothly the problem will operate. The trainer is responsible for developing the referral sources appropriate for the type of peer helping program he/she supervises. For example, drug information, venereal disease information, and pregnancy information may be helpful to teenagers. Hotline numbers may be helpful to individuals of all ages. A list of agencies with addresses and telephone numbers is provided in a book entitled *Not With My Life I Don't: Preventing Your Suicide and That of Others* by Rosenthal (1988).

Awareness of Other Peer Helping Programs. Peer helpers can learn about their function by visiting other peer helper programs. Personnel of one crisis center may want to visit and observe the operation of another crisis center to gather ideas for new techniques. Peer helpers in one school should visit with peer helpers in another school to observe new techniques in terms of implementing their own program.

Drug and Alcohol Abuse: Intervention and Prevention Training. Chemical abuse is one of the leading problems in America. Most trainees are not aware of the problems with chemicals and what to do with them. This area will assist trainees in becoming aware of their own use and in beginning to make life-style changes. For specifics, see Module XIV in *Peer Power, Book 2, Workbook.*

Wellness/Stress Management. Wellness implies leading a healthy life, putting into balance the body, mind, and emotions. Stress management is a technique that demonstrates how to manage more effectively those stressors that impact the individual. For specifics, see Module XV in *Peer Power, Book 2, Workbook.*

Enhancing Self-esteem. Enhancing self-esteem focuses on assisting the peer counselors/helpers with focusing on strengths and potential of themselves and beginning to feel better about themselves and gaining confidence. For specifics, see Module XVI in *Peer Power, Book 2, Workbook.*

Leadership Training. Leadership training assists the individual in becoming an effective leader with individuals and with tasks. For specifics, see Module XVII in *Peer Power, Book 2, Workbook.*

Goal Setting. Peer helpers need to participate in goal setting during advanced training. Each peer helper may set goals for the following week that he/she wishes to accomplish.

Facilitating Small Group Discussion. Small group discussion can be useful in helping any age group discuss topics and problem solving. Peer helpers are often called upon to lead small discussion groups. Exercises in this can be found in Module XIX in *Peer Power, Book 2, Workbook.*

Classroom Presentations. Classroom presentations can be made by peer helpers using a structured lesson plan and materials. These topics can range from health issues to wellness issues to prevention issues. Many of the exercises from *Book 2* can be adapted for classroom groups. For specifics, see Module XX in *Peer Power, Book 2, Workbook.*

Suicide Prevention. Suicide prevention is needed in today's schools and work sites. Assisting others with learning about the problems of suicide can be very helpful. Assisting peer helpers with learning to recognize the signs of a potential suicidal person often can lead to needed referral and help. Peer helpers often are called upon to help the survivors of suicide through listening and caring. An entire institution, school, church, and community can be immobilized as a result of a suicide. For specifics, see Modules XXII and XXIII in *Peer Power, Book 2, Workbook.*

Eating Disorders. Eating disorders are prevalent in today's society. Equipping the peer helper with the skills to recognize the symptoms of an eating disorder can help individuals get referred and obtain the help needed. Also, with the ability to lead small and large groups concerning eating problems, peer helpers can help prevent unhealthy eating problems. For specifics, see Module XXI in *Peer Power, Book 2, Workbook.*

Coping with Loss. Practically all individuals, helpers and helpees, face loss. Loss often can change their lives. Learning skills in coping with loss can be helpful throughout one's life. For specifics, see Module XXIII in *Peer Power, Book 2, Workbook.*

Understanding Self and Others. As the peer helpers go through training, they need to understand themselves in terms of personality type, values, leadership styles, work styles, and time management skills. This is addressed in *Peer Power, Book 1, Workbook.*

This can be done throughout the training through exercises found in both *Peer Power Workbooks 1* and *2.* You also may want to use formal assessment instruments such as the *Myers-Briggs Type Indicator.* One caution when using formal instruments—the trainer must possess the training and expertise to administer and interpret the testing. Therefore, a trainer may want to use a psychologist or a professional counselor.

Helping Self and Others through Sharing. Throughout all of the training (*Book 1* and *Book 2*) trainees should be encouraged to use their own personal experiences in the role-playing. An extremely important aspect of the program is to provide sufficient time for peer helpers to share their own concerns and receive help from others. This can be done at regularly scheduled times or done spontaneously in the training.

Ethical Considerations in Peer Helping. Ethical issues will be faced by peer professionals and peer helpers during training as well as during their projects. An important aspect of a good peer helper program is the development of and utilization of a local "code of conduct" and "ethics" for peer helpers (see Module XXIV in *Peer Power, Book 2, Workbook* and Chapter XII in this book for lengthy presentations). Ethics should be discussed and dealt with throughout the training. The issue of confidentiality, for example, is important in the training sessions, as is the application of these skills with the helpees.

Feedback Flow Sheet

Peer helpers are asked to complete flow sheets and return them to the peer professional at the next advanced training session. The purpose of the flow sheet is to determine how each skill is used by the peer helper and to plan the necessary training to overcome areas of weakness. (See "Flow Sheet for Peer Helper Contact" in *Peer Power, Book 1, Workbook*, p. 322.)

MY PLAN

After reviewing how peer helpers have been utilized in various situations and after recognizing the training that will be needed, consider various questions that must be answered. Form 9.1 is provided to assist in raising questions and providing space for recording responses.

MY UTILIZATION OF PEER HELPERS

1. Who will receive the peer helping assistance?

2. What is the outcome of the assistance?

3. What is the plan?

4. What will the peer helpers do?

5. What skills do they need?

6. What procedures do they follow?

7. What is the time line?

8. What other support do I need?

9. What are the logistics?

10. How will I assist others?

Form 9.1. Questions to consider as plans are made for utilizing peer helpers.

> One of the most beautiful compensations
> of this life is that no man can sincerely help another
> without helping himself.
> Shakespeare

Chapter

EVALUATION OF THE PROGRAM

Evaluation needs to be done on the program, the peer helping professional and peer helper(s), and the community. Program evaluation is necessary for any peer helper training if the venture is to be considered a competent one with continuing value. Evaluation is often a difficult task to complete effectively because certain built-in "booby traps" are difficult to avoid. If the evaluator does not avoid them, many distorted and incomplete results are accepted as valid outcomes.

Three traps exist that weaken or distort evaluation procedures. *One is the peer professional's bias to demonstrate positive outcomes.* The amount of effort that a peer helping professional invests in planning, training, and organizing the peer helpers creates pressure either to (1) distort the outcomes of effective evaluation procedures or (2) cause the trainer to omit evaluation of the program altogether for fear of failure to meet goals. The need to have a successful program is a strong one in most of us, and the fear of failure can cause unprofessional behaviors when evaluation procedures and outcomes are involved.

A second trap is the **lack of peer professional's skills in effective evaluation procedures.** Insufficient skills in evaluation procedures can create many minor or gross errors when attempting to evaluate a program. Evaluation procedures can become very technical and require expertise far beyond the average trainer. As a result, when those procedures are used by unskilled trainers, the evaluations frequently lack the quality needed to make valid judgments concerning the effectiveness of the program.

A third trap that negatively affects evaluation attempts is **timing.** Evaluation occurs after considerable effort has been invested in a focused direction. Outcomes that would suggest change of focus, reworking parts, or other major revision of the program can have deleterious effects on evaluation procedures or results if incentive is lacking on the trainer's part to make the needed changes.

In spite of several possible pitfalls, evaluation needs to be an integral part of the peer helper training program. Evaluation should take place on two levels: one, overall program evaluation and, two, constant evaluation of each trainee's progress in each learned step of the program.

PROGRAM EVALUATION

When considering overall program evaluation, many subjective evaluation procedures can be used. Objective evaluations are less available and not as easily used. Careful subjective evaluation procedures are valid for most programs, and "eyeball" (looking at it) evaluations can give much worthwhile information regarding effectiveness of a program.

In program evaluation, goals need to be identified clearly. These goals can be stated in general terms but should have a focus. For example, two goals would be "to complete an accurate needs assessment for the use of peer helpers in a system," and the second would be "to train a specific number of people to do peer helping in the system." In this way, the outcomes reflect the goals.

Program objectives established in the program development stages can help in the evaluation by providing a guide that helps trainers identify outcomes. Program objectives should answer the questions *how, when,* and *how much change* is expected. When goals (broad concepts) and objectives (specific outcomes) are included in program planning, evaluation procedures can be established to meet both goals and objectives. When evaluation of the total program is included, the program itself feeds vital information to the trainer, which includes a review of all phases of program development and essentially resembles a single feedback system in itself as shown in Figure 10.1.

Questions to be Asked

Someone involved in evaluation may want to formulate questions. For example,

Did the trainees learn the communication skills?

Did the tutees improve academically?

Did the peer helpers grow emotionally?

From these questions, certain instruments and control groups may be developed.

EVALUATION OF GOALS AND OBJECTIVES

The *goals* of a program, stated as general concepts, can be evaluated after the training procedure has completed one cycle. Since goals are general, broad non-evaluative constructs will identify how well the goals have been met. For example, one easily can identify how well the goal to train 15 peer helpers by the end of the training sessions has been reached by counting the ones who have completed the program.

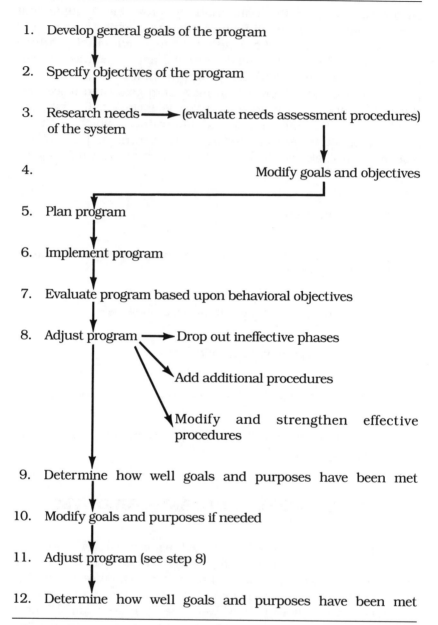

1. Develop general goals of the program

2. Specify objectives of the program

3. Research needs ⟶ (evaluate needs assessment procedures)
   of the system

4.   Modify goals and objectives

5. Plan program

6. Implement program

7. Evaluate program based upon behavioral objectives

8. Adjust program ⟶ Drop out ineffective phases

   Add additional procedures

   Modify and strengthen effective procedures

9. Determine how well goals and purposes have been met

10. Modify goals and purposes if needed

11. Adjust program (see step 8)

12. Determine how well goals and purposes have been met

Figure 10.1. Total review of program development.

Whether or not the program reached its *purposes* is evaluated best by having purposes initially stated by the trainer in as specific behavioral terms as is possible. Often humanistic concepts and objectives, such as this program teaches, can be stated in behavioral terms. For example, in teaching a person empathy skill, one can effectively state the objectives in terms of how frequently the trainee reflected accurately helpee feelings and meaning when in the role of helper. By stating behavioral objectives in frequency and quality of a particular behavior, a trainer can identify how well the objectives of that phase of training are being met.

Evaluating Purposes and Objectives

In this book are listed general purposes for each of the training modules from which one could form a basis for evaluation of each skill being taught. Those purposes listed are to be used as a basis for developing one's own specific objectives.

This book does not intend to teach people behavioral objective writing but simply to point out that if the trainer would write the objectives of a program in trainee-outcome terms, the process of evaluation of the program would be simplified. When an objective is written in terms of outcomes relating to the behavior desired, an evaluation process is built into the written objective.

Frequently when objectives are stated in specific behavioral terms, these objectives describe the procedures needed to achieve them. However, behavioral objectives must be distinguished from the procedures; otherwise, one can easily superimpose process on results. Behavioral objectives need to state clearly what outcome is expected as the result of the training: how much change is expected and who or what is to change. Procedures will spell out what change is to be accomplished and what experiences are going to be given trainees to reach the behavioral objective.

Evaluating Needs Assessment Procedures

In all probability, the concept of initiating a peer helping program was born as the result of some recognized need within the system and with some goals, objectives, and possible procedures to meet the needs emerging concomitantly. As a result, the needs of the system probably will be assessed in close proximity to the development of goals and program purposes. Evaluating the effectiveness of the needs assessment procedures is best completed before the final program assessment and evaluation of the assessment procedure's effectiveness and accuracy can decidedly change the goals and purposes of a program. For example, when a needs assessment or feasibility study has been completed competently and evaluated effectively, the results are used to establish specific and attainable goals. By using accurate information gathering to establish specific goals and purposes, one is able to establish the format for a formal and final proposal. When a plan of action or procedure is added to the information gathered, the entire proposal reflects organization. By stating goals and objectives with specific action parameters and areas of responsibility clearly defined, including the names of people responsible, one has a complete and saleable program format.

EVALUATION OF TRAINING

In order to evaluate well the training program, several aspects must be examined as to how well they meet the program's goals and objectives. The following training components must be evaluated:

1. Selection of trainees

2. Effectiveness of training in each module (Did the trainees learn the goals of the module?)

3. How well the trainees' skills are developing
   a. within each module and
   b. within each of the eight skills.

4. How the peer helpers are working with the helpee
   a. by trainer evaluation,
   b. by other staff evaluations,
   c. by helpee evaluations,
   d. by research, and
   e. by advanced training evaluations.

Evaluation of the training aspect of the program is on two levels. The first level is concerned with the effectiveness of each segment of the training procedure in doing what is required of that segment. The second level of evaluation has to do with developing skills of the trainees. Evaluation procedures for the first level are accomplished by an assortment of procedures initiated by the peer professional, other staff members, and research strategies. Evaluation procedures for the second level are identified almost wholly through the use of the feedback or rating process used by the peer professional or trainees during practice sessions.

Selection of Trainees

Evaluation of the selection process can be done only upon completion of the basic training. However, selection procedures can be established in such a way that research can be done on the effectiveness of any one of several selection means. To establish these procedures requires that prior to trainee selection, an evaluation (research) design be developed for producing the kind of information at the end of the program that will identify the best selection procedures. For example, a design that selects three groups from three different populations can be developed. By giving a pre- and posttest and comparing the rates of changes on a pre-selected behavioral criteria, an assessment can be made. Another selection design is to pretest a population and then divide the training and control groups by skill level, academic achievement, or any one of a variety of criteria. A posttest will assess changes based upon selection procedures. A third design would be to have selected groups chosen based upon specific criteria and compare them with groups that were volunteer groups.

Evaluation of Training Module

Each module in the training program contains stated goals. Also contained in each module are evaluation procedures and outcomes that are to be measured. An evaluation process for each module is thus built into the training procedure. If module goals are changed, then the evaluation procedures and outcome measurements need to be altered to reflect new goals.

EVALUATION OF TRAINEES' SKILLS

In evaluating the skills learned by the trainees, the peer professional is heavily dependent upon the feedback mechanism in which the trainer or trainee rated the quality of responses during practice sessions. The rating sheets in *Peer Power, Book 1, Workbook* function as learning experiences as well as evaluation devices. The peer professional can observe the skill of the trainees and use observation and review of the homework as a form of evaluation.

Each skill of the eight needs to be critiqued and evaluated during all practice sessions by both the peer professional and the trainees.

Evaluating Attending Skill

The peer professional should establish a minimum acceptance level for effective attending behaviors of the trainees when in the role of helper. When raters (trainees) give feedback during practice sessions, attending should always be one of the qualities critiqued. The most effective criteria for the helper are to have good eye contact, to be squared and open to the helpee, and to lean slightly toward the helpee. These behaviors can be evaluated consistently and easily.

Evaluating Empathy and Discriminating Skill

Evaluation of discrimination is accomplished by identifying how accurately the rater was perceiving both the feelings of the helpee statements and the accuracy of the responses of the helper to those feelings. Discrimination is a quality that the rater must have both as a rater and as a helper. The ability to discriminate precedes the ability to provide helping communication and depends upon how accurately each person perceives feelings and meaning. Evaluation of empathy skill is subjective, and variations among ratings are to be expected. Nuances of feeling cause discrepancies in how several trainees may perceive feelings or meaning. Discrimination abilities of the trainees become more consistent with practice.

In evaluating empathy, three conditions are rated:

1. helper's accuracy of identifying feelings communicated by the helpee,

2. helper's accuracy of identifying meaning communicated by the helpee, and

3. the degree of interchangeability between the helpee's statements and helper's responses.

High levels of attending are included in evaluating (rater's feedback) empathic responses. When helper initiative or summary responses are included in the evaluation critique, the rater also will use criteria for summarizing and questioning skills to determine the helper's effectiveness in questioning and/or summarizing responses.

Evaluating Summarizing Skill

Evaluation of the summarizing skill is easily accomplished by rating a helper's ability to organize separate and discrete statements made by the helpee into a response that shows the integral relationship between those statements. Although the evaluation of the trainee's ability to summarize is subjective, it is valid enough to identify summarization skills effectively. See the preceding paragraphs on evaluating empathy in the previous section. The following question serves as an example.

Did the response tie together various aspects of the helpee's concern so as to help the helpee see how all parts relate to one another?

Evaluating Questioning Skill

Evaluating questioning responses takes some practice and experience but can be accomplished by following criteria listed earlier in this chapter under "Evaluating Empathy and Discriminating Skill." Questioning responses widen a helpee's awareness, thereby creating greater understanding of the concern and identifying the goals to be gained. When these characteristics are present in a helper's responses, they can be rated high on initiative:

1. Did the initiative response expand the helpee's awareness of self or concern?

2. Did the initiative response identify where the helpee wanted to be?

3. Did the initiative response personalize the concern? Was it focused on the person rather than the problem?

Evaluating Genuineness Skill

Evaluating the quality of genuineness skill or non-phony behavior is more difficult than evaluating empathy. Genuine helper feelings cannot be identified until communicated either verbally or nonverbally. Therefore, a helper may be feeling a reaction to what a helpee is saying but may choose not to reveal these feelings for a variety of reasons. The most common reason for not revealing genuine feelings is self-protection or perceived threat by the helper if the helper's real feelings were revealed.

In evaluating helper genuineness, the rater identifies verbal and nonverbal cues that show discrepant characteristics. For example, a helper may show nonverbal signs of retreating when a sensitive subject matter is explored by the helpee. This withdrawal can be a physical closing off by the use of nonverbal behaviors or actually moving away from the helpee. Verbal signs of retreat and nongenuine behavior can be identified when a helper withdraws from sensitive helpee concerns by not responding to feelings, asking irrelevant questions, or by other verbal behaviors that show a desire on the helper's part to move away from the subject being discussed. Evaluating the level of genuineness can be done only by raters when they are able to discriminate discrepant behaviors by the helper that may indicate that the helper's internal feelings and external behaviors are not the same. Genuine behaviors are identified rather easily when both nonverbal and verbal behaviors communicate the same message and when the helper reveals feelings that relate to the helpee that are risky for the helper to reveal but affect the helpee-helper relationship.

Evaluating Assertiveness Skill

Assertiveness is as difficult to evaluate as is genuineness. Assertive behavior cannot be identified until the trainee has practiced both verbally and nonverbally.

In evaluating helper assertiveness, the rater identifies verbal and nonverbal cues that show these specific characteristics. Use the material in *Peer Power, Book 1, Workbook* to assess the assertive skills of the trainees.

Evaluating Confrontation Skill

Evaluating confrontation effectively relies upon the rater's ability to identify whether or not the helper was able to point out discrepancies in the helpee's discrepant behavior as well as the helper's before the helper's confrontation skill can be evaluated. Three basic criteria of discrepant helpee behavior need to be confronted effectively by the helper:

1. Discrepancies between the helpee's real self and ideal self.

   Example: "I am very much interested in tennis, but I haven't played in over two years."

2. Discrepancies between self and others.

   Example: "You say you are a very gentle person, but your wife says she is terrified by your temper."

3. Discrepancies between self and helper.

   Example: "You tell me you want to be different, but you refuse to try any new behaviors we have decided would help you change."

When a helper identifies and clarifies discrepant behavior in a helpee, the helper can be rated high on confrontation skills. If helpers do not, they must be rated low on the same skill. Effective evaluation, however, depends upon the rater being able to identify discrepant helpee behaviors before the rater can rate the helper's ability to confront. In order to produce growth, confrontation should enhance the relationship, and evaluation of its effectiveness should be made on that basis.

Evaluating Problem-solving Skill

Evaluating a helper's ability to problem solve with a helpee can be accomplished in either of two ways. One is based upon the adequacy of the devised solution. The other evaluation can be made regarding the helper's skill in following problem-solving procedures. Ultimately, the solution of the problem becomes the criterion for determining the quality of the helper's behaviors.

Evaluating Conflict Resolution Skills

Evaluating the helper's ability to resolve conflicts can be done in a variety of ways. For example, one way is based on observation of the trainer and how well the trainee can solve conflicts. The second way is when the skills are being utilized with real conflicts. You may get feedback from those who were in conflict and how well the trainees did. The other area you may want to look at is how conflict was reduced in the environment. For example, fighting at school was reduced by 50%, or referrals to the office were reduced by 80%.

Evaluating Integration of Skills

The degree to which the eight skills are integrated into the normal behavior of the peer helper can be measured in several ways. Measuring the total integration of skills requires general evaluation procedures and the increased involvement of other people.

1. One method of evaluating the level of skill integration is to provide a composite rating sheet for raters to use during training sessions. The complete rating of all skills comes only near the end of the training program.

2. Self-rating (from a rating sheet) is another way to measure the degree of helper/skill integration.

3. Peer evaluation (from rating sheets) will add additional awareness as to how well the skills are being integrated by the peer helper.

4. Trainer evaluation is a final process to determine the degree of integration of the basic communication skills. Other advanced skills that may be taught later need to be evaluated by the trainer also.

Assessment of the helper skills being taught is an ongoing process that takes place during basic training and advanced training sessions by the peer professional and other trainees.

EVALUATING BEHAVIORS OF PEER HELPERS

Continued appraisal of the program is done most effectively by additional ongoing evaluation procedures carried out by a variety of people. Evaluating peer helper effectiveness is essentially a process with great dependency on "eyeball" or subjective measures. Difficulty arises in making highly objective appraisals of subjective responses or in rating highly subjective material such as how I "feel" about something. Therefore, the evaluation procedures for effectiveness of the peer helpers after training is more subjective than evaluating procedures of the program but not necessarily less valuable material.

Evaluation by Peer Helping Professional

Advance training is needed to maintain contact with peer helpers and their follow-through in using skills. By checking out skill levels of peer helpers through means previously identified, a trainer can identify weaknesses and strengths in both the program and the peer helper skill levels.

In advanced training, a trainer can assess program effectiveness by working with the peer helper in examining his/her helping goals. How well the goals are met is a reflection on the effectiveness of the training. Reasons for peer helpers not meeting their helping goals are varied. The peer helper can reflect insufficient training, ineffective skills, lack of understanding, or unrealistic goals. By examining the reasons for success or lack of success, the trainer can adapt either the program, peer helper goals, the target population, or future training so as to meet the emerging needs of each peer helper.

Observing a peer helper at work is an effective evaluative procedure. By using criteria for evaluating empathy, genuineness, attending, and other skills learned during training, a trainer can rate the peer helper directly and the program indirectly. These observations can be made through audio or videotapes or through role-playing with other peer helpers. Actual observation, if conditions permit, is an excellent way to evaluate the continued progress of peer helpers.

Evaluations by Other Staff Members

Other members of the staff may have an opportunity to observe peer helpers in action. Staff observation could take place in the classroom, in a church school room with staff members participating in multiple counseling situations, or in any number of other situations where other trained or untrained staff personnel could be called upon to evaluate the performance of peer helpers. If staff members are in a position to evaluate, then they must be given some training, if only briefly, to identify the behaviors to be rated and how they are to be rated. If this brief training is not given, staff evaluations will be scattered and diverse and will be of little value in assessing the trainee's effectiveness. A worksheet that identifies the behaviors and attitudes that are to be evaluated, the qualities needing to be assessed, and in what manner they should be assessed could be an aid to the evaluation by the staff members. Using such a device, the staff observations will more consistently evaluate similar behaviors. Qualities that would be important to include on an evaluation form are the following: the quality of attending behavior, empathic responses, genuineness, and problem-solving skills. Evaluation of advanced training peer helpers also could include group discussion behaviors, values clarification experiences, and leadership responsibilities by staff members.

Another easily followed procedure is to request a short prose evaluation of helper behaviors observed by staff members. To do so may necessitate staff orientation as to peer helper behaviors that are to be evaluated. Also discuss *how* peer helpers are to be evaluated, which will be necessary in order to gain consistency in the reporting.

Evaluation from the Population Served

If one of the goals of your peer helping program is to serve a specific population, you will need to obtain feedback from them. For example, if the program is in a school, a simple questionnaire can be given to a random tenth-grade class to check whether or not they are aware of the program, if they used the available peer helper, and if so how effective was the help. Individual interviews can be performed by an unbiased outside agent.

Overall changes can be looked at in terms of reducing areas that are targeted. Examples might be increased scores on standardized testing (tutoring), reduced drug use (prevention), reduced smoking (prevention), reduced drop-out rate (helping the lost and lonely person), increased attendance, productivity (special friend, big sister/brother project, focus group, quality check groups), and increase in wellness (through information relative to diet, smoking, exercise, etc.). This type of evaluation may be difficult, but it is important to do to change training or refocus.

Evaluation of Personal Growth

The peer helper goes through a growing period. Feedback to each trainer as well as important information for the peer professional might be from formal and informal feedback from the peer helpers themselves. Such formal instruments ought to be the Pretesting Yourself Communications Exercise (Module I, Exercise 1.1 of *Peer Power, Book 1, Workbook*), and/or the Posttest Communications Exercise (Module XIII, Exercise SD 1.1 of *Peer Power, Book 1, Workbook*). Formal instruments such as the Self-evaluation for the Peer Helper, as found at the back of *Peer Power, Book 2, Workbook,* may be important not only for the peer helper but also for the trainer to give pretraining and posttraining. Observation of outside behavior may be helpful—for example, increased GPA, attendance, reduced conflict with friends and family, happier person, and so forth.

Evaluation through Research

Formal and informal research designs are excellent evaluation procedures. Researching a program provides the most useful feedback on the quality and effectiveness of a program. The methods previously mentioned are worthwhile and can give general information regarding the progress of the training, but serious research will give the best kind of information to answer questions about the program's ultimate value to the people involved.

When researching the program, two areas will prove to be most fruitful for program development and public relations. They are ***program design*** and ***effects of training on trainees.*** Although the basic training design is well supported by research, much work remains to be completed in improving on teaching techniques and procedures. The effects of the training on the trainees or on those people whom they attempt to help is described by considerable research data, but, as is usually the case, the data have opened up many questions that need to be answered.

Taking pre- and post-measurements on one or more characteristics of behavior provides data that allow the drawing of conclusions regarding the merits of a program. Using schools as an example, pre- and post-measurements can be taken on grades of trainees, grades of the people with whom they work, school attendance, a variety of student attitudes, discipline referrals, or parental attitudes toward the children who participated in the program before and after training.

More complex research can be done, but experience frequently shows that time and working conditions do not allow for highly sophisticated research designs. Some trainers who develop programs will be close enough to colleges and universities so that, with assistance, more complex studies can be attempted. Help from the *National Peer Helpers Association* (NPHA) also can be requested for suggestions in needed research design. In studying peer helping programs, the researcher may want to look at the impact of the program on classroom behavior, attendance, changes in academic grades, self-concept, discipline, referrals, and property damage. Researchers may want to simply chart types of problems and number of contacts.

Elements of Evaluation

As you can see, evaluation can involve many aspects. It can relate to the program goals, to the training, to how the peers are utilized, to feedback from staff and environment. Indeed all aspects of the program can be part of the evaluation.

Evaluation Process

A process of the evaluation needs to be decided on from the beginning. For example:

focus on the evaluation,

collect the information,

organize the information,

analyze the information,

administer the evaluation,

summarize the information,

report the information to other peer professionals or your organization (school or other), and

write up the evaluation.

You may want to team up with a university to conduct some formal research, such as comparing your peer helpers to a group that has not had training (control group), or you may compare those who received the services (experimental) vs. those who did not receive the services (control group).

Some of the variables that may be topics for evaluation are

academic achievement,

grade changes,

cognitive development,

self-concept changes,

locus of control,

school climate,

work climate,

attitude changes,

communication skills,

attendance,

alcohol and drug use,

behavior changes,

programs through student services,

reduction in conflict, and

reduced tension.

There are several commercial assessments available, or you can develop your own.

Public Relations as an Evaluation Process

Programs such as peer helper training need consistent and effective public relations work. Emphatically, the results of program evaluation give much valuable material that can be used to sell the program and to insure that the program remains acceptable to those who have supported the program.

Staff members can sabotage programs unless they are involved in the feedback. Specifically, counselors, teachers, and parents need to be asked for their feedback. Teachers and administrators also can be important friends for you and your program. Therefore, if the projects that your peer helpers are doing meet the addressed needs of the school, you will gain a lot of support.

Other staff members, administrators, and the public need to know the results of any evaluation that is undertaken. The importance of continued evaluation and reporting of that evaluation to many people should be stressed to those interested in developing programs. Informing the public once at the onset of the program is not adequate if continued support is expected from people not directly involved. Conditions and people change, and as a result, they need to be reminded periodically of the work that the program is accomplishing. Without such follow-up, one may lose support for the program. The reporting of program results can be accomplished by speaking to any number of groups or reporting results through news media. Public relations can be in the form of posters, flyers announcing the program, letters to other staff members, or articles from publications given to targeted audiences (e.g., parents, teens, administrators, C.E.O.s).

Also, a unique program of this nature involves sharing program results with other professionals in the field. The helping profession grows through the sharing of resources and experiences. Exchange can be effected through seminars in which people involved with peer helpers meet to discuss common concerns and problems. Giving programs at professional meetings or writing in journals or newsletters are two additional means of reaching other professionals. Another option is to inform other professionals about a peer helping program and invite them to attend the training sessions. Much can be learned by observing such a program in action.

Feedback from the public is one of the best criteria of intent of acceptance of the peer helping program. Consider the public relations aspect as a two-way flow: (1) sharing with the public what is being done and what the evaluation supports as accomplishments, and (2) asking for and listening to what the public has as perceptions. Feedback gives information on how well goals and objectives are being reached and whether or not changes are needed in training, goals, objectives, criteria for trainees selected, and/or places where trainees practice/apply their skills.

EVALUATION PLANS

You are now in a position to develop your own blueprint for evaluation that will guide change. A "blueprint for education" is provided in Form 10.1 to provide a framework for you to consider as you make evaluation plans.

BLUEPRINT FOR EVALUATION				
	Who Is Respon-sible	To Do When	What Is Needed	How (Design)
NEEDS	————	————	————	————
GOALS	————	————	————	————
RECRUITMENT	————	————	————	————
SELECTION	————	————	————	————
BASIC TRAINING	————	————	————	————
ADVANCED TRAINING	————	————	————	————
TARGET POPULATION	————	————	————	————
CHANGES IN ENVIRONMENT	————	————	————	————
PERSONAL GROWTH	————	————	————	————
RESEARCH	————	————	————	————
OTHER				
————	————	————	————	————
————	————	————	————	————
————	————	————	————	————

Form 10.1. Blueprint for evaluation: Items to consider as evaluation plans are developed.

> "Our youth comprise about 25% of our population
> and 100% of our future."

Chapter

BUILDING A TEAM

In starting a peer helping program and in enhancing a program, building a team is essential for the long term of the program. Even if you are just doing a program by yourself, you still need a team for support and guidance. If you are in a large system, you may need support from others to be able to operate. If you are trying to make peer helping part of several components in your system, you may have to develop an organizational structure with an administrator, support staff, and professional staff along with organizational guidelines.

TEAMS VERSUS GROUPS

Several groups call themselves teams, when in fact they are not. Groups that are not teams may include people who meet daily for coffee break but who have no defined goals, or a monthly coin club in which people merely have similar interests. Some of the differences between groups and teams are shown in Figure 11.1.

GROUPS	TEAMS
Members are together for administrative purposes only and work independently.	Members recognize their interdependence because both personal and team goals are best accomplished by mutual support.
Individuals focus on self, see themselves as hired hands.	Members feel ownership for their job.
Members have no commitment to overall goal.	Members are committed to overall goal.
Members do not participate in decision making.	Members contribute to decision making.
Members are told what to do.	Members contribute to each other.
Communication is closed.	Communication is open.
Members get training, but can't apply it.	Members are encouraged to develop skills and learn to apply them.
Members distrust others.	Climate of trust exists with questions being welcomed.

Figure 11.1. Differences between groups and teams.

First it is important to decide if you want to develop a team. Next is to determine the effectiveness of a team. Typically an effective team has the following characteristics:

Goals—members mutually decide goals on which they will work together.

Interdependence—members have designated assignments.

Commitment—team members can be relied on to complete a group task.

Accountability—the larger organization holds them accountable.

One example is an athletic team because it has a reason to work together. Individual players have specific assignments for which they must each be responsible. Finally, the team usually operates within the framework of a higher organization such as a league.

The team members often have similar objectives, values, and characteristics such as the following:

understand and are committed to group goals;
are friendly, concerned with others on the team;
confront conflict openly;
listen to others empathetically;
involve others in decision making;
respect individual differences;
contribute ideas and solutions;
reward team efforts; and
appreciate comments about team performance.

The leaders of effective teams see their role as "unifying a diverse group of people to work effectively as a team toward a common purpose under varied and often difficult conditions." Often leaders are needed to put an effective team together.

STAGES OF TEAM DEVELOPMENT

To help you understand some of the stages of team development, I have borrowed ideas from Kormanski (1985), Tuckman (1965), Tuckman and Jensen (1977), Woodcock (1979), Woodcock and Francis (1981), Yalom (1970), and others. Teams are rapidly replacing individuals as the primary unit of focus in many aspects of society. Many companies, schools, and agencies are learning how to build, nurture, lead, and dismantle teams. Team building is often used to improve the effectiveness of work groups.

As you move from starting a team to performing effectively, it is important to understand the stages of team development. The five stages of team development are listed in Figure 11.2.

Forming—This stage identifies who each team member is and how he or she will enhance the overall team.

Norming—This stage identifies how the structure of the team is set up and how roles are established.

Storming—This stage involves disagreement and problem solving, empowering team players to participate in constructive conflict.

Mourning—This stage helps the team lose a sense of competitiveness, a sense of backroom politics, a tendency toward one-up-manship, old leadership styles and patterns, and the way it was.

Performing—This stage demonstrates a team that is effective and productive in its responsibilities.

Figure 11.2. Five stages of team development. (Based on Rohen & Tindall, 1991)

An effective leader will help the team members through all of the stages, and the team members will understand the different phases of team development and work to move in that direction.

The effective leader knows that in the beginning, the **Forming Stage,** it is important to gain commitment and acceptance of the values of the group, develop a common mission, and envision the future. During the **Norming Stage,** norms and roles are established. During the **Storming Stage,** the skills of flexibility, creativity, and kaleidoscopic thinking will assist the movement toward the next stage. The **Mourning Stage** often involves separation and ways of celebrating the old way and looking at the new way. The skills of **Performing** involve multicultural awareness, mentoring, and tutoring. The *Myers-Briggs Type Indicator* and *MBTI-EAR-TDI* have been utilized effectively to help groups move from one stage to another.

TEAM BUILDING THROUGH SELF-UNDERSTANDING

Peer helping professionals are often so busy developing their own programs and helping the peer helpers that they forget about themselves. This often puts them in a very stressful environment, and they may find themselves not working effectively with the rest of the team.

Lack of team spirit and high stress levels are obvious to the peer helpers. A support staff member who is frustrated by poor communication gives the peer helpers the message that something is wrong. When you have a disagreement with another peer professional, you are concerned with that issue and may not be able to focus on your training group.

If you want to be effective with your trainees, and reduce stress in your organization, you should learn something about your own style of working and about the work styles of the other people on your team. This understanding can help reduce stress, increase communication, increase productivity, reduce conflict, and contribute overall to a happier environment in which people enjoy working.

As peer helping professionals, we spend our lives helping others to self-understanding, but we often fall short when it comes to understanding ourselves. Once we understand ourselves, we can begin to have our own needs met; when our needs are met, we have even more to give to the peer helpers. So how can we put our skills together to help ourselves and those we work with?

Awareness

The first essential to self-understanding is an awareness of the individual's strengths and weaknesses, ways he or she wants to be appreciated, ways of communication, problem-solving style, leadership style, working style, values, needs, and operational style under stress. One methodology used to promote this self-understanding is a self-assessment instrument such as the *Myers-Briggs Type Indicator*, *16PF*, *Values survey*, *MMPI*, *LIFO*, and others. To show the value of using such instruments with the team, let us consider the *MBTI* as a measure of personality type. It is based on the theory of C.G. Jung and was developed and refined by a mother-daughter team, Isabel Myers and Katherine Briggs.

Interaction

The *MBTI* gives four general categories of personality preferences. The first category has to do with how we interact with work and how we get our energy. This characteristic is measured on the Introversion-Extraversion scale and is referred to as either an "E" or the "I" preference. Introverts get energy from quiet inner reflection, while extroverts get energy from interacting with people.

World View

The second category of preferences has to do with how we perceive the world. The two ends of the continuum are "Sensing" and "Intuition" ("S" and "N"). Sensing types prefer practical, detailed approaches to situations and use their five senses to gather data. Intuitive types, on the other hand, prefer using their "sixth sense" and tend to trust their hunches.

Decisions

The third pair of preferences are called "Thinking" and "Feeling" ("T" and "F") and describe how we make decisions. Thinking types are logical, matter-of-fact and stay focused on the issue. Feeling types are much less concerned with the facts and more concerned with how decisions affect people.

Processing

"Judging" and "Perceiving" ("J" and "P") are the fourth set of preferences and have to do with how we utilize our time and process our decisions. Judges tend to like things planned, organized, and on a schedule. Perceivers are more spontaneous and flexible and will delay a decision while they search for more data.

Categories

The various combinations of preferences give us 16 distinct categories of personality types. They are commonly referred to as ESFP, (Extraverted, Sensing, Feeling, Perceiving), ISTJ, (Introverted, Sensing, Thinking, Judging), and so forth.

Groups and organizations often take on a collective personality, usually influenced by key individuals in the organization, both past and present. This collective personality is often called the "Team Culture." It usually comes about because a key individual with a certain work style (say, an ESFP type) likes to have others of the same type around him, and chooses similar individuals for hiring and promotion. After a while, there is a distinct ESFP feeling about the team, and individuals with slightly different work styles may adapt slightly to take on the team culture themselves.

Mismatches

Introducing a skilled individual with a radically different personality type (INFJ) to this atmosphere can make the new person feel like the proverbial square peg in a round hole. The new team member prefers a quiet office with a closed door to work behind; the old team members see this as snobbish or secretive. Unless all team members understand each other and each other's needs, frustration and dissatisfaction will build.

Assessment

Using the *MBTI* to assess personality types, you can become aware of the strengths and the weaknesses of others on your team. It is important that you have someone skilled in interpreting the *MBTI* to analyze the results. For example, if one person has the ability to analyze a situation, organize and find flaws in a plan in advance, that person should be the first to examine any suggestions for radical expansion, etc. If someone is good at persuasion and arousing enthusiasm, when the group needs someone to sell a program, that person would be the obvious choice.

On the flip side, if you learn that one of your weaknesses is to miss details and to skip over the fine print, it is important to recognize this. When it is time to examine a contract, you can either ask for help from someone else (whose strong point is analysis), or remind yourself that you are weak in this area and that you must concentrate on the task to perform it adequately.

Appreciation

It is also important to know and to share the ways in which we need appreciation. Some of us like lots of hugs, some of us like to be recognized for a competent job, and others like to be sent cards and gifts. What is important to you? How can you help others understand how you need to be appreciated? Again, this area is open to misinterpretation. A hearty hug of congratulations from someone who is physically expansive could be misconstrued as sexual harassment by someone with a more reserved style.

Communication

Communication patterns are also important to understand. For example, if you are an extravert, you like for people to show energy and enthusiasm, and for people to respond quickly without long pauses. You have a high tolerance for talking without reaching definite conclusions. If you are an introvert, you will like to know ahead of time what the agenda is; you may like to have more one-to-one interactions, and you may need to have other people understand that you may be slow to respond because you are processing information. Extroverts often need others in order to brainstorm. Introverts often need time to themselves to think through things. If you are an extravert working with introverts, it is important to have your co-workers understand your communication needs.

Problem Solving

It is also important to understand problem-solving style. Do you solve problems best by talking with others, following your guts, figuring them out logically, or getting lots of information before deciding?

Stress

How do you operate under stress? Do your team members understand that your preferred way of operating is different if you feel under stress? For example, if you change suddenly from being very loose to being very controlling, it helps if your team members realize that this means you are under stress. Then they can try to help you cope with the stress. The *LIFO, 16PF* and *MBTI* are instruments that help you understand how you operate under stress.

Resolving Conflicts

What is your method of resolving conflict? Do you avoid conflict or see it as essential for growth? Skill practice will assist you through the "storming stage."

Leadership Style

What about leadership style? Does your manner of operation put other people under stress? Are you too laid-back for new team members? Are you too controlling for older team members? The *MBTI* and *16PF* help you get in touch with your preferred leadership style.

Needs

Understanding your needs is also important. For example, if you need a lot of fun and humor in your life but work primarily with troubled youth, then finding a balance in your leisure life will help you maintain your equilibrium.

Team members should clarify their values and beliefs. If you value your family life and the team wants to work weekends and evenings, it is important that all of you are aware of each other's values and can understand and accept the value systems of the others.

Taking Care of Yourself

In trying to set up a program, don't forget to take care of yourself. How you do this depends on your personality type and some of your current life events. It is important to be a model and practice stress management.

Remember that it is essential to set limits and establish boundaries between yourself and the peer program. Many peer professionals feel that the program is their whole life. Hopefully, you will see this as just a part of your professional life that is helping others. For several ideas on taking care of yourself, please refer to past issues of the *Peer Facilitator Quarterly* in which columns appear regularly on this topic.

Self-understanding is the first stage of team building. Once these components are shared with others on the team, the team members will become better able to understand you and also to help when needed. Acceptance of different styles is critical for a smoothly operating organization. Once differences are seen as acceptable and needed for the organization, then the team will problem solve more effectively.

Figure 11.3 contains an outline for considering yourself and your team members.

MY PEER HELPING TEAM

My team includes ———————————————————

————————————————————————————

Characteristics of my team are ———————————

————————————————————————————

My team culture is ———————————————————

————————————————————————————

Strengths of our team are ———————————————

————————————————————————————

Weaknesses of our team are ——————————————

————————————————————————————

Growth areas of our team include ————————————

————————————————————————————

Stage of our team (explain)

Forming ——————————————————————

————————————————————————————

Norming ——————————————————————

————————————————————————————

Storming ——————————————————————

————————————————————————————

Mourning ————————————————————

————————————————————————

Performing ————————————————————

————————————————————————

What I need from a team is ————————————

————————————————————————

How do I take care of myself? ——————————

————————————————————————

How do I communicate with the team? ————————

————————————————————————

How do I problem solve with the team? ——————

————————————————————————

How do I appreciate others on the team? ——————

————————————————————————

How do I handle stress on the team? ——————————

————————————————————————

How do I solve conflict? ——————————————

————————————————————————

What does our team need? ——————————————

————————————————————————

Figure 11.3. Outline of items for consideration about team members.

CREATIVE RESOURCES
OF PEER HELPING PROFESSIONAL

Everyone has some creative ability with which to approach a given situation in a different way. Using this book as a base, the next step is to supplement parts of the training with plans to meet one's own particular area of need with individual talents. This *Peer Programs* book was designed only for a structured base so that **the Peer Helping Professional may add his/her own creative supplementary material.** However, **the program model and training session model should be followed exactly.** Procedures to implement the models need to be suitable to trainees.

The implementation of the program may involve one individual helping the other person on a one-to-one basis. On the other hand, implementation of the program may require peer counselors to lead "rap groups" in which the groups talk about everyday, common concerns. The groups are designed to allow people to air some of their concerns with someone who is interested in listening and to help them through use of other helping skills learned in the peer helping program.

"YOUR BALL GAME, GO GET THEM!"

The hope is that this book has planted ideas and methods that will bring about the initiation and development of a peer helping program.

Hopefully, this written communication will encourage others to try new risk-taking behavior with their own approaches for helping others. Actually, this book calls on individuals to train lay populations in helping skills. The concept is to develop mentally healthy people who can listen, communicate, and problem solve. Individuals have the potential to train people in schools, churches, and community organizations, and the authors of this book are extremely interested in learning about successes and/or failures you may have with your peer helping program. Please write or call us. Written communication can be sent through the publisher. Only by sharing successes and failures will the process of developing a more workable peer helping model be feasible. I am throwing the ball to you, so go with it, and see what programs evolve.

You will be thanked by peer helpers for a long time. The following is a letter written to a peer helper from one of the youth who received the help. You will be able to add your own stories of appreciation for the help you give.

Thank You for Helping Me

What would I do without your point of view? I have come to rely on your perspective. So many times, you've helped me see the big picture. You're able to come up with a different angle on each new problem. You challenge my assumptions, yet support my goals and feelings. You help me sort out when I have the right to be angry, or when I'm just overreacting. You remind me of my strengths when I've forgotten I even had any. So many times, your insights have made a difference in my life. And from my point of view, that makes you someone pretty special.

Thank You For Helping Me,

Signed (Name removed to protect individual)

Chapter

PROGRAMMATIC STANDARDS AND CODES OF ETHICS

Peer programs are designed to be helpful to others. As such, each peer helper and peer professional needs to assure himself/herself that the highest standards are upheld at all times. Each helpee has the right to hold an expectation of being assisted in a manner consistent with local, state, and national guidelines for peer helpers.

To assure that high standards will be met and maintained, national guidelines not only need to be reviewed, but peer helpers and peer professionals also need to fully understand and be able (skilled) to implement guidelines. Included will be the need to assure that each peer helper knows his/her limits and knows how to ask for assistance and/or make a referral. This necessitates training of peer helpers to the degree that they can learn skills and become aware of their limitations. Also, referral sources must be identified and procedures outlined as to which helpees and/or types of assistance, when needed, should be referred, when, and by what procedures.

Included in this chapter are five nationally accepted guidelines for use with peer helpers. The five and their major components and/or uses are as follows:

1. *ASCA Position Statement on Peer Helping*—This statement was prepared by the American School Counselor Association. Although designed for school use, the content is applicable for community agencies, businesses, and industries. It defines peer helping and identifies what a peer helper does.

   Peer helping values are identified, and peer helping roles are detailed. Peer helpers need to obtain training offered by peer professionals and to have ongoing supervision from a peer professional. Thus, responsibilities need to be spelled out. *The ASCA Position Statement* provides a list of responsibilities for the peer professional.

2. *Programmatic Standards, National Peer Helpers Association*—This set of standards pertains to the program and, as such, it lists specifics to consider when implementing a program. If the standards cannot be met, then the program needs to be delayed until a time when those standards can be met.

   The standards are specified for program maintenance including evaluation, public relations, and long-range planning.

3. *Programmatic Standards, National Peer Helpers Association: Checklist for a Peer Helper Program*—This is a checklist to use as the program is considered, initiated, maintained, and evaluated. Each checklist item is explained in full in the *Programmatic Standards* listed in item 2 above.

4. *National Peer Helpers Association Code of Ethics for Peer Helping Professionals*—This short list identifies components that need to be in any code of ethics for peer helping professionals.

5. *National Peer Helpers Association Code of Ethics for Peer Helpers*—This list of six items identifies components that need to be in any code of ethics for peer helpers (e.g., a locally produced code should include these six items).

ASCA POSITION STATEMENT ON PEER HELPING

(The following position statement was originally approved by the Governing Board of the American School Counselor Association in December of 1978 and later revised.)

It is the position of the American School Counselor Association that Peer Counseling Programs enhance the effectiveness of the helper program by increasing outreach programs and expanding guidance services. Through proper selection, training, and supervision, peer helpers can be a positive force within the school and the community, one that will meet the needs of a sizable segment of the student body.

Teenagers often communicate their problems to their peers rather than to parents, administrators, or counselors. There exists in every school community a segment of the student population that rejects adult relationships. In our society, peer influence may be the strongest single motivational force in a teenager's life. Peers can be selected and trained by professional counselors in communication and counseling skills through a carefully planned peer counseling program and can produce additional guidance services that otherwise might never have been realized.

Peer Helping Defined

Peer helping is defined as a variety of interpersonal helping behaviors assumed by nonprofessionals who undertake a helping role with others. Peer helping includes one-to-one helping relationships, group leadership, discussion leadership, advisement, tutoring, and all activities of an interpersonal helping or assisting nature. A peer helper refers to a person who assumes the role of a helping person with contemporaries. Peers are individuals who share related values, experiences, and life-styles and who are approximately the same age.

Peer Helping Roles

Peer helpers can provide a variety of useful and helpful services for schools, depending on the individual school's needs. It should be emphasized that peer helpers should not be used as mere clerical assistants since they have been trained to function in an interpersonal capacity.

The most obvious role of peer helpers is that of one-to-one counseling. Talking with students about their personal problems, referring peers to other sources of help in the community, giving information about drugs, sex, and venereal diseases, and helping students with their school problems are some of the types of assistance given by peer helpers on a one-to-one basis.

Peer helpers can be effective in group settings. Their training enables them to be used as group leaders, assistants in counseling groups, or as communications skills trainers in the classroom. They can also help to train new groups of peer counselors/peer helpers.

There are several educational functions that peer helpers can perform effectively such as tutoring students in academic areas, serving as readers for nonreaders, and assisting Special Education consultants in working with learning and behaviorally disabled students.

Peer helpers can be helpful in many guidance capacities. They are very effective in greeting new students and their parents and in making them feel welcome. They can be used to help with the registration process by aiding students in the selection of their classes and serving as assistants and runners on registration nights. Other guidance functions that peer helpers can perform are serving as career center helpers, being open house guides, writing the guidance newsletter, helping with organizational details of testing, and engaging career program speakers.

Professional Counselors' Responsibilities in Peer Counseling

The professional counselor must accept the responsibility for adequately meeting the needs of the school population and for writing a peer counseling program designed to meet those needs. The counselor must then accept the additional responsibilities of:

1. Devising a plan for selection of peer helpers that is compatible with the population to be served.

2. Coordinating the leadership of an adequate training program for the peer helpers selected.

3. Planning the professional helper's time budget so that adequate time is scheduled for work with the peer helpers.

4. Constructing a support system through positive, factual, and honest public relations.

5. Providing time for meeting with the peer counseling group on a weekly basis for continued training, supervision, sharing, and personal growth.

6. Continually monitoring and evaluating the training and the impact of the program, and instituting any necessary changes to help the program meet the assessed needs of the population it serves.

The professional counselor must serve as a support and a resource person to peer helpers. The counselor must have a broad, reliable awareness of competent resources, and support professionals in the community who can and will accept referrals when needed.

The professional counselor should accept responsibility for the design and completion of research on the program.

Follow-up studies and program effectiveness must be conducted and studied in an objective manner. Results should be reported to the population served and to interested professionals; it is the responsibility of the counselor to share information, research, and expertise with other interested counselors.

How Peer Helpers Help the Professional Counselor

After training and with ongoing supervision, peer helpers can work as important members of the guidance team. Peer helpers often are able to help accomplish things that the professional cannot do alone or cannot do as quickly alone. Therefore, peer helpers help increase the services of the counseling center. They are able to serve in an outreach function and be of help to any population that may feel uncomfortable talking with a professional counselor.

The peer helpers may assist peers with a variety of problems by serving as listeners. As listeners, they are able to help others to stay healthy mentally and to reduce crisis situations by alerting professional counselors to serious problems.

As peer helpers are trained with helping skills, they grow as individuals and become more functional at a higher level. The experience of counseling peers also may help them decide if they want a future occupation in the helping profession. Peer helpers are trained to become more effective adults.

It is imperative that all guidance and counseling departments in the schools plan, initiate, and implement a peer counseling program. Well-trained peer helpers can have a positive effect on students such as no one else can provide. Students sometimes relate and accept alternative patterns of behavior from peers who are struggling with similar feelings and problems. Peer helpers can create a tremendous positive impact on the student population.

PROGRAMMATIC STANDARDS
NATIONAL PEER HELPERS ASSOCIATION

(Reproduced with permission from National Peer Helpers Association)

The National Peer Helpers Association believes the following standards are essential for any quality peer program:

I. PROGRAM START-UP

A. PLANNING
Prior to program implementation, careful planning should be conducted to address such issues as the following:

1. Rationale: There is a clear and compelling rationale for the development of the program; frequently, this is accomplished through conducting a formal or informal needs assessment in the setting in which the program is to be implemented.

2. Purpose: The purpose of the program derives logically from its rationale, and is typically summarized in a formal mission statement.

3. Goals and Objectives: Programmatic goals and objectives are
   (a) reflective of the rationale and purpose of the program; and
   (b) clear, realistic, and achievable.

4. Procedures: The procedures and activities through which programmatic goals are to be accomplished are laid out in clear and systematic fashion.

5. Compliance: The program is planned and implemented in a manner consistent with local, state, and national guidelines for programmatic standards and ethics (see *NPHA Code of Ethics for Peer Helpers* and *Peer Helping Professionals*).

B. COMMITMENT
The program should enjoy not simply the permission, but the active commitment and involvement of those

to solicit and maintain its services. Such commitment is reflected particularly in the following areas:

1. Tangible evidence of a high level of administrative, staff, and community support; in many cases, this includes the formation of a program advisory committee. Committee members may or may not be directly involved in program implementation, but they provide valuable input to program staff, and help to maximize a sense of program ownership.
2. Sufficient financial and logistical support for effective program implementation; such support includes the provision of necessary curricular and training resources.

C. STAFFING

Program staff should possess appropriate background, training, and characteristics to enable them to carry out their responsibilities in an effective manner. Among professional staff who work directly with peer helpers, the following skills are essential:

1. Strong positive rapport with the population from which the peer helpers are selected.
2. Educational and practical experience that is relevant to the nature and goals of the program.
3. Understanding of, and commitment to, fundamental principles of peer helping; this includes a readiness to maximize the level of programmatic ownership and involvement on the part of the peer helpers themselves.
4. Close familiarity with the setting in which the program is to be implemented.
5. Clear grasp of program needs and goals, and ability to articulate effectively the nature and purpose of the program to peer helpers, other staff, the sponsoring agency, and the broader community.
6. Recognition of the importance of serving as a positive role model, both personally and professionally.
7. Familiarity with different learning styles and teaching strategies, including both experiential and didactic approaches.

8. Ability to work effectively with groups.
9. Mastery of concepts and skills necessary for effective training and supervision of peer helpers.
10. Sufficient time and energy in order to be able to carry out programmatic responsibilities.

D. ORGANIZATIONAL STRUCTURE
The program should be organized and structured in a logical and consistent manner that provides clear lines of authority, responsibility, and communication; and is reflective of the nature and purpose of the program.

II. PROGRAM IMPLEMENTATION

A. SCREENING AND SELECTION
The program should employ a clear, systematic, and careful procedure for the screening and selection of peer helpers. Typically, this procedure includes the following:
1. Establishing appropriate criteria as to the characteristics being sought among prospective peer helpers. Among those characteristics are helpfulness, trustworthiness, concern for others, ability to listen, and potential to serve as a positive role model.
2. Conducting a formal or informal survey in the program setting, in order to determine which individuals are felt to possess the desired characteristics.
3. Making application to the program, soliciting recommendations from others in the program setting, and structuring an interview with program staff.

Programs may differ as to whether final selection of peer helpers should occur prior to or after peer helping training. But in either case, the selection process should be guided by the following criteria:
1. Demonstration of appropriate helping characteristics and skills.

2. Evidence of emotional security.
3. Understanding of the type(s) of services to be provided.
4. Commitment to and availability for the provision of those services.
5. Ability to be reflective of and sensitive to the characteristics of the population to be served.
6. Manageability of the size of the group selected, in order to ensure quality training and supervision.

B. TRAINING

Once peer helpers have been selected, they should be provided with quality training in the knowledge and skills they will need to be effective in the peer helping role. The training program that is implemented should be reflective of the nature and goals of the program; should take into account the age, needs and characteristics of the population to be served; should utilize appropriate curricular resources and training strategies; and should be consistent with local, state, and national guidelines on ethics and standards. Trainees should commit to participate in all aspects of training, and to maximize opportunities for both skill development and personal growth. Finally, training should be viewed as an ongoing process, one which is never truly completed.

While specific features of training may vary somewhat from program to program, the following elements are characteristic of effective peer helping training models:
1. Role of the Peer Helper Training in the peer helping role includes, but may not be limited to, the following:
   a. Program orientation.
   b. Characteristics of the helper (caring, acceptance, genuineness, understanding, trustworthiness).
   c. Self-awareness.
   d. Positive role modeling; maintaining a healthy lifestyle.
   e. Avoidance of temptation to offer advice, propose solutions, or impose skills.

f. Positive listening skills.

g. Recognition of limitations.

h. Development of individual and group trust.

i. Creation of a support system of peer helpers for each other, as well as for helpees.

j. Development of a code of ethics and standards of behavior.

2. Confidentiality/Liability Issues
While communications between peer helpers and helpees are typically confidential, there are two important exceptions to this general rule:

a. Potential threats to the personal safety or well-being of the peer helper, helpee, or others;

b. Situations or problems beyond the personal experience level or expertise of the peer helper.

It is an essential component of any peer helping training program that peer helpers know how to recognize such situations, are aware of their limitations and responsibilities, and have ready access to professional staff and appropriate referral resources.

3. Communication Skills

a. Basic principles of verbal and of nonverbal communication.

b. Active listening skills (attending, empathizing, etc.).

c. Facilitative responding (questioning, clarifying, summarizing, etc.).

4. Problem-Solving/Decision-Making Strategies
Steps in principled decision-making (identifying the problem; brainstorming alternatives; predicting consequences; carrying out action plan; evaluating results).

5. Additional Issues and Topics
Depending upon the nature and goals of particular programs, additional specialized training may be provided in areas such as the following:

a. Basic concepts of human behavior. While not expected to function as amateur therapists, peer helpers should have some degree of familiarity with concepts such as the following:
   1. The role of motivational and reinforcement factors in behavior.
   2. Sociocultural influences and differences.
   3. Individual and group dynamics.
b. Group facilitation techniques.
c. Peer tutoring strategies.
d. Crisis management.
e. Conflict resolution.
f. Special needs populations.
g. Telephone "hotline" management.
h. Specific problem areas (substance abuse, dropouts, depression and suicide, teen pregnancy, child abuse, sexually transmitted diseases, gangs and cults, family relations, etc.).
i. Knowledge of referral resources, services, and programs.

C. SERVICE DELIVERY
Subsequent to training, peer helpers should be provided with structured opportunities to engage in a variety of meaningful, productive helping roles within the program setting. The peer helping services which are provided should:
   1. Be consistent with and reflective of program goals.
   2. Enable peer helpers to apply the knowledge and skills they have acquired during training.
   3. Enhance the personal growth and positive development of peer helpers and helpees alike.
   4. Recognize and accommodate the need for ongoing opportunities for continued learning and training.
   5. Establish safeguards to protect peer helpers from burnout, role confusion, inappropriate assignments, or manipulation.

D. SUPERVISION
Once peer helpers have begun to provide services, it is imperative that they receive regular, ongoing

supervision from program staff. In addition to regularly-scheduled sessions, staff should be available to provide supplemental supervision and support as needed. Major goals of supervision include the following:

1. Enable program staff to monitor program-related activities and services.
2. Enhance the effectiveness and personal growth of peer helpers.
3. Encourage peer helpers to share with, learn from, and support each other in the performance of their helping roles.

III. PROGRAM MAINTENANCE

Once the program has been established, program staff should take steps to ensure its continued survival, improvement, and success. These steps include the following:

A. EVALUATION

In order to document program-related activities and services, to assess the impact of the program with reference to its goals, and to provide grounds for future revisions, the program should develop and implement a formal evaluation plan. The evaluation plan typically includes two components:

1. Formative Evaluation

Formative evaluation provides an accurate picture of what happened in connection with the program. Formative data includes information in such areas as number of peer helpers and helpees involved; program staffing and organization; selection procedures; nature and extent of training; amount and types of services provided; and other program-related activities.

2. Summative Evaluation

Summative evaluation determines the degree to which the program has been successful in achieving its goals, and typically assesses the impact of program participation upon both peer helpers and those who have received program services. Such assessment can be qualitative (questionnaires, opinion surveys, etc.) and/or can employ "hard" quantitative indices of program impact. In a school-based program, for example, summative evaluation might assess impact in such areas as student attitudes or behavior, grade point average, absenteeism and dropout rates, or incidence of disciplinary referrals.

Both formative and summative evaluation data should be utilized by program staff in a periodic effort to determine whether and how the program needs to be revised for future improvement.

B. PUBLIC RELATIONS
Program staff should make a concerted, ongoing effort to keep those in the program setting, as well as interested individuals and organizations in the broader community, well-informed about the program, and supportive of its goals. Techniques for strengthening programmatic public relations might include production of a program brochure or newsletter; maintenance of media contacts; involvement of community representatives in training or program services; and community outreach projects.

C. LONG-RANGE PLANNING
Program staff should engage in long-range planning to ensure that in the future, the program does not die, but rather becomes stronger and more firmly integrated within the program setting as time goes by. Key factors to consider include the following:

1. Staffing: It is important that the success of the program not be dependent upon the particular person, or personality, who happens to be coordinating it at any give time. In this regard, a sense of program ownership should be maximized through such strategies as the formation of a program advisory committee, and there should always be at least one individual within the program

setting who is prepared to assume coordination responsibilities in the event of staffing changes.

2. Funding: The program should (a) have a secure and consistent funding base, and/or (b) have contingency plans to provide for continued operation in the event of reduced or nonexistent funding.

3. Peer Ownership: The program should strive to maximize the level of ownership and involvement on the part of the peer helpers themselves; if peers feel directly responsible for the success and survival of the program, they are unlikely to allow it to perish.

PROGRAMMATIC STANDARDS
NATIONAL PEER HELPERS ASSOCIATION
CHECKLIST
FOR A PEER HELPER PROGRAM

(Reprinted with permission from National Peer Helpers Association)

I. PROGRAM START-UP:

A. Planning
— Rationale
— Purpose
— Goals and Objectives
— Procedures
— Compliance

B. Commitment
— Program Advisory Committee
— Administrative Support
— Financial Support
— Resources

C. Staffing
— Positive rapport with population to be helped
— Experience with and knowledge of program needs and goals
— Knowledge of fundamental principles of peer helping
— Positive public relations links
— Positive role model to various publics
— Knowledge of different teaching/learning skills
— Ability to teach didactic and experiential lessons
— Ability to work with groups
— Participation in an on-going training program
— Skills necessary for supervision
— Time to train, plan, evaluate, and supervise

D. Organizational Structure
    — Clear lines of authority, responsibility, and
      communication
    — Structure congruent with program purposes

II. PROGRAM IMPLEMENTATION

    A. Screening and Selection
        — Establish appropriate criteria
        — Seek prospective peer helpers who are helpful,
          trustworthy, concerned for others, good listeners,
          and positive role models
        — Develop and distribute criteria to potential applicants
          who represent the population that they serve
        — Apply to the program in a formal way
        — Solicit recommendations
        — Structure interview
        — Demonstrate appropriate helping characteristics and
          skills
        — Ensure emotional security
        — Understand services provided
        — Commit to the provision of services
        — Be sensitive to population being served

    B. Training
        — Role of the peer helper
        — Confidentiality—Liability Issue
        — Listening and Communication skills
        — Problem Solving/Decision Making Strategies
        — Additional issues and topics
        — Represents nature and goals of a particular program

    C. Service Delivery
        — Appropriate variety of meaningful, productive helping
          roles within the program setting

    D. Supervision
        — On-going regular supervision

III. MAINTENANCE

A. Evaluation
— Formative Evaluation
— Summative Evaluation

B. Public Relations
— Well-informed community
— Program brochure or newsletter
— Media contacts
— Community involvement in training or program services
— Community outreach projects

C. Long-range Planning
— Staffing
— Funding
— Peer ownership

NATIONAL PEER HELPERS ASSOCIATION CODE OF ETHICS FOR PEER HELPING PROFESSIONALS

(Reproduced with permission from National Peer Helpers Association)

Professionals who are responsible for implementing peer helping programs shall be people of personal and professional integrity. As a minimum, the NPHA believes the *Code of Ethics for Peer Helping Professionals* shall contain the following and be evidenced by commitment to and pursuit of:

1. A philosophy which upholds peer helping as an effective way to address the needs and conditions of people.

2. The individual's right to dignity, self-development, and self-direction.

3. Excellence in program development and implementation through: Strong positive rapport with peer helpers. Appropriate background, training, and skills. Personal commitment and energy. The use of professionals with expertise and experience in human relations training. The use of a proven curriculum for training, supervising, and supporting peer helpers.

4. The development of a nurturing personality which: Reflects a positive role model and healthy lifestyle. Rejects the pursuit of personal power or gain at the expense of others. Respects copyright and acknowledgement obligations as they pertain to peer helping resources and ideas. Adheres to the ethical and legal obligations of confidentiality. Strives to exemplify the peer helping philosophy in all life situations.

5. The promotion of a realistic understanding by both internal and external audiences of the benefits and limitations of a peer helping program.

NATIONAL PEER HELPERS ASSOCIATION CODE OF ETHICS* FOR PEER HELPERS

(Reprinted with permission from National Peer Helpers Association.)

Peer Helpers shall be people of personal integrity. As a minimum, the NPHA believes the peer helpers *Code of Ethics* shall contain the following and be evidenced by a commitment to and pursuit of:

1. A philosophy which upholds peer helping as an effective way to address the needs and conditions of people.

2. The individual's right to dignity, self-development, and self-direction.

3. Supervision and support from professional staff while involved in the program.

4. The development of a nurturing personality which: Reflects a positive role model and healthy lifestyle (i.e., development and observation of a set of norms which guide behavior while in the program). Rejects the pursuit of personal power, elitist status, or gain at the expense of others. Strives to exemplify the peer helping philosophy in all life situations.

5. Maintenance of confidentiality of information imparted during the course of program-related activities. While confidentiality is the norm, certain exceptions shall be referred immediately to the professional staff. These exceptions include the following:

   - Situations involving real or potential danger to the safety or well-being of the peer helper, helpee, or others.
   - Child abuse, sexual abuse, and other situations involving legal requirements of disclosure.

- Severe family dysfunction, psychotic behavior, extreme drug or alcohol abuse, and any other problems beyond the experience and expertise of the peer helper.

6. Personal Safety

Peer helpers must recognize, report, and know techniques to deal with potential threats to their emotional or physical well-being.

*A CODE OF ETHICS IS AN AGREEMENT AMONG THOSE WHO COMMIT TO THE PROGRAM AS TO THE NORMS WHICH SHALL GUIDE THEIR BEHAVIOR DURING THEIR INVOLVEMENT IN THE PROGRAM.

APPENDICES

A. PRETEST AND POSTTEST POSITIVE VALUES CONTINUUM

B. TEACHER EVALUATION FORM FOR DISCUSSION GROUPS

C. RAP GROUP EVALUATION

D. VOCATIONAL EXPLORATION GROUP

E. SAMPLE TRAINING FOR JUNIOR HIGH

F. SAMPLE TRAINING FOR HIGH SCHOOL
   Section 1
   Section 2

G. ST. CHARLES HIGH SCHOOL PEER FACILITATOR PROGRAM SOCIOGRAM

H. NOMINATIONS OF PEER HELPERS

I. ST. CHARLES HIGH SCHOOL PEER HELPING APPLICATION

J. PAL APPLICATION FORM

K. ADDITIONAL QUESTIONS TO USE WHEN INTERVIEWING PROSPECTIVE PEER HELPERS

L. TEACHER RECOMMENDATION FORM: PEER HELPING CLASS

M. PEER FACILITATOR TRAINEE SELF-RATING SHEET

N. INTERVIEWER RATING SHEET OF PROSPECTIVE PEER HELPER

APPENDIX A

PRETEST AND POSTTEST
POSITIVE VALUES CONTINUUM

Part One

The words listed below are examples of values that one may or may not have. Some words represent ways one behaves, some one's abilities. Put an X on the continuum at the appropriate place for each behavior or ability. Use **own personal opinion** about each one.

Behavior or Ability	Important	Sometimes Important	Never Important	Don't Know
Physical Ability	.	.	.	.
Intellectual Ability	.	.	.	.
Learning	.	.	.	.
Attractiveness	.	.	.	.
Honesty	.	.	.	.
Considerate of Others	.	.	.	.
Able to Take Criticism from Others	.	.	.	.
Independence	.	.	.	.
Being a Friend	.	.	.	.
Close to Family	.	.	.	.
Having Money	.	.	.	.

Part Two

Now that these values have been rated according to how important they are, let us see how it is felt about these values as they pertain to daily living. Think carefully about the way one believes in what he/she does and how he/she does it.

Read the following carefully. The statement may describe how you behave all of the time, some of the time, or never, or the statement may describe how you feel about your abilities. Mark an X on the continuum at the spot which best describes your behavior or ability on each item.

Behavior or Ability	Always	Sometimes	Never
I am physically fit.	.	.	.
I learn easily.	.	.	.
I am a person who is getting a lot from my education.	.	.	.
I am a person who plans for the future.	.	.	.
I work hard at my appearance.	.	.	.
I am honest.	.	.	.
I am considerate of others' feelings.	.	.	.
I am able to listen to criticism from others without anger or fear.	.	.	.
I am independent.	.	.	.
I am a friendly person.	.	.	.
I am a good family member.	.	.	.
I can make (will make) a lot of money.	.	.	.

Part Three

In Part Two, you described your own behaviors and abilities as you see them. In Part Three, we would like you to look at yourself the way that others look at you. Read the following statements carefully. These statements may describe you as others think of you all the time, some of the time, or never. Mark an X on the continuum at the spot which best describes *how you feel others feel about you* regarding each item.

I Feel	Always	Sometimes	Never
People believe that I am in good physical condition.	.	.	.
People believe that I am intelligent.	.	.	.
People believe that I am getting a lot from my education.	.	.	.
People believe that I am good-looking.	.	.	.
People believe that I am honest.	.	.	.
People believe that I am considerate of others' feelings.	.	.	.
People believe that I am a person who can accept criticism without anger or fear.	.	.	.
People believe that I am an independent person.	.	.	.
Many people want to be my friend.	.	.	.
People believe that my family is important to me.	.	.	.
People believe that money is important to me.	.	.	.

APPENDIX B

TEACHER EVALUATION FORM
FOR DISCUSSION GROUPS

TEACHER _____

DATE _____ HOUR _____

In order to develop a group discussion procedure, an evaluation of this program seems important to improve future discussions. The rating may be used to give feedback to the peer helper. Please rate each peer helper on his/her communication and discussion skills. Rate on a five (5) point scale with one (1) being not effective and five (5) being very effective.

Peer helper's name _____

Item Rated	Not Effective			Very Effective
Attending Behavior	. . .	.	.	.
Empathic Behavior	. . .	.	.	.
Genuine Behavior	. . .	.	.	.
Problem-solving Behavior	. . .	.	.	.
Group Management	. . .	.	.	.
Leadership (Promptness)	. . .	.	.	.
Overall Rating	. . .	.	.	.

APPENDIX C

"RAP" GROUP EVALUATION

(To be completed by participants)

1. How often has your group met? _____

2. Leader's name _____

3. Do you think the same leader each week is important?
   Yes _____
   Depends on the discussion _____
   No _____

4. Your feeling toward the discussion group in general is that it is

   a waste of time. _____
   just to get out of class work. _____
   sometimes worthwhile. _____

5. Your "rap" leader

   doesn't understand what you say. _____
   most of the time understands what you say. _____
   really understands what you say. _____

6. Benefits from the "rap" group:

   Doesn't help _____
   Helps some _____
   Is very helpful _____

7. Did the group get you to think about yourself?

   All the time _____
   Sometimes _____
   Rarely _____

8. Would you like to continue with the same group?

   Yes _____
   No _____

9. Do you feel the program should be continued and expanded to include other peers?

   Yes _____
   No _____

APPENDIX D

VOCATIONAL EXPLORATION GROUP
(To be completed by participants)

Leader Survey

		Yes	Don't Know	No
1.	Did your leader seem interested?	———	———	———
2.	Did your leader explain the material well?	———	———	———
3.	Did your leader keep the group busy with the activity?	———	———	———
4.	Did the game get you to consider occupations you had not considered?	———	———	———
5.	Did the leader listen to you?	———	———	———

APPENDIX E

SAMPLE TRAINING FOR JUNIOR HIGH

PAL Training

A meeting was held prior to the onset of training to discuss the training schedule and answer any questions in realation to the beginning of PAL training. Training sessions were scheduled twice a week during the trainees' homeroom and recess time. In addition to these times, there was a 2-hour afterschool session once a week. This time was designed to provide practice, feedback, and reinforcement of newly introduced skills.

All training sessions were conducted with the trainees seated in a circle. Each of the training sessions was videotaped. This was done for three purposes: First, the tapes were used in the training to point out behaviors that trainees needed to improve and to reinforce behaviors they were doing well. Second, this method was extremely useful because it allowed the trainer to assess trainee performance and at the same time maintain trainee interest because they enjoyed seeing themselves on tape. Third, the tapes were valuable for future peer counseling training programs and further development of the program.

PAL PROGRAM TRAINING OUTLINE

Session 1 (1 hour) Group introductions and icebreaker exercises are used (e.g. students had to interview each other for 3 minutes each and then tell the group as much as they could about that person in one minute). Brief explanations of training program, plans, and expectations are used.
Exercise: Knowing Others.

Session 2 (1 hour) Students read the handout on helping behavior.
Exercise: How Do I Help.
Discussion and feedback are provided.

Session 3 (1 hour)	Exercise: Exploring Helping Behaviors. Discussion and feedback are provided.
Session 4 (2 hours)	Students read the handout on attending skills. Exercise: Becoming Aware of My Attending Behavior. Role plays practicing attending behavior are incorporated.
Session 5 (1 hour)	Exercise: Becoming Aware of Others' Nonverbal Behavior. Exercise: Attending Skill—Rating the Helper.
Session 6 (1 hour)	Students read a handout on communication stoppers. Exercise: Identifying Communication Stoppers.
Session 7 (1 hour)	Exercise: Discriminating and Responding by Paraphrasing (role playing).
Session 8 (1 hour)	Exercise: Empathy Skills & Feeling Words. Exercise: Empathy Skills & Responding to Feelings. Exercise: Empathy Skills & Feelings and Emotions.
Session 9 (2 hours)	Exercise: Empathy Skills & Describing Feelings. Trainers role play examples. Exercise: Attending and Empathy.

Note: More time was spent on this skill because the trainees have difficulty addressing feelings and emotions rather than content. Trainees practiced this skill through role playing, alternating roles as the helper and helpee with trainers providing feedback after each role play.

Session 10 (1 hour)	Students read a handout on Facilitative and Non-Facilitative Dialogue. Exercise: Choose the Best Empathic Response.

Session 11 (1 hour)   Students read handouts on Summarizing Skills.
                                 Exercise: Open-ended Questions.

Session 12 (2 hours)   Exercise: Open-ended Questions.

Near the end of the training program, a day-long final training session was scheduled on a Saturday. This session was designed (a) to reinforce skills, (b) to introduce one final skill (problem-solving), and (c) to put closure on the training program.

At the conclusion, helping activities were discussed with the new PALS. Group discussion centered on fears and apprehensions students had in helping their peers as well as ideas the students had learned throughout the training program. During the initial training session and throughout the program, issues of confidentiality and ethics were discussed with PAL trainees and were reemphasized during the final training session.

Day-long PAL Training Session

Session 13   8:50 to 9:00:   Arrival.

                9:00 to 10:00:   Handout on problem solving.

           10:00 to 10:45:   Problem-solving dialogue.

           10:45 to 11:30:   Teamwork time!

           11:30 to 12:00:   Pizza break!

           12:00 to 1:00:   Role-playing practice in problem-solving skills.

             1:00 to 1:45:   Preparing for PAL activities.
                                   a) Group facilitating.
                                   b) Individual help.
                                   c) Theme weeks.

             1:45 to 2:00:   Discussion and wrap up.

USE OF EXERCISES AND SELF-DISCLOSURE

All of the exercises in the training program should be designed to be as life-like or realistic as possible. In the PAL training program, as many exercises as possible were designed in this format; simply reading and reciting material is not sufficient. Role plays used in the PAL training program simulated actual helping situations. In these role plays, PALS were encouraged to use issues that they were struggling with in their own lives. This achieved a number of things. First, those being helped had to identify areas in their lives that they wanted to improve. This enabled the students to identify issues and concerns and allowed them to problem solve with other individuals, thus encouraging personal growth.

Second, it allowed those being helped to experience how a helper-helpee relationship feels. Experiencing both sides of the helping relationship enabled the PAL students to become better listeners and to understand more fully how others can become comfortable with them. Early in the PAL program, students were taught to give appropriate feedback. During role plays, the students shared their reasons for wanting to disclose or not disclose. This allowed trainees to become more aware of skills they needed to develop and skills that they did well. The importance of this type of experience was stressed and related to the development of healthy relationships.

CONCLUSION

Overall, the program has been a success and will be expanded next fall. Preliminary research has shown that both grade point averages and behavioral classroom ratings have improved for the peer leaders and group participants. Feedback from students, faculty members, and administrators has been extremely positive. Faculty members and administative personnel were pleased with the program and impressed with the positive behavioral changes demonstrated by the students. Upon the request of the school principal, several PALS served as guest speakers with elementary students who were scheduled to attend the junior high school the next year to help these students make a better adjustment at a new environment.

Student interest and participation in the program has also increased greatly since the inception of the program.

Like any new program, however, there are still problems that must be corrected if the program is to continue to be effective. There are always scheduling difficulties when implementing programs of this nature in a school setting. Students had to use homeroom times and intramural periods to participate in the program. Certainly the intent in the future is to make the program a regular part of the curriculum and school day with the possiblity of academic credit for the past leaders.

Garner, Martin, and Martin (1989, October). Reprinted from *Elementary School Guidance & Counseling*, 24(1), 71-75. © ACA. Reprinted with permission. No further reproduction authorized without written permission of the American Counseling Association.

APPENDIX F

SAMPLE TRAINING FOR HIGH SCHOOL STUDENTS

Section 1
Peer Counseling Training Curriculum for High School Students

First Semester Course Content for High School Students:

I. Awareness and appreciation of self and others in the group (4 weeks)
   A. Journal keeping
   B. Value and Belief system
   C. Exercise patterns-relaxation
   D. Dietary habits
   E. Interpersonal relationships
   F. Self-esteem
   G. Reach course
   H. Plan and conduct newcomers' groups

II. Helping skills (4 weeks)
   A. Helper attitudes and values
   B. Establishing a helping relationship
      1. Empathy
      2. Nonverbal behavior
      3. Door openers
   C. Ways of listening and responding
      1. Paraphrasing
      2. Summarizing
      3. Clarifying
      4. Reflecting feelings
      5. Nondirective leading
   D. Feedback
   E. Confronting skills
   F. Decision-making skills

III. Grief and loss (3 weeks)
   A. Recognizing change and loss as part of life
   B. Understanding grief
   C. Death and dying

1. Personal perspectives
2. Cultural perspectives and customs
3. Death by self-destruction: suicide
4. Care settings for the dying
D. Helping yourself. . .helping others through grief
E. Community resources for loss and grief
F. The art of grieving: healing and growing through change
IV. Group facilitation skills (4 weeks)
A. Groups and group behavior
1. Definition of a group
2. Theory of group development
3. Membership issues in a group
4. Group norms
5. Group versus individual goals
6. Leadership styles and behaviors
B. Group leadership
1. Establishing ground rules
2. Setting group goals
3. Energizing structured group activities
4. Designing structured group activities
5. Conducting a group discussion
6. Conducting a group process
7. Diagnosing group problems
8. Handling problem behaviors
9. Closure
10. Evaluation
C. Understanding early adolescence
1. Physical
2. Emotional
V. Understanding effect of disrupted families on teenagers (2 weeks)
A. Psychological tasks of children of divorce
B. Coping with family changes
1. Redefining the family
2. Single-parent families
3. Stepparents and blended families
C. How teenagers survive divorce
1. The first year
2. The long run
VI. Making lesson plans (1 week)

Second-Semester Course Content for High School Students:
(Typical second-semester week of training activities)

Monday: Planning seminar led by classroom teacher for all 24 students in Experimental Groups I and II.

Tuesday: Peer leaders co-lead groups at middle school group.

Wednesday: Peer leaders in Experimental Group I meet with counselor for guided reflection. Peer leaders in Experimental Group II lead middle school group.

Thursday: Peer leaders co-lead middle school groups.

Friday: Guided reflection led by classroom teacher for all 24 students in Experimental Groups I and II.

Section 2

Journal Excerpts for High School and Middle School Students

High School Student Entries: *Student 1*

November Entry: I really like co-leading the group of new high school students today—good practice for next semester. Mostly I just feel good and comfortable about this class. I feel closer to the students in here than to anybody else at school. But _____, I would like to talk to you about my dad at lunch tomorrow about _____, okay?

April Entry: I'm glad we meet together at least once a week in here, but it sure feels different from when we met every day.

We tried your suggestions about changing everybody's seat yesterday. It helped some with more kids talking. They liked the "talking to an empty chair" lesson a lot! _____ and _____ really got angry talking to their pretend stepsisters, but then the group discussed what happened and looked okay with it. _____ didn't seem to like anything but the pizza, but we've got 4 more weeks. Maybe he'll lighten up. I want to talk to you after class about his pain.

Student 2

December Entry: This Grief and Loss stuff is almost too heavy.   Here's the poem I want you to read to the class:

COMES THE DAWN

After a while you learn the subtle difference
Between holding a hand and chaining a soul,
And you learn that love doesn't mean security,
And you begin to learn that kisses aren't contracts
And presents aren't promises
and you begin to accept your defeats
With your head up and your eyes open,
With the grace of a woman, not the grief of a child,
And you learn to build all your roads
On today because tomorrow's ground is too uncertain,
And futures have
A way of falling down in midflight,
After a while you learn that even sunshine burns if you get
   too much.
So you plant your own garden and decorate your own soul,
   instead of waiting
And you learn that you really can endure...
That you really are strong,
And you really do have worth
And you learn and learn
With every goodbye you learn.

May Entry: I can't believe how _____ and _____
are so upbeat in the group when I know how bad it is for
them without their dads even living in this town. It does
seem like the group really helps and just being friends of
each other helps. _____ wrote in her journal that she
is glad just to see _____ and me on Tuesdays to see
how we look. But _____ and I know there's more going
on, lots more.

Student 3

October Entry: I trust some people in the group, but
not all of them. Hope you don't mind if I don't have much
to say about what I think right now.

May Entry: Today _____ and I led the group off the subject (as usual) and talked about risks. They really liked it and opened up so that I think the level of trust is much better. I shared a simple risk with them but this is the one I thought about—what happened with me and my car... . I had it out one day, minding my own business and was driving with traffic. Everyone knew about this car that lived in town. Then, this old Camaro, of course, he wanted to race, shot out in front of me and I went after him. I was going at least 80 mph in the rain having some fun, I thought. When I got a hold on myself, I slowed down and was lucky I didn't get a ticket. I won by the way. I was ashamed and hadn't proved a thing.

The kids in the group had a lot of show-off risks to tell about but I did not know if it was "appropriate"—your word— to share mine. What do you think?

Student 4

September Entry: Yes, communication skills are what it's all about. My family communicates with each other well but I don't know if we communicate well with other people.

March Entry: Seems like I communicate better with these middle school kids than with some of my high school friends. My family doesn't have much in common with these kids' families but I think I do... .

Yesterday we were talking in Psychology about religion. It got really involved. I don't usually come out and talk about my religion since I'm a Mormon. A lot of people have a lot of harsh views towards Mormons, so I never really talk about my religion unless I know the person real well. After class yesterday I went up to my teacher and asked him what he thought about Mormons. To me that was scary. He seemed to know a lot about religion though, and I wanted to know his views on Mormonism. We had a nice talk. He wasn't hostile at all. I really enjoyed the talk. It helped me to overcome a little fear I had of telling people what I believe. I'm not ashamed of my religion, but I was afraid of the way some people react when I tell them I'm a Mormon.

Student 5

October Entry: Why am I in this class? You wonder why I don't talk probably. I'm scared I'll look and sound silly. I like kids but if that's the only reason I'm here, that's not enough. I'm so different from the rest of these kids.

March Entry: Today, two things were better. First, I took leadership of the group—not _____. We did that "Common Feelings about Divorce" lesson and discussed guilty, sad, angry, disappointed. Mostly the kids talked, but I knew I kept it directed.

Middle School Student Entries: Student 1

What I really enjoyed about this class was when _____ and _____ could always give good advice anytime you need it. And they always seem to be there when you need them. I hate to see them go because they're really special even if _____ always likes to say "chill-out." But it never bothered me. There is nothing I never liked about this class. I think this class has really helped me out mentally. It made me realize what me and my family really is and can be. I hope when I join this class next year they'll be the leaders.

Student 2

Liked talking about what I did on weekends. Kool getting drinks and things.

Student 3

I already am helping my family get better by understanding and listening. I am close to my stepmother.

Student 4

The most important reason I see in marrying is to live in happiness and not be lonely.

Student 5

I am learning to work on my troubles when things come up.

Student 6

I really like this group. It was fun, and I felt free to talk about things, and I learned how other people feel about divorced parents and what they did in problem situations.

Student 7

I like this group because it helps me with family problems and is relaxing. I would like to lead a group like this when I'm a junior in high school—with somebody else.

Sprinthall, Hall, and Gerler (1992, April). Reprinted from *Elementary School Guidance & Counseling, 26*(4), 279-304. © ACA. Reprinted with permission. No further reproduction authorized without written permission of the American Counseling Association.

APPENDIX G

ST. CHARLES HIGH SCHOOL
PEER FACILITATOR PROGRAM SOCIOGRAM*

The purpose of this sociogram is to determine the three or four most trusted students at each grade level, ninth through twelfth, for the Peer Facilitator Program, which will begin at the high school next fall. The students with the most votes will not necessarily be the peer facilitators: first, they may not be interested, and second, they may not be selected in the final interview. The survey is confidential and anonymous, so please do not sign your name. Your serious considerations are greatly appreciated.

1. If you had a problem and wanted to talk with one of your fellow students about it, someone whom you know

   a. You could trust.
   b. Would care about and try to help you.
   c. Would keep your problem between the two of you.

   Who would you go to? (SELECT THREE)

   First choice: _____

   Second choice: _____

   Third choice: _____

---

*Used with permission from Gale Horn and Charles Meeker, St. Charles High School, St. Charles, Missouri.

APPENDIX H

TO: Faculty

FROM: Peer Helper Advisors

DATE: February 22, 1994

RE: NOMINATIONS OF PEER HELPERS FOR 1994-1995

We are beginning the process of selecting Peer Helpers for the new Peer Facilitators class for next year. Please give me the names of any of your sophomore or junior students who would be good Peer Helpers.

A good nominee is one who shows caring and concern for others, has leadership qualities, is willing to take responsibility, is respected by other students, and shows a high level of maturity.

Thank you for your help.

Gayle Horn, Charlie Meeker
Peer Helping Advisors

STUDENTS RECOMMENDED:

_____

_____

_____

_____

_____

This list will be kept confidential. If you would be willing to have us contact you for further information, please sign your name below.

_____

Please return this memo to the Guidance Office by Monday, February 25.

APPENDIX I

ST. CHARLES HIGH SCHOOL
PEER HELPING APPLICATION

Name: _____ Phone: _____

Address: _____

1. List the various groups to which you belong both in school and out of school.

2. Of the groups listed above, which one is the most satisfying and why?

3. List two experiences that you have had that would be useful to you as a peer group leader (e.g., camp counselor, Sunday School teacher).

4. List two things that you have done that make you feel proud.

5. List two values or principles that are important to the way you conduct your life.

6. What three qualities do you look for in a friend?

7. What contributions do you feel that you can personally add to the Peer Helping Program?

8. If you could change one thing about St. Charles High School, what would it be?

9. My description of me as a person (what kind of person):

10. A stranger's first impression of me would include...

11. I would like others to see me as...

12. I spend too much time...

13. What I have done lately that really turned people off...

14. What I have done lately that really turned people on...

15. Do my friends confide in me? Why or why not?

16. My reputation includes

17. Things I value...

18. The best advice I ever got...

19. The worst advice I ever got...

20. When I have a problem I handle it by...

21. When someone criticizes me, I...

22. When someone becomes angry with me, I...

23. When I become angry, I...

24. I like me because...

25. Describe what your idea of a Peer Helper is and what a Peer Helper does.

APPENDIX J

PAL APPLICATION FORM

Thanks for picking up a PAL application form! In order to be considered for selection as a PAL you must return this application form to the office by the end of the school day on Thursday, January 14. Be sure to fill out all parts of the application form before you turn it in. We will announce the students who are being selected for PAL training on Tuesday, January 19. Good Luck!

Name _____ Age _____

Birthdate _____

Homeroom _____ Homeroom Time _____

Extra-Curricular Activities: _____

_____

_____

_____

_____

Why would you like to be a PAL? (write only in the space provided)

What qualities do you think might be hard to do when you are a PAL?

What do you think you would gain from being a PAL?

Have you had any experiences that you think would help you be a good PAL? (If so, explain.)

List two people that support your application to be a PAL. One person should be a teacher, principal, or counselor at Edison.

*Note—You should ask the people that you list as references before listing them on your application.

1) _____

2) _____

Signature _____

Date _____

Thank you for applying to be a PAL. You will be notified Tuesday, January 19.

APPENDIX K

ADDITIONAL QUESTIONS TO USE WHEN INTERVIEWING PROSPECTIVE PEER HELPERS

1. What do you do when individuals tell you that they have a problem?

2. What does confidentiality mean to you? Are there any exceptions?

3. Do you have any duties or chores at home? Do you have to be reminded to do them?

4. Have you ever been in charge of a project? If so, how did you feel? If not, how do you think you would feel?

5. How do you feel in front of other people (younger, same age, older)?

6. Examples of dependability, honesty:

7. Any unusual experiences, trips, and so forth:

8. Name a significant person in your life and explain why that person is significant.

APPENDIX L

TEACHER RECOMMENDATION FORM
PEER HELPING CLASS

Name of Student: _____

    In your recommendation, please include the student's attitude, sense of responsibility, leadership potential, commitment, honesty, and genuine willingness to help others. Because the peer helper will be trained to help students with problems, the student whom you are recommending should possess the ability to listen and to understand others.

Signed: _____

Dated: _____

Recommendation must be complete and returned by March 7. Please return to Mrs. Horn's mailbox or the Guidance Office.

APPENDIX M

PEER FACILITATOR TRAINEE
SELF-RATING SHEET

_____

Name of Student

Codes (CIRCLE ONE):

SA = Strongly Agree
A = Agree
U = Uncertain
D = Disagree
SD = Strongly Disagree

1. Concern for the welfare of others   SA A U D SD

2. Ability to listen to and understand others   SA A U D SD

3. Flexibility: ability to adjust to new situations   SA A U D SD

4. Self-confidence   SA A U D SD

5. Dependability: responsible and able to follow
   through with assigned tasks   SA A U D SD

6. Honesty   SA A U D SD

7. Potential for leadership   SA A U D SD

8. Ability to keep confidential information   SA A U D SD

9. Ability to work without constant supervision   SA A U D SD

APPENDIX N

INTERVIEWER RATING SHEET
OF PROSPECTIVE PEER HELPER

Name of Interviewer: _____

Name of Nominee: _____

Code:

5 = The statement is completely and consistently descriptive of the nominee and your rating is outstanding (top 5%).

4 = It is almost always descriptive and your rating is excellent (top 15%).

3 = It is almost always descriptive and your rating is good (top third)

2 = It is occasionally descriptive and your rating is average (middle third).

1 = It is not descriptive at all and your rating is poor (bottom third).

DK = you do not feel that you can evaluate the candidate on the item.

Concern for welfare of others	1	2	3	4	5	DK
Ability to listen and to understand others	1	2	3	4	5	DK
Ability to keep confidential information	1	2	3	4	5	DK
Ability to work without constant supervision	1	2	3	4	5	DK
Potential for leadership	1	2	3	4	5	DK
Self-confidence	1	2	3	4	5	DK
Dependability	1	2	3	4	5	DK
Honesty	1	2	3	4	5	DK
Sense of humor	1	2	3	4	5	DK
Energetic	1	2	3	4	5	DK
Self-initiative and motivation	1	2	3	4	5	DK
Diversity of experience and background	1	2	3	4	5	DK
Good rapport with other students	1	2	3	4	5	DK
Good rapport with teachers	1	2	3	4	5	DK

My overall recommendation:

_____ Recommend without reservation

_____ Recommend

_____ Recommend as an alternate

_____ Do not recommend

COMMENTS:

_____

_____

_____

_____

_____

_____

_____

_____

_____

_____

_____

_____

_____

_____

_____

REFERENCES

Akita, J., & Mooney, C. (1982). *Natural helpers: A peer support program—naturally, A leader's guide.* Seattle, WA: Robers and Associates.

Akridge, R., Farley, R., & Rice, B. (1987). An empirical evaluation of the effects of peer counseling training on sample of vocational rehabilitation facility clients. *Journal of Applied Rehabilitation Counseling, 18*(3), 20-24.

Alexander, V. (December, 1990/January, 1991). Black women and HIV/AIDS. *Siecus Report,* 8-10.

Allbee, R. (1976). *A comparison of the effects of two variations of micro-counseling paradigm on the development of human relations skills of students in community college setting.* Unpublished doctoral dissertation, Saint Louis University, St. Louis, MO.

Alpaugh, P., & Haney, M. (1978). *Counseling the older adult: A training manual for paraprofessionals and beginning counselors* (rev. ed.). San Diego, CA: California Press.

Arkin, R. M., Roemhild, H. J., Johnson, C. A., Luepker, R. V., & Murray, D. M. (1981). The Minnesota smoking prevention program: A seventh grade health curriculum supplement. *Journal of School Health, 51*(19), 616-661.

Armstrong, E., & Waszak, C. (1990). *Teenage pregnancy and too-early childbearing: Public costs, personal consequences* (5th ed.) N.P. Atlanta, GA: Center for Population Options.

Attili, G., (1990). Successful and disconfirmed children in the peer group: Indices of social competence within an evolutionary perspective. *Human Development, 33,* 238-249.

Avis, J., & Bigelow, E. (1987). Group problem solving to promote integration in a desegregated high school: A case study. *International Journal for the Advancement of Counseling, 10*(2), 111-121.

Bandura, A. (1977). *Social learning theory.* Englewood Cliffs, NJ: Prentice-Hall.

Becker, K. F., & Zarit, S. H. (1978). Training older adults as peer counselors. *Educational Gerontology, 3*(3), 241-250.

Benson, P. L. (1990). *The troubled journey: A portrait of 6th-12th grade youth.* Minneapolis, MN: Search Institute.

Bernard, B. (1991, April). *Moving toward a "just and vital culture": Multiculturalism in our school.* San Francisco, CA: Western Regional Center for Drug-free Schools and Community.

Bernard, B. (1992, March). Peer programs: A major strategy for fostering resiliency in kids. *Peer Facilitator Quarterly, 9*(3).

Best, J. A., Thomas, S., Santi, S., Smith, E., & Brown, K. S. (1988). Preventing cigarette smoking among school children. *Annual Review Public Health,* 161-201.

Bishop, J. (1992, April). Correspondence. Greensboro, NC: Guilford County Peer Programs.

Boan, R. P., & Myrick R. D. (1987). Effects of an elementary school peer facilitator program on children with behavior problems. *The School Counselor, 34*(5).

Boehm, K., Chessare, J., Volko, T., & Sager, M. (1991). Teen line: A descriptive analysis of peer telephone listening service. *Adolescence, 26*(103), 643-648.

Booth, R. (1990, April). A short-term peer model for treating shyness in college students: A note on an exploratory study. *Psychological Reports, 66*(2), 417-418.

Botvin, G. (1986). Substance abuse prevention research: Recent developments and future directions. *Journal of School Health 56*(9), 369-374.

Botvin, G. J., Baker, E., Renick, N. L., Filazzola, A. D., & Botvin, E. M. (1984). A cognitive-behavioral approach to substance abuse prevention. *Addictive Behavior, 9,* 137-147.

Botvin, G., & Williams, C. (1980). Preventing the onset of cigarette smoking through life skills training. *Preventive Medicine 9,* 135-145.

Botvin, G. J., & Wills, T. A. (1985). Personal and social skills training: Cognitive behavioral approaches to substance abuse prevention. In Bell et al. (Eds.), *Prevention research: Deterring drug abuse among children and adolescents.* NIDA Research Monograph 63. Washington DC: USGPO 8-49.

Bowman, R. (1986). Peer facilitator programs for middle graders: Students helping each other grow up. (Special Issue: Counseling middle-grade students.) *The School Counselor, 33*(3), 221-229.

Bowman, R. P. (1982). *A student facilitator program: Fifth graders helping primary-grade problem-behavior students.* Unpublished doctoral dissertation. University of Florida, Gainesville, FL.

Bowman, R. P., & Myrick, R. D. (1980). I'm a junior counselor having lots of fun. *The School Counselor, 28,* 31-38.

Bowman, R. P., & Rotter, J. C. (1983). Computer games: Friend or foe? *Elementary School Guidance & Counseling, 18,* 25-34.

Brannon, J., & Troyer, R. (1991). Peer group counseling: A normalized residential alternative to the specialized treatment of adolescent sex offenders. *International Journal of Offender Therapy and Comparative Criminology, 35*(3), 225-234.

Bratter, B. (1986). Peer counseling for older adults. *Generations, 10*(3), 49-50.

Briskin, A. S., & Anderson, E. M. (1973). Students as contingency managers. *Elementary School Guidance & Counseling, 7,* 262-268.

Bronfenbrenner, A. (1986, February). Alienation and the four worlds of childhood. *Phi Delta Kappan, 67*(6) 456-467.

Brookman, B. (1988). Parent to parent: A model for parent support and information—Topics in early childhood. *Special Education, 8*(2), 88-93.

Brown, W. F. (1974). Effectiveness of paraprofessionals: The evidence. *Personnel and Guidance Journal, 53*(4), 257-264.

Buck, C. B., & Pineda, C. (1985). *A peer counseling training module for campus outreach and support services.* Paper presented at annual meeting of California Counseling and Development, San Diego, CA.

Burke, M., & Hayes, R. (1986). Peer counseling for elderly victims of crime and violence (special issue). *Support Groups, 11*(2), 107-113.

Burns, J. (1990). *Resource guide on peer support training.* Prepared by the planning committee for the National Conference on Peer Support Training for Genetic Support Groups. March 31-April 1. Washington DC: Alliance of Genetic Support Groups.

Caning, J. (1983). Peer facilitator projects for elementary and middle schools. *Elementary School Guidance & Counseling, 18*(2), 124-129.

Caplan, G. (1964). *Principles of preventive psychiatry.* New York: Basic Books.

Carbarino, J. (1992). *Children in danger: Coping with the consequences of community violence.* San Francisco CA: Jossey-Bass.

Carkhuff, R. R. (1969). *Helping and human relations* (Volume 1). New York: Holt, Rinehart, and Winston.

Carkhuff, R. R. (1971). *The development of human resources.* New York: Holt, Rinehart, and Winston.

Carkhuff, R. R. (1972). New directions in training the helping professions: Toward a technology for human and community resource development. *Counseling Psychologist, 3*(3), 12-30.

Carkhuff, R. R. (1987a). *The art of helping.* Amherst, MA: Human Resource Development Press.

Carkhuff, R. R. (1987b). *The art of helping student workbook.* Amherst MA: Human Resource Development Press.

Carkhuff, R. R., & Truax, C. B. (1969). Lay mental health counseling. *Journal of Consulting Psychology, 29*(5), 5-10.

Carnegie Council on Adolescent Development. (1989). *Turning points: Preparing youth for the 21st century.* New York: Carnegie Corporation of New York.

Cary, L. (1989, January). Social support: Peer counselling and the community counsellor. *Canadian Journal of Counseling, 23*(1), 92-102.

Centers for Disease Control. (1992, August). Interview with hotline staff, Atlanta, GA. Clinical Review.

Children's Defense Fund. (1990). *S.O.S. America! Children's defense fund budget.* Washington, DC: Children's Defense Fund Association.

Children's Defense Fund. (1992). *The state of America's children.* Washington, DC: Children's Defense Fund.

Ciborowski, P. (1984). *The changing family.* Port Chester, NY: Stratman Educational systems.

Clark, J. H., MacPherson, B., Holmes, D. R., & Jones, R. (1986). Reducing adolescent smoking: A comparison of peer-led, teacher-led, and expert interventions. *Journal of School Health, 56*(2), 106.

Cohen, B., & Livneh, H. (1986). The self-help movement: Evolution of a dystonia chapter. *Rehabilitation Literature, 47*(1-2), 8-11.

Cohen, R. M. (1978). The effect of employment status change on self-attitudes. *Social Psychology 41,* 81-93.

Combs, A. W. (1974). *Professional education of teachers.* Boston: Allyn and Bacon.

Cooker, P., & Cherchia, P. (1976). Effects of communications skill training on high school students' ability to function as peer group facilitators. *Journal of Counseling Psychology, 23*(5), 117-126.

Cooper-White, P. (1990). Peer vs. clinical counseling: Is there a place for both in the battered women's movement? *Response to the Victimization of Women and Children, 13*(3), 2-6.

Creange, N. (1982). *The effects of individual and peer group counseling on a sample of disruptive high school students.* Unpublished doctoral dissertation, University of the Pacific, Stockton, CA.

Diver-Stamnes, A. C. (1991). Assessing the effectiveness of an inner-city high school peer counseling program. *Urban Education, 26*(3), 269-284.

Egan, G. (1986). *The skilled helper.* Monterey, CA: Brooks-Cole Publishing.

Eisdorfer, C., & Golann, S. E. (1969). Principles for training of new professionals in mental health. *Community Mental Health Journal, 5*, 239-257.

Farran, D. C., & Margolis, L. H. (1983). *The impact of paternal job loss on the family.* Presented at the Annual Meeting of the Society for Research in Child Development, Detroit, MI.

Fatum, W. R. (1993). Project OPTION: Peer leadership training for the incarcerated delinquent adolescent. *Peer Facilitator Quarterly, 10*(3), 26-27.

Federal Bureau of Investigation. (1989). *Uniform crime report, 1989.* Washington, DC: U.S. Government Printing Office.

Feldman, R. A., & Caplinger, T. E. (1983). *The St. Louis conundrum: The effective treatment of anti-social youth.* Englewood Cliffs, NJ: Prentice-Hall.

Finn, P. (1981, February). Institutionalizing peer education in the health education classroom. *Journal of School Health,* 91-95.

Flax, E. (1991, October). Peer counseling programs keep lines of communications open. *Education Week,* 7.

Flay, B., (1985a). Are social-psychological prevention programs effective? The Waterloo study. *Journal of Behavioral Medicine, 8*(1), 37-59.

Flay, B. (1985b). What do we know about the social influence approach to smoking prevention? Review and recommendations. In C. Bell et al. (Eds.), *Prevention research: Deterring drug abuse among children and adolescents.* Washington, DC: U.S. Government Printing Office, U.S. Department of Health and Human Services, Publication No. (ADM) 85.

Forrest, J. D., & Singh, S. (1990). The sexual and reproductive behavior of American women, 1982-1988. *Family Planning Perspectives, 22,* 206-214.

Foster, E. (1991). A case for emotional development through elementary peer helping programs. *Peer Facilitator Quarterly, 8*(4), 17-20.

Foster, E. (1992). *Tutoring: Learning by helping* (revised ed.). Minneapolis, MN: Educational Media.

Foster, G., Wadden, T., & Brownell, K. (1985). Peer-led program for the treatment and prevention of obesity in the schools. *Journal of Consulting and Clinical Psychology, 53*(4), 538-40.

France, M. H. (1989). Residents as helpers: Peer counseling in a long-term care facility. *Canadian Journal of Counselling, 23*(1), 113-119.

Frisz, R. H., & Lane, R. J. (1987). Student user evaluations of peer adviser services. *Journal of College Student Personnel, 287*(3), 241-245.

Galanter, M. (1988). Zealous self-help groups as adjuncts to psychiatric treatment: A study of Recovery, Inc. *American Journal of Psychiatry, 145*(10), 1248-1253.

Galanter, M., Castaneda, R., & Salamon, I. (1987, October). Institutional self-help theory for alcoholism. *Alcoholism Clinical and Experimental Research, 11*(5), 424-429.

Gant, G. (1992). Peer power in the workplace. *EAPA Exchange, 22*(8), 22-25.

Gardner, J. (1990). *On leadership.* New York: The Free Press.

Garner, R., Martin, D., & Martin, M. (1989). The PALS program: A peer counseling training program for junior high school (Special Issue: Preventive and development counseling.) *Elementary School Guidance & Counseling, 24*(1), 71-75.

Gartner, A., & Riessman, F. (1974). The paraprofessional movement in perspective. *Personnel and Guidance Journal, 54*(4), 253-256.

Gazda, G. M. (1973). *Human relations development: A manual for educators.* Boston: Allyn and Bacon.

Girls, Inc. (1991). *Truth, trust and technology.* Indianapolis, IN: National Resource Center.

Glanz, K., Marger, S., & Meehan, E. (1986). Evaluation of a peer educator stroke education program for the elderly. *Health Education Research, 1*(2), 121-130.

Goldstein, A. (1991). *Delinquent gangs: A psychological perspective.* Champaign, IL: Research Press.

Goldstein, A., Reagles, K., & Amann, L. (1990). *Refusal skills: Preventing drug use in adolescents.* Champaign, IL: Research Press.

Gonzales, L. (1991). *Gang-free zones. A training program for prevention of school violence and disruptions related to gangs and drugs.* Oakland CA: Center for Gang-free Schools and Communities.

Gordon, T. (1970). *Parent effectiveness training.* New York: Peter H. Wyden.

Gordon, T. (1978). *Leader effectiveness training (L.E.T.).* New York: Banram Books.

Gordon, D. A., & Arbuthot, J. (1988). The use of paraprofessionals to deliver home-based family therapy to juvenile delinquents. *Criminal Justice and Behavior, 15*(3), 364-378.

Gray, H. D., & Tindall, J. (1974). Communications training study: A model for training junior high school peer counselors. *The School Counselor, 22*(2), 107-112.

Greenwood, C. R., Terry, B., Arrega-Mayer, C., & Finney, R. (1992). The classroom peer tutoring program: Implementation factors moderating student achievement. *Journal of Applied Behavioral Analysis, 25,* 101-116.

Gumaer, J. (Ed.). (1976). Special issue: Peer facilitators. *Elementary School Guidance & Counseling, 11*(1), 26-36.

Hamburg, B. A., & Varenhorst, B. B. (1972). Peer counseling in the secondary schools: A community mental health project for youth. *American Journal of Orthopsychiatry, 42*(4), 566-581.

Hanson, W., & Graham, R. (1991). Preventing alcohol, marijuana, and cigarette use among adolescents: Peer pressure resistance training versus establishing conservative norms. *Preventive Medicine, 20,* 414-430.

Hazouri, S., & Smith, M. (1991). *Peer listening in the middle school.* Minneapolis, MN: Educational Media.

Hein, K. (1989). AIDS in adolescence. *Journal of Adolescent Health Care,* *10,* 105-355.

Hendin, D. (Winter, 1987). Students as teachers: A tool for improving school climate and productivity. *Social Policy,* 24-27.

Henriksen, E. M. (1991, January). A peer helping program for the middle school. *Canadian Journal of Counselling, 25*(1), 12-18.

Hensley, B., & Mickelson, E. (1978). *You give a little for great return with peer counseling.* The Guidance Clinic, New York: Parker Publishing Co.

Hetherington, E. M. (1984). Families in transition: The processes of dissolution and reconstruction. In R. Parke (Ed.), *Review of child development research.* Paper presented at the Society for Research on Adolescence, Atlanta, GA.

Hodgkinson, H. (1990, November). *Guess who's coming to work.* Northwest Regional Educational Laboratory, Education and Work Conference, Institute for Educational Leadership, Portland, OR.

Hodgkinson, H. (1992, March). *Drug demographics: A look at the future.* 8th Annual DASA Prevention Conference, Lisle, IL.

Holly, K. A. (1987). Development of a college peer counselor program. *Journal of College Student Personnel, 28*(3), 285-286.

Ivey, A. (1971). *Microcounseling: Innovations in interviewing training.* Springfield, IL: Charles C. Thomas.

Ivey, A. E. (1973). Microcounseling: The counselor as a trainer. *Personnel and Guidance Journal, 51,* 311-316.

Ivey, A. E., & Alschuler, A. S. (1973). Editors psychological education: A prime function of the counselor. *Personnel and Guidance Journal, 51*(9), 586-682.

Ivey, A., & Gluckstern, N. (1984). *Basic influencing skills.* North Amherst, MA: Microtraining Associates.

Ivey, A., Gluckstern, N., & Ivey, M. B. (1982). *Basic attending skills.* North Amherst, MA: Microtraining Associates.

Jakubowski-Spector, P. (1973a). Facilitating the growth of women through assertive training. *The Counseling Psychologist, 4*(1), 75-96.

Jakubowski-Spector, P. (1973b). *An introduction to assertive training procedures for women.* Washington, DC: American Personnel Guidance Association Press.

Johnson, D., & Johnson, R. (1987, November). Research shows the benefits of adult cooperation. *Education Leadership,* 27-30.

Johnson, W. B. (1987). *Workforce 2000: Work and workers for the twenty-first century.* Indianapolis, IN: Hudson Institute.

Jones, E. (1985, March/April). Teenage pregnancy in developed countries: Determinants and policy implications. *Family Planning Perspectives, 18*(2), 53-63.

Jones, J. (1991). *Preemployment honesty testing.* Westport, CT: Quarum Books.

Jourard, S. M. (1971). *The transparent self* (revised ed.). New York: Van Nostrand Reinhold.

Jovick, F. (1989). Cool schools on the Sunshine Coast. Teacher: *News Magazine of the British Columbia Teachers' Federation, 2*(2), 14-15.

Keboyan, V. A. (1992). *Partners for change.* Rolling Hills Estate, CA: Jalmar Press.

Kellam, S. (1982, December). *Social adaptation and psychological antecedents in first grade adolescent psychopathology ten years later.* Paper presented at Research Workshop on Preventive Aspects of Suicide and Affective Disorders among Adolescents and Young Adults. Boston: Harvard School of Public Health.

Kiersey, D., & Bates, M. (1978). *Please understand me.* Del Mar, CA: Prometheus Press.

Kirkley, B., Battaglia, L., Earle, L., & Gans, K. (1988). Health education as a component of bulimia treatment programs. *Journal of American College Health, 37*(1), 40-43.

Klepp-Knut, I., Halper, A., & Peery, C. (1986). The efficacy of peer leaders in drug abuse prevention. *Journal of Social Health, 56*(9), 407-411.

Kohlberg, L. (1971). The concept of developmental psychology as the central guide to education: Examples from cognitive, moral, and psychological education. In M. C. Reynolds (Ed.), *Proceedings of the conference on psychology in the next decade: Alternative concepts.* Minneapolis: University of Minnesota Press.

Kormanski, C. L. (1985). A situational leadership approach to groups using the Tuckman model of group development. In L. D. Goodstein & J. W. Pfeiffer (Eds.), *The 1985 annual: Developing human resources* (pp. 217-227). San Diego, CA: University Associates.

Kottman, T., & Wilborn, B. (1992). Parents helping parents: Multiplying the counselor's effectiveness. *The School Counselor, 40*(1), 10-15.

Krantz, P. J., Ramsland, S., & McClannahan, L. E. (1989). Conversational skills for autistic adolescents: An autistic peer as prompter. *Behavioral Residential Treatment, 4*(3), 171-189.

Kroger, O., & Thuesen, J. (1988). *Type talk.* New York: Delacorte Press.

Kum, W., & Gal, E. (1976). Programs in practice. *Elementary School Guidance & Counseling, 11,* 74.

Lawrence, J. (1987). Reports of child abuse, neglect up 55% in five years, study says. *Anchorage Daily News,* March 3, A1.

Lister, L., & Ward, D. (1985). Youth hospice training. *Death Studies, 9*(4-5), 353-363.

Lobitz, W. C. (1970). Maximizing the high school counselor's effectiveness: The use of senior tutors. *The School Counselor, 18*(2), 127-129.

Locke, D. C., & Zimmerman, N. A. (1987). Effects of peer counseling training on psychological maturity of Black students. *Journal of College Student Personnel, 28*(6), 525-532.

Loevinger, J, (1976). *Ego development.* San Francisco: Jossey-Bass.

Loevinger, J., Wessler, R., & Redmore, C. (1970). *Measuring ego development II: Scoring Manual for women and girls.* San Francisco: Jossey-Bass.

Luepker, R. V., Johnson, C. A., & Murray, D. M. (1983). Prevention of cigarette smoking: Three-year follow-up of an educational program for youth. *Journal of Behavioral Medicine, 6*(1), 53-62.

Lukens, H. C. (1983). Training paraprofessionals: Christian Counselors— A survey conducted. *Journal of Psychology and Christianity, 2,* 51-61.

Lynn, D. (1986). Peer helpers increasing positive student involvement in school. *The School Counselor, 34*(1), 62-66.

Mack, D. (1989). Peer counseling: Increasing Mexican American and Black student contact with a university counseling center. *Journal of College Student Development, 30*(2), 187-188.

Maslow, A. H. (1968). *Toward a psychology of being* (2nd ed.). New York: Van Nostrand Reinhold.

Mathur, S., & Rutherford, R. (1991). Peer mediated interventions promoting social skills of children and youth with behavioral disorders. *Education and Treatment of Children, 14*(3), 227-242.

McArdle, G. E. H. (1993). *Delivering effective training sessions.* Menlo Park, CA: Crisp Publications, Inc.

McCann, G. B. (1975). Peer counseling: An approach to psychological education. *Elementary School Guidance & Counseling, 9*(3), 180-187.

McGill, C., & Patterson, C. (1990). Former patients as peer counselors on locked psychiatric inpatient units. *Hospital and Community Psychiatry, 41*(9), 1017-1019.

McGuire, W. J. (1964). Inducing resistance to persuasion. In L. Berkowitz (Ed.), *Advances in experimental social psychology* (1st ed.) New York: Academic Press.

McLaughlin, M. S., & Hazouri, S. P. (1992). *Tutoring, leading cooperating: Training activities for elementary school students.* Minneapolis, MN: Educational Media.

Mendel, R., & Lincoln, C. (1990). *Guiding children to success: What schools and communities can do.* Chapel Hill, NC: MDC, Inc.

Miller, K. L. (1989). Training peer counselors to work on a multicultural campus. *Journal of College Student Development, 30*(6), 561-562.

Miller, R., & Metz, G. (1991). Union counseling as peer assistance. *Employee Assistance Quarterly, 6*(4), 1-21.

Mogtader, E., & Leff, P. (1986). Young healers: Chronically ill adolescents as child life assistants. *Children's Health Care, 14*(3), 174-177.

Molloy, D. (1989). Peer intervention: An exploratory study. *Journal of Drug Issues, 19*(3), 319-336.

Morey, R., Miller, C., Rosen, L., & Fulton, R. (1993). High school peer counseling: The relationship between student satisfaction and peer counselors' style of helping. *The School Counselor, 40,* 293-300.

Muller, W. (1992). *Legacy of the heart: The spiritual advantages of a painful childhood.* NY: Simon and Schuster.

Murphy, F. L. (1975). *A study of the effects of peer group counseling on attendance at the senior high level.* Unpublished doctoral dissertation. George Washington University, Washington, DC.

Murray, D. M., Richards, P. S., Luepker, R. G., & Johnson, C. (1987). Peer teaching and smoking prevention among junior high students. *Adolescence, 15,* 277-281.

Myrick, R. D., & Bowman, R. P. (1981). *Children helping children: Teaching students to become friendly helpers.* Minneapolis: Educational Media.

Myrick, R. D., & Bowman, R. P. (1983). Peer helpers and the learning process. *Elementary School Guidance & Counseling 18,* 111-117.

Myrick, R., & Folk, B. (1991). *Peervention: Training peer facilitators for prevention education.* Minneapolis, MN: Educational Media.

Myrick, R., & Sorenson, D. (1992). *Helping skills for middle school students.* Minneapolis, MN: Educational Media.

Newman, L. (1990). *Preventable causes of learning impairment.* Denver, CO: Education Commission of the States.

Newman, W. (1985). Multi-cultural peer counselling programs. *The B. C. Counsellor, 7*(2), 13-18.

Noddings, N. (1992). *The challenge to care in schools: Alternative approach to education.* New York: Teachers College Press.

Nowicki, S., & Strickland, B. (1973). A locus of control scale for children. *Journal of Consulting and Clinical Psychology, 40,* 148-154.

Olsen, C. (1974). *The base church.* Atlanta, GA: Forum House.

Otto, H. (1970). *Group methods to actualize human potential: A handbook.* Beverly Hills, CA: Holistic Press.

Painter, C. (1989). *Friends helping friends.* Minneapolis, MN: Educational Media.

Pallas, A. (1989, June-July). The changing nature of the disadvantaged population: Current dimensions and future trends. *Educational Researcher,* 16-22.

Palmer, J., Davis, E., Sher, A., & Hicks, S. (1989). High school senior athletes as peer educators and role models: An innovative approach to drug prevention. *Journal of Alcohol and Drug Education, 35*(1), 23-27.

Perry, C., & Grant, M. (1991). A cross cultural pilot study on alcohol education and young people. *World Health Quarterly, 44*(2), 70-73.

Perry, C. L. & Kelder, S. H. (1992). Models for effective prevention. *Journal of Adolescent Health, 13,* 355-363.

Perry, C., Killen, J., & Slinkard, L. A. (1980). Peer teaching and smoking prevention among junior high students. *Adolescence, 15*(58), 277-281.

Perry, C., Klepp, K., Halper, A., Hawkins, K. G., & Murray, D. (1986). A process evaluation study of peer leaders in health education. *Journal of School Health, 56*(2), 62-67.

Perry, C., Klepp, K., & Sillers, C. (1989). Community-wide strategies for cardiovascular health: The Minnesota Heart Health Program youth program. *Health Education Research,* 4(1), 87-101.

Peterson, A., & Peppas, G. (1988). Trained peer helpers facilitate student adjustment in an overseas school. *The School Counselor,* 36(1), 67-73.

Petty, B., & Cusack, S. (1989). Assessing the impact of a seniors' peer counseling program. *Educational Gerontology,* 15(1), 49-64.

Pine, G., & Hilliard, A. (1990, April). Rx for racism: Imperatives for America's schools. *Phi Delta Kappan,* 593-600.

Rapp, H. M., Dworkin, A. L., & Moss, J. L. (1978). Student-to-student helping program. *Humanistic Educator,* 18, 88-98.

Reardon, M. T. (1991, June 8). Effectiveness of peer counseling on high school students who failed two or more classes in a nineweek quarter. *Peer Facilitator Quarterly,* (4), 9-13.

Redburn, D., & Juretich, M. (1989). Some considerations for using widowed self-help group leaders. *Gerontology and Geriatrics Education,* 9(3), 89-90.

Reeves, M. S. (1988, April 27). Self-interest and the common weal: Focusing on the bottom half. *Education Week,* 14-21.

Rest, J. R. (1986). *Moral development.* New York: Praeger.

Rice, R. (1991, January). An intervention program for older than average students. *Journal of College Student Development,* 32(1), 88-89.

Riessman, F. (1987). Paper presented at the National Peer Helpers Conference, St. Louis, MO.

Riessman, F. (1990). Restructuring help: A human services paradigm for the 1990's. *American Journal of Community Psychology,* 18(2), 221-230.

Robinson, S., Morrow, S., Kigin, T., & Lindeman, M. (1991, September). Peer counselors in a high school setting: Evaluation of training and impact on students. *The School Counselor,* 39(1), 35-40.

Rogers, C. H. (1980). *A way of being*. Boston: Houghton Mifflin.

Rohen, T., & Tindall, J. (1991, October). *The TDI and teambuilding: Forming, norming, storming, mourning, and performing*. Presentation at the ADVANCED technology conference on the MBTI-EAR-TDI, Princeton, NJ.

Roper, V. (1991). *HELP Network manual*. Fort Worth, TX: Texas Christian University.

Rosenthal, H. (1988). *Not with my life I don't: Preventing your suicide and that of others*. Muncie, IN: Accelerated Development.

Rubenstein, E., Panzarine, S., & Lanning, P. (1990, March). Peer counseling with adolescent mothers: A pilot program. *Families in Society*, (3), 136-141.

Russel, J., & Thompson, D. (1987, July). Evaluation of a program of peer helping for 1st year students. *Journal of College Student Personnel, 28*(4), 330-336.

Sachnoff, I. S. (1984). *High school peer resource programs: A director's perspective*. San Francisco, CA: Peer Resource Programs.

Sachnoff, I. (1992). Correspondence.

Salmon, S. (1992a). Program presentation, NPHA, Chicago.

Salmon, S. (1992b). Correspondence concerning sexual activity of middle school students.

Samuels, D., & Samuels, M. (1975). *The complete handbook of peer counseling*. Miami, FL: Fiesta Publishing.

Sasso, G., Hughes, G., Swanson, H., & Novak, C. (1987). A comparison of peer initiation interventions in promoting multiple peer initiators. *Education and Training in Mental Retardation, 22*(3), 150-155.

Scales, P. (1988, Fall). Helping adolescents create their futures. *FLEducator*, 4-10.

Schalzman, B. (1992). *Professional, paraprofessional, peer counseling*. Unpublished dissertation. St. Louis, MO: Jefferson Barracks Veterans Administration Medical Center.

Schrumpf, R., Crawford, D., & Usadel, H. C. (1991). *Peer mediation: conflict resolution in the schools.* Champaign, IL: Research Press.

Scott, S. (1985). *Peer pressure reversal.* Amherst, MA: Human Resource Development Press.

Scott, S. H., & Warner, R. W., Jr. (1974). Peer counseling. *Personnel and Guidance Journal, 53*(3), 228-231.

Sergiovanni, T. (1992). *Moral leadership: Getting to the heart of school improvement.* San Francisco: Jossey-Bass.

Sesan, R. (1988-89). Peer educators: A creative resource for the eating disordered college student. *Journal of College Student Psychotherapy, 3*(2-4), 221-240.

Sexuality Today Newsletter. (1986, July 7). Startling new study shows one in six women incestuously abused before age 18, pp. 3-4.

Shorey, A. E. (1981). *Peer counseling and achievement motivation: A comparison of two counseling approaches to an urban middle school.* Chicago: Northwestern University.

Skogan, W. G. (1989). Social change and the future of violent crime. In T. R. Gurr (Ed.), *Violence in America: Volume 1, The history of crime.* Newbury Park, CA: Sage.

Slap, G., Plotkin, S., Khalid, N., Michelman, D., & Forke, L. (1991). A human immunodeficiency virus peer education program for adolescent females. *Journal of Adolescent Health, 12*(6), 434-442.

Sobey, G. (1970). *The nonprofessional revolution in mental health.* New York: Columbia University Press.

Solberg, C., & Whitford, E. (1989). Elementary peer support: Developmental issues. *Peer Facilitator Quarterly, 6*(3), 14-17.

Spergel, I. A., Ross, R. E., Curry, G. D., & Chance, R. (1989). *Youth gangs: Problem and response.* Washington, DC: Office of Juvenile Justice and Delinquency Prevention.

Sprinthall, N. A., & Blum, R. (1980). *Promoting social and psychological development for mainstream classes: Peer and cross-age teaching in the social environment of the schools.* Reston, VA: Council for Exceptional Children.

Sprinthall, N. A., Hall, J. S., Gerler, E. R. (1992, April). Peer counseling for middle school students experiencing family divorce: A deliberate psychological education model. *Elementary School Guidance & Counseling, 26*(4), 279-304.

St. Louis Post Dispatch. (1992, September 10). A.C.T. Scores, p. 1.

Steinhausen, G. W. (1983). Peer education programs: A look nationally. *Health Education, 14*(7), 7-8, 10.

Sullivan, L. (1992, January 27). Remarks at a press conference to the release of the National High School Senior Drug Abuse survey, Executive Office Building, Washington, DC.

Telch, M. J., Kellen, J. D., & McAlister, A. L. (1982). Long term follow up of pilot project on smoking prevention with adolescents. *Journal of Behavioral Medicine, 5,* 1-8.

Telch, M., Miller, L., Killen, J., Cooke, S., & Maccoby, N. (1990). Social influences approach to smoking prevention: The effects of videotape delivery with and without same-age peer leader participation. *Addictive Behaviors, 15,* 21-28.

Thompson, R. (1986, February). Developing a peer group facilitation program on the secondary school level. An investment with multiple returns. *Small Group Behavior, 17*(1), 105-112.

Tindall, J. (1978). *A partial replication of effects of communication skill training on high school students' ability to function as peer group facilitators.* Unpublished study, Saint Louis University, St. Louis, MO.

Tindall, J., & Gray, H. D. (1978). *Peer counseling.* Muncie, IN: Accelerated Development.

Tindall, J., & Salmon-White, S. (1990). *Peers helping peers: Program for the preadolescent, leader manual and student workbook.* Muncie, IN: Accelerated Development.

Tobler, N. (1986). Meta-analysis of 1,433 adolescent drug prevention programs: Quantitative outcome results of program participants compared to a control or comparison group. *Journal of Drug Issues, 16*(14), 537-567.

Toepfer, E. (1991). Peer helping in higher education: Literature and resources. *Peer Facilitator Quarterly, 8*(3), 21-23.

Toole, J., & Toole, P. (1992, June). *Youth as resource.* Presentation at the National Peer Helping Conference, Chicago.

Toseland, R. W., Rossiter, C. M., & Labrecque, M. S. (1989). The effectiveness of peer-led and professional led groups to support family care givers. *Gerontologist, 29*(4), 465-479.

Truax, C. B., & Carkhuff, R. R. (1967). *Toward effective counseling and psychotherapy: Training and practice.* Chicago: Aldine Co.

Tuckman, B. W. (1965). Developmental sequence in small groups. *Psychological Bulletin, 63,* 384-399.

Tuckman, B. W., & Jensen, M. A. (1977). Stages of small group development revisited. *Group & Organization Studies, 2*(4), 419-427.

Turney, T. (1988). *Peer leadership.* Mountainside, NJ: Author.

USA Weekend, (1994, February 25-27). p. 1.

Ursone, D. (1990). Parental divorce during childhood: In-school programming, outside of school support, and effects on perceived social relationships of young adults. Unpublished master's thesis, North Carolina State University, Raleigh.

Varenhorst, B. (1987, May). Research and publications. *Peer Facilitator Quarterly, 4,* 3.

Varenhorst, B., & Sparks, L. (1988). *Training teenagers for peer ministry: A step by step program—Teaching kids how to care for each other.* Loveland, CO: Group Books.

Vijayalakshmi, S., & Mythili, S. P. (1985, January). Effect of human relations training on the students' ability to function as peer counselors. *Journal of the Indian Academy of Applied Psychology, 11*(1), 31-38.

Vijayalakshmi, S., Mythili, S. P., Rao, P., & Krishna. (1986, July 5). Effect of peer counseling training on helping skills and certain psychological factors: An exploratory study. *Journal of Indian Psychology, 5*(2), 50-62.

Vriend, T. J. (1969). High performing inner-city adolescents assist lower performing peers in counseling groups. *Personnel and Guidance Journal, 47*(9), 897-904.

Waas, L. L. (1991). *Imagine that.* Rolling Hills Estates, CA: Jalmar Press.

Ware, C., & Gold, B. (1971). *The Los Angeles City College peer counseling program.* O.E.O/A,A,J.C. Report, -2. Washington, DC: American Association of Junior Colleges.

Watstein, S., & Laurich, R. (1991). *AIDS and WOMEN: A sourcebook.* Phoenix, AZ: Oryz Press.

Werner, E., & Smith, R. (1992). *Overcoming the odds: High-risk children from birth to adulthood.* Ithaca, NY: Cornell University Press.

Williams, Mary B. (1986). Peer counseling for teenage victims: A student proposal. *Response to the Victimization of Women & Children, 9*(2), 22-23.

Wilson, M. (1992). Peers helping peers: PHP program reduces violence and vandalism. *Peer Facilitator Quarterly, 9*(3), 27-28.

Wolin, S. (1993). *The resilient self: How survivors of troubled families rise above adversity.* New York: Villard Books.

Woodcock, M. (1979). *Team development manual.* New York: John Wiley.

Woodcock, M., & Francis, D. (1981). *Organization development through team building: Planning a cost effective strategy.* New York: John Wiley.

Yalom, I. D. (1970). *The theory and practice of group psychotherapy.* New York: Basic Books.

Zwibelman, F. (1977). Effects of training. *Journal of Counseling Psychology, 24*(4), 359-364.

ADDITIONAL READINGS

Ackerman, R. J. (1983). *Children of alcoholics* (2nd ed.). Homes Beach, FL: Learning Publications.

Baiss, A. (1989). A peer counseling program for persons testing H.I.V. antibody positive. *Canadian Journal of Counselling 23*(1), 127-132.

Bandura, A. (1969). *Principles of behavior modification.* New York: Holt, Rinehart, and Winston.

Bell, C. M. (1977). *Changes in self-concept and academic achievement of peer counselors in an urban school district.* Unpublished doctoral dissertation, University of Maryland, College Park, MD.

Bell, C. S., & Battjes, R. (Eds.). (1985). Prevention research: Deterring drug abuse among children and adolescents. *NIDA Research Monograph 63.* Washington, DC: DHHS, PHS, Alcohol, Drug Abuse, and Mental Health Administration.

Bell, N.K. (1989). AIDS education and women: Remaining ethical issues. *AIDS Education and Prevention, 1*(1), 22-30. Chicago, IL: Guilford Press.

Benson, H. (1975). *The relaxation response.* New York: Avon Publishers.

Bernard, B. (1988, January 6-12). *Peer programs: The lodestone to prevention.* Prevention Forum (Illinois Prevention Resource Center).

Bernard, B. (1991). The case for peers. *Peer Facilitator Quarterly, 8*(4), 20-27.

Bernard, B. (1991, December). Peer programs: Essential to school restructuring. *Peer Facilitator Quarterly, 9*(2).

Black, C. (1982). *It will never happen to me!* Denver, CO: MAC Publications.

Brendtro, L., Brokenleg, M., & Van Bockern, S. (1990). *Reclaiming youth at risk: Our hope for the future.* Bloomington, IN: National Education Service.

Caplan, G., & Killilea, M. (1976). *Support systems and mutual help: Multidisciplinary explorations.* New York: Grune and Stratton.

Carr, R. (1992). Street youth often bridge the gap in aids services. *Peer Counselor, 9*(1).

Carroll, M. (Ed.). (1973). Special feature: Psychological education. *The School Counselor, 20*(5), 332-361.

Cary, L. (1989, January). Social support, peer counselling and the community counsellor. *Canadian Journal of Counselling, 23*(1), 92-102.

Children and Teens Today Newsletter. (1987, February), p. 3.

Covey, S., & Farnsworth, C. (1991). *Learning how to learn.* Provo, UT: Executive excellence.

Delquadri, J., Greenwood, R., Whorton, D., Carta, J., & Hall, R. V. (1986). Classwide peer tutoring. *Exceptional Children, 52*(6), 535-42.

Ellickson, P., Bell, R. (1990). Drug prevention in jr. high: A multi-site longitudinal test. *Science 247*, 1299-1305.

Emmert, B. A. (1977). *An analysis of the effectiveness of large group peer-helper training with pre- and early adolescents in the middle school.* Unpublished doctoral dissertation, University of Northern Colorado, Greely, CO.

Feuer, B. (1992). An innovative behavioral health care and model. *E.A.P. Association Exchange, 22*(10), 28-33.

Foster, E., & Tindall J. (1992, Fall). Establishing a peer helping program . . . step by step. *Schools in the Middle, 2*(1), 40-45.

Gartner, A., Kohler, M., & Riessman, F. (1971). *Children teach children.* New York: Harper and Row.

Gazda, G. M. (1969). *Theories and methods of group counseling in the schools.* Springfield, IL: Charles, C. Thomas.

Glick, P., & Norton, A. (1978). Marrying, divorcing, and living together in the U.S. today. *Population Bulletin, 32*, 3-38.

Golin, N., & Safferstone, M. (1971). *Peer group counseling: A manual for trainers.* Miami, FL: Dade County Public Schools.

Guttman, M. (1987). Verbal interactions of peer led group counselling. *Canadian Journal of Counselling, 21*(1), 49-58.

Hamilton, S. F., & Hamilton, M. A. (1992, March). Mentoring programs: Promise and paradox. *Phi Delta Kappan, 73*(7), 546-650.

Hofferth, S. L., & Hayes, C. (Eds.). (1987). Risking the future: Adolescent sexuality, pregnancy and childbearing. *National Academy Press, 11,* 290-291.

Johnson, D., & Johnson, R. (1983). The socialization and achievement crises: Are cooperative learning experiences the solution? In Leonard Bickman (Ed.), *Applied social psychology annual* (4th ed.) (pp. 119-164). New York: Sage Publications.

Koch, J. J. (1973). Counselor power. *The School Counselor, 20*(4), 288-292.

Landis, J. (1987). Teens find pregnancy is not child's play. *Guidepost, 29*(16), 1.

Lawrence, G. (1993). *People types and tiger stripes: A practical guide to learning styles* (3rd ed.). Gainesville, FL: Center for the Application of Psychological Type.

Loevinger, J. (1979). Construct validity of the sentence completion test of ego development. *Applied Psychological Measurement, 3,* 281-311.

Maheady, L., Sacca, M., & Harper, G. (1988). Classwide peer tutoring with mildly handicapped high school students. *Exceptional Children, 55*(1), 25-29.

Mastroiani, M., & Dinkmeyer, D. (1980). Developing an interest in others through peer facilitation. *Elementary School Guidance & Counseling, 14,* 214-221.

McAnarney, E., & Hendee, W. (1989). The prevention of adolescent pregnancy. *Journal of the American Medical Association, 262*:78.

McCarthy, B. W. (1975). Growth and development of a university companion program. *Journal of Counseling Psychology, 22*(1), 66-69.

McKay, M., Davis, M., & Fanning, P. (1983). *Messages: The communication book.* Oakland, CA: New Harbinger Publications.

Mentoring Training Curriculum. (1991). Alexandria, VA: United Way of America.

Mizell, M. H. (1978). Designing and implementing effective in-school alternatives to suspension. *Urban Review, 10,* 213-226.

Murray, M., & Owens, M. (1991). *Beyond the myths and magic of mentoring.* San Francisco, CA: Jossey-Bass.

Perry, C., Grant, M., Ernberg, G., Florenzano, R., Langdon, M., Myeni, A., Waahlberg, R., Berg, S., Anderson, K., Fisher, K., Blaze-Temple, D., Cross, D., Saunders, B., Jacobs, D., & Schmid, T. (1989). WHO collaborative study of alcohol education and young people: Outcomes of a four-country pilot study. *The International Journal of Addictions, 24*(12), 1145-1171.

Raths, L., Harmon, M., & Simon, S. (1966). *Values and teaching: working with values in the classroom.* Columbus, OH: Merrill.

Rice, D. P., Kelman, S., Miller, L. S., & Dunmeyer, S. (1990). *The economic costs of alcohol and drug abuse and mental illness.* Rockville, MD: National institute on Drug Abuse.

Riessman, F. (1991, June 5). Plotting a "thematic" third stage of reform. *Education Week,* p. 3.

Rosenroll, D., Saunders, G., & Carr, R. (1993). *The Canadian stay-in-school mentor strategy.* Victoria BC: Peer Systems Consulting Group.

Sciacca, J., & Seehafer, R. (1986, Spring). College peer health education: Program Rationale, support, and example. *Wellness Perspectives, 111*(2), 3-8.

Schinke, S., & Gilehrist, L. (1985). Preventing substance abuse in children and adolescents. *Journal of Consulting and Clinical Psychology, 53*(5), 596-602.

Selye, H. (1974). *Stress without distress*. NY: J. B. Lippincott.

Selye, H. (1978). *The stress of life* (rev. ed.). New York: McGraw-Hill.

Sexuality Today Newsletter. (1986, July 23). Short takes, p. 4.

Simon, S. (1973). *I am lovable and capable* (IALAC). Allen, TX: Argus communications. (Also available as a filmstrip.)

Simon, S., Howe, L., & Kirschenbaum, H. (1972). *Values clarification: A handbook of practical strategies for teachers and students*. Denver, CO: Harat Publishing.

Sprinthall, N. A. (1973). A curriculum for secondary schools: Counselors as teachers for psychological growth. *The School Counselor, 29*(5), 361-369.

Sprinthall, N. A., & Burke, S. M. (1985). Intellectual, interpersonal, and emotional development during childhood. *Journal of Humanistic Education and Development, 24*(2), 30-32.

Thomas, L., & Yates, R. (1974). Paraprofessionals in minority programs. *Personnel and Guidance Journal, 53*(4), 285-288.

Tindall, J. (1982). *The effectiveness of a wellness program: Coping with stress in schools*. Unpublished doctoral dissertation, Saint Louis University, St. Louis, MO.

Toseland, R., Rossiter, C., & Labrecque, M. (1989). The effectiveness of three group intervention strategies to support family caregivers. *American Journal of Orthopsychiatry, 59*(3), 420-429.

Turning points: Preparing American youth for the 21st century. (1989). Washington, DC: Carnegie Council on Adolescent Development.

Turney, T. (1994). *Peer leadership* (2nd ed.). Mountainside, NJ: Author.

Turney, T. (1994). *Peer leadership: Resource book*. Mountainside, NJ: Author.

U.S.D.H.H.S. (1990). Tobacco. Chapter three in health people: National health promotion and disease prevention objectives. *DHHS Publications* (PHS 91-50212).

United Way of America. (1990). *Wrap-around services for high-risk children and their families: Responding to national crisis.* Alexandria, VA: Author.

Varenhorst, B. (1973). Middle junior high school counselors' corner. *Elementary School Guidance & Counseling, 8*(1), 54-57.

Walters, J. L., Feemas, M. E., & Remstrom, D. (1990). *Volunteer coordinators' handbook: Volunteer mentor training program.* Tulsa, OK: National Resource Center for Youth Service.

Warr, P. (1984). Job Loss, unemployment and psychological well-being. In V. L. Allen & E. van de Vilert (Eds.), *Role transitions* (pp. 263-285). New York: Plenum.

Wasserman, D., & Derion, J. (1968). *Man of La Mancha.* New York: Dell.

Whitely, W., Dougherty, T., & Dreher, G. (1991). The relationship of career mentoring and socioeconomic origin to managers' and professionals' early career progress. *Academy of Management Journal, 34*(2), 331-351.

Woititz, J. (1983). *Adult children of alcoholics.* Hollywood, FL: Health Communications.

Woititz, J. (1984). *Struggle for intimacy.* Pompano Beach, FL: Health Communications.

Zabin, L. S., Hirsch, M. B., Smith, E. A., Streett, R., & Hardy, J. B. (1986). Evaluation of a pregnancy prevention program for urban teenagers. *Family Planning Perspectives, 18,* 119-126.

Zapka, J., & Mazur, D. (1977). Peer sex education training and evaluation. *American Journal of Public Health, 67*(5), 450-454.

INDEX

INDEX

Brown, W.F. 60, 319
Brownell, K. 93, 323
Buck, C. B. 79, 319
Budget drafting 151, 154, *Forms* 151-4, 155-6
Burke, M. 98, 320
Burke, S.M. 341
Burns, J. 98, 320
Business
changing role of counseling 58

C

Caning, J. 208, 320
Caplan, G. 13, 320, 338
Caplinger, T.E. 95, 322
Carbarino, J. 46, 320
Care of self 248
Career Center 208
Carkhuff, R.R. 3, 13, 15, 66, 71, 77, 107, 110, 123, 139, 170, 177, 189, 193, 320, 335
Carnegie Council on Adolescent Development 39, 320
Carr, R. 338, 340
Carroll, M. 338
Carta, J. 338
Cary, L. 80, 320, 338
Castaneda, R. 69, 323
Categores in Myers-Biggs Type Indicator 245
Center for Disease Control 40, 321
Chance, R. 29, 333
Characteristics of peer helping professional
ability to motivate 115
adaptability 115-6
dedication 114
flexibility of approach 115-6
intellectual curiosity 111
knowing self 116
optimism 112-3
physical fitness 111
pragmatic outlook 112
problem-solving skills 113-4
role model 114-5
understanding helpers and helpees 115
understanding values 116-7
Cherchia, P. 71, 72, 75

Chessare, J. 78, 318
Children and Teens Today Newsletter 338
Children's Defense Fund 22, 26, 27, 36, 321
Ciborowski, P. 68, 321
Clark, J.H. 35, 321
Class discussions
leading 207
Classroom groups
leading 18
Code of Ethics 253, 254, 271-3
National Peer Helpers Association 254, 271-3
Cohen, B. 98, 321
Cohen, R.M. 42, 321
Combs, A.W. 213, 321
Communication
definition 11
patterns 246
Communication Index 71
Community agency
changing role of counseling 59-62
Comparison group method 67-72
Components
peer helping 7-19
Conflict and violence 27-8
Conflict mediation definition 16
Conflict resolution 205
skill, evaluation 230
Confrontation
definition 16
skill, evaluation 229-30
Contract
peer helpers, *Form* 178
Cooke, S. 92, 334
Cooker, P. 71, 72, 75, 321
Cooper-White, P. 97, 321
Counseling, changing roles in
business 58
community agency 59-62
industry 58
juvenile justice system 59
prevention 58-9
religious setting 55-7
school 51-5
self-help groups 59
Counselor
how peer helpers help 258

Hall, R.V. 338
Halper, A. 23, 327
Hamburg, B.A. 74, 77, 324
Hamilton, M.A. 339
Hamilton, S.F. 339
Haney, M. 99, 317
Hanson, W. 93, 342
Hardy, J.B. 342
Harmon, M. 340
Harper, G. 339
Hawkins, K.G. 23, 330
Hayes, C. 339
Hayes, R. 98, 320
Hazouri, S. 75, 324, 328
Hein, K. 93, 325
Helpee definition 10
Helping definition 11
Helping process
    definition 11
Hendee, W. 339
Hendin, D. 30, 325
Henriksen, E.M. 69, 325
Hensley, B. 74, 325
Hetherington, E.M. 42, 325
Hicks, S. 81, 330
Hilliard, A. 38, 331
Hirsch, M.B. 342
Hodgkinson, H. 36, 37, 46, 47,
    325
Hofferth, S.L. 339
Holly, K.A. 79, 325
Holmes, D.R. 35, 321
Homework 195-6
Howe, L. 341
Hughes, G. 91, 97, 332
Human potential experience 134-5

I

Icebreakers 127
Implementation
    checklist 269
    program 261-5
Industry
    changing role of counseling 58
Integration of skill
    skill, evaluation 230-1
Interaction 244
Interview
    prospective peer helpers 309

rating sheet 315-6
Interviewer
    rating sheet 315-6
Ivey, A. 14, 110, 123, 189, 325
Ivey, A.E. 14, 52, 325
Ivey, M.B. 14, 325

J

Jacobs, D. 340
Jakubowski-Spector, P. 14, 326
Jensen, M.A. 241, 335
Johnson, C.A. 92, 93, 317, 328, 329
Johnson, D. 22, 23, 326, 339
Johnson, R. 22, 23, 326, 339
Johnson, W.B. 27, 326
Jones, E. 39, 326
Jones, J. 28, 33, 326
Jones, R. 35, 321
Jourard, S.M. 110, 326
Journal excerpts
    high school student 296-9
    middle school student 299-300
Jovick, F. 91, 326
Juretich, M. 99, 331
Juvenile justice system
    changing role of counseling 59

K

Keboyan, V.A. 75, 95, 326
Kelder, S.H. 93, 330
Kellam, S. 23, 326
Kellen, J.D. 93, 334
Kelman, S. 340
Khalid, N. 94, 101, 333
Kiersey, D. 126, 326
Kigin, T. 66, 331
Killen, J. 92, 93, 330, 334
Killilea, M. 337
Kirkley, B. 79, 326
Kirschenbaum, H. 341
Klepp, K. 23, 92, 93, 330, 331
Klepp-Knut, I. 23, 327
Koch, J.J. 339
Kohlberg, L. 176, 327
Kohler, M. 338
Kormanski, C.L. 241, 327
Kottman, T. 100, 327
Krantz, P.J. 96, 327

ABOUT THE AUTHOR

Judith A Tindall, Ph. D.

ABOUT THE AUTHOR

Judith A. Tindall, Ph. D., consultant, psychologist, Licensed Professional Counselor, and author has been in private practice with Rohen and Associates Psychological Center as a psychologist, L.P.C., and consultant to business, schools, government agencies, hospitals, social service agencies, professional associations, and churches for the past 14 years. She has assisted those groups through assessment, consulting, and training on a wide range of topics such as team building, leadership, peer helping, communication skills, TQM strategic planning, sexual harassment, and cultural diversity.

Prior to this, Dr. Tindall worked in public schools for 18 years as a teacher, counselor, and guidance director. She has taught courses at the graduate level at University of Missouri-St. Louis, Webster University, and Lindenwood College.

Typical of her E.N.T.J. (*Myers-Briggs Type Indicator*) personality, Dr. Tindall has served in a variety of leadership roles over the years. She has been an officer in local, state and national professional associations. She is past president of Missouri Association of Counseling and Development and past president of St. Louis Association of Counseling and Development. She was past legislative chairperson and middle school Vice President of Missouri School Counselors Association. She was Vice President Middle School of American School Counselors Association. She currently serves on the national American Counselors Association (ACA) committee of Interprofessional/Interpersonal Relations representing American Mental Health Counselors Association (AMHCA). Two years ago, she was asked to present at Princeton on the *MBTI-EAR-TDI* on team building and counseling. She is the current president of the National Peer Helpers Association and start-up president for Missouri Peer Helpers Association. She previously served on NPHA Programmatic Standards and Ethics, co-chaired development. She is an approved NPHA Trainer.

In June of 1993, Dr. Tindall presented a pre-conference workshop at the Association of Psychological Type on "Team Building: Forming, Norming, Storming, Mourning, Performing" utilizing the *MBTI-EAR-TDI*. She also has been recognized by her peers and received service awards from professional counseling associations.

She has published several books and numerous articles on peer helping, communication, team building, stress management, leadership, eating disorders, wellness, taking care of you, and type development. She has been on TV and radio concerning a variety of topics, and has presented locally and nationally on the *MBTI-EAR-TDI*.

Dr. Tindall has a Ph.D. from St. Louis University, an Ed.S. in counseling and psychology from Southern Illinois University at Edwardsville, an M.Ed. in counseling from University of Missouri at Columbia, and a B.S.Ed. in speech and political science from Southeast Missouri State University. She is married and has two sons and enjoys playing golf, spending time with friends, and surviving college tuition payments.